TOO MUCH MAGIC

Pulling the Plug
on the
Cult of Tech

*Secrets They Won't Tell You
About Your Digital Life*

by

Jason Benlevi

Contrarian Books

Too Much Magic: Pulling the Plug on the Cult of Tech
Copyright 2011 by Jason Benlevi

Published by Contrarian Books - San Francisco
ISBN 978-1-936790-10-4 (paper)
ISBN 978-1-936790-12-8 (Kindle)
ISBN 978-1-936790-14-2 (ePub)

Front cover art by Bill Groshelle

"Any sufficiently advanced technology is indistinguishable from magic."

— Arthur C. Clarke

"Everybody's got a cell phone that makes pancakes so they don't want to rock the boat. They don't want to make any trouble. People have been bought off by gizmos and toys in this country. No one questions things anymore."

— George Carlin, October 2007

Contents

Too Much Magic

Jason Benlevi

Preface:
It's Personal

For me, computing has always been personal.

When I was a teenager, I engaged in vain attempts to string together wires and bits of circuitry to build a computer, but in those days having a personal computer was a fantasy. There was also the personal conflict between being both a "creative type" and a nerd. The humanist and the technologist in me were often at odds.

I was the sole student at my university who, while attending the artsy film school, also sneaked off to computer-programming classes. While Jobs and Wozniak were putting a rainbow apple on their first computers, I had just completed what may have been the first screenplay ever written about hacking. Needless to say, their venture was somewhat more successful than mine.

Nonetheless, as a resident of the San Francisco Bay Area, I was fortunate to find my storytelling skills and an affinity for technology to be a useful combination. For more than two decades, I have been helping Silicon Valley companies articulate and envision the future, putting words in the mouths of executives and engineers, and scripting videos portraying magical visions of digital life.

I have been at tech ground zero in Silicon Valley and Redmond, Washington, working on teams that introduced Java, Sony PlayStation, Windows XP, and the latest from Apple, as well as less successful ventures including at least five failed attempts at interactive TV. I have lived in both dotcom land and "dot-bomb" land, and I am witnessing "Web 2.0" as it unfolds and inevitably folds. Then, as always, it's on to the "next big thing." These have been interesting times and, for me, more fun than having a real job.

Too Much Magic

As much as I love technology, I have never been dazzled by devices or bamboozled by tech biz-speak, partly because I was among the ones who wrote it. At times, my value has been as a B.S. filter for a business sorely in need of one. Sometimes it was appreciated; at other times it was apostasy. Like anything, the more you know about something, the more likely you are going to see its faults.

While there are abundant critics of technology, they generally come at it from two opposite sides. There are those who rant, rave, and blog about the minutiae of that interface, this gadget, or that new app, which is great if you are only trying to figure what mobile phone or big-screen display to buy. At the other end of the spectrum are the social critics who are certain that technology is responsible, to varying degrees, for our doom. Often they disdain technology because they don't have the time or inclination to grasp it, and they remain flummoxed and clueless even though, that doesn't dissuade them from gabbing into cell phones or watching TiVoed movies from the comfort of their couch.

I am a different kind of critic. As always, I find myself at the intersection of technology and humanity. Criticisms of technology can bring on charges of "heresy" or, worse, "Luddism." Luddites were those 19th century British weavers who tried to hold back the wheel of mechanization in the textile mills by trashing the machines with pitchforks and axes. Their attempts obviously did little to stem the industrialization that would change the world order forever. (Of course, they did give us a terrific-sounding term for those who oppose technology;. could we have picked a better sound than Ludd-ite to represent the forces of regression?) They did have a legitimate point, but their methodology, though visceral and emotionally cathartic, was ineffective.

I truly believe that technology has the capacity to improve the lives of many people. It is instead the trajectory of digital life that I find increasingly troubling. When I was starting my non-job, computers had just evolved from huge corporate IBM machines into personal-empowerment tools. The Mac/PC revolution was in full swing, and there was a feel-good, changing-the-world mentality among people in the tech business and the grass-roots community of newly empowered users.

Then, sometime in the 90s, I saw it change. It wasn't about empowering individuals anymore. Just as in the bad old days, there were powerful, ominous forces driving our new dependence on digital technology, only these were dressed up in hip new attire. With a fawning press and a bamboozled public, this shift was hardly noticed as the brilliance of digital technology took a darker turn. Being close to the business I realized that the goals of these new tech titans were at odds with what is good for the rest of us.

As the parent of one of the first digital-generation children, I have seen a new human life and the digital life grow and develop in parallel, deeply intermingled. This gifted child had precociously received early and full exposure to all the toys/tools of digital life and has now grown to adulthood cocooned by technology. In order to remain free-thinking and independent people, her generation must learn to emerge from the digital cocoon with which we have surrounded them.

While everyone is becoming aware of the dangers of unleashing too much carbon into the atmosphere, we also need, metaphorically speaking, to be aware of unleashing too much silicon into the process of daily life.

As a humanist, technologist, and parent, my goal is to help people become better informed about how "being digital" impacts them and the choices they need to make to live self-determined and happy lives. This book offers what is required to make informed decisions on buying into the digital lifestyle that you are being sold.

Too Much Magic

Jason Benlevi

The Twilight Zone

There was a Twilight Zone show I remember from my childhood. It was the story of a common hoodlum, a 60s TV show-style street tough. While escaping the pursuing cops, he tumbles from a fence. After a significant fall and a presumed loss of consciousness, he rises to find the portly and elegantly bearded actor, Sebastian Cabot, helping him to his feet. In due time, Mr. Cabot reveals himself as a supernatural being and tells the thug that he has, alas, passed. Disbelieving at first, he is invited by the Cabot character to a casino, where the perp wins every roll of the dice and every turn of the wheel.

Partying on, every beautiful woman he encounters showers him with affection. Everything he wants is his, effortlessly. Easy Street. Soon, the tough finds himself getting bored. There is no challenge. All uncertainty has been drained. Deeply disappointed, the outlaw complains to his host that he thought heaven would be more "kicks" than this. It is only then that his host roars with demonic laughter and says, "Heaven? My dear man! No, no — this is that other place."

When everything is possible (or at least appears to be possible) what would still be thrilling, or special? A genie granting only three wishes is a more compelling story than genie granting infinite wishes. Three wishes are more precious and the selections made are of colossal significance. Each wish has a huge value and power because it is finite. Too much magic becomes no magic at all.

For at least a century, technology has become our magic. We have come to believe that by applying enough technology (and usually money) there is nothing that can't be accomplished. Yet does having our wishes fulfilled easily create a new paradise, or a sophisticated high-tech hell that threatens our privacy, individuality, and humanity?

Too Much Magic

Isn't it strange that consumers, itching to buy the newest tech gadget, will stand in line overnight, while, at the same time, our movies generally portray a tech-laden future that is bleak and dystopic? There is a telling disconnect.

Are we fated to a tech heaven or a tech hell? That answer requires a greater understanding of technology than can be found quickly browsing product reviews on a website. You need to know who is pushing this technology upon us and for what reasons. You need to know about The Cult of Tech and how it is influencing your daily life without your informed consent.

Section One

LEARNING
THE TRICKS

Too Much Magic

Jason Benlevi

1.1

That Old Black Box Magic

Though we'd like to believe that it exists, we know there is no such thing as real magic — the supernatural kind, that is. Magic is something that was made up to fool people. It is made of a deft move of the hand, a misdirection, perhaps a mechanically articulated illusion. It is entertainment and a means of income generation for the skilled practitioner of deception. Even if you are innocent enough to suspect a supernatural basis, the chances are that you will not be harmed by this delusion. So believing, if even for just a moment, is not a dangerous indulgence.

The digital revolution has everything a good magic act should have: deft moves, misdirections, and technically achieved illusions. There is no shortage of deceptive practitioners; with an income-generation potential that is unlike anything the world has ever seen.

The illusionists — The Cult of Tech — behind the digital revolution want you to believe that technology will only improve your life. There are only pluses and no minuses. Slowly, in steps, you are buying in. Every facet of human life has become a tech encounter. Familiar activities such as dating, sending letters, banking, taking pictures, making movies, and selling music have all gone digital. Digital magic is becoming central to your life, your job, your spare time, and your relations with your family. Even voting has been digitized.

The fundamental problem is that when we adopt digital technology into our lives, we introduce a "medium" to facilitate it. Your digital interactions are mediated relationships. These relationships require intermediaries that provide you with services and make devices for you to use. Unless you are telepathic you can't send instant messages or images across distances without an electronic device, the appropriate software, and a network for the message to travel upon. So, right away, you are playing by their rules.

As your life becomes more "digital," you become more dependent upon these intermediaries to hook you into your new life, and these hooks reach deeper into your activities all the time. Businesses are motivated to offer you a digital lifestyle for one simple reason: money. At times these businesses are in direct conflict with your personal interests and rights. For example: The nation's phone companies handed over your private records to the executive branch of the U.S. government without a court order because they wanted to do business with the government on other issues that were in alignment with their business plans. You were for sale without your knowledge. But who could or would give up their mobile or home phone in protest? You are hooked.

You used to vote by checking a box on a paper ballot, which fellow citizens would see with their own eyes and count by hand. In the digital age you are entrusting private companies to convey your vote to your government. People (that's us) have been removed from the process. There is no one to check ballots nor anything for anyone to check. It's a black box, a company secret. Black magic. What has been gained? Convenience? Speed? We elected Jefferson, Lincoln, and two Roosevelts with paper ballots, human eyes, and weeks of counting. In 2004, electronic voting delivered George W. Bush's "victory" overnight in a cloud of uncertainty. Do you choose not to vote at all in disgust and protest? Not a wise choice. Once again you are hooked.

There are two things to always remember about digital magic:

• Those who are in the business of providing the technology and services will serve their own agenda (money and power) before they will serve yours.

• Every time we apply a technology, or add an intermediator to a human endeavor, we change our inter-human processes at a both a micro and macro level.

That Old Black Box Magic

We are not the same people as when we were happy to move at a horse's pace and could wait days for a message to reach us. Our senses of time and space have been altered. We can do more in less time. We move faster. Have shorter attention spans. Have less patience. Need faster food. Need faster cycles of new things. We grow more dependent on technical devices and more vulnerable to their malfunction. As tech companies offer us more, we keep buying, regardless of the human price. The question is, are we really any better off?

The irony is that this current digital revolution started with a great act of liberation, the advent of personal computers. The goal was to empower individuals to be creative and independent. It was a great idea in the beginning, but things have changed. The personal computer and mobile phone have now become a backdoor to attach those deep hooks into your personal and private life. You are showing up on radar screens everywhere and you are a juicy target for those illusionists looking for fortune at your expense, not just the spammers and scammers, but the legitimate Fortune 500 players, too.

Silicon Valley has become synonymous with fast companies and outrageous fortune. The Valley itself morphed from a collection of brilliant, curious people in love with science and technology into a collection of merchants and bankers who are motivated by the prospect of building ridiculous wealth overnight.

Product designers and electrical engineers, the true geniuses, are too busy inventing stuff on an accelerated track to think about human impacts, and venture capitalists are voracious for the next big thing to cash in on early and fast. Consumers are always looking for something new with which to run up their credit-card balance. With this codependent triad of engineers, investors, and consumers securely in place, technology adoption continues to gain momentum.

Even the most inept tech marketeers can't dampen the appeal of brilliant new devices sporting shiny new buttons and illuminated screens. The magic of wireless adds a seductive appeal to even the most mundane appliance. Just think how your phone changed from a box on the wall to the sleek "Swiss Army" device in your pocket that does thousands of things as of this writing. So, objectively, is technology good or bad? Just like humanity itself, it's a blend of both.

Technology and humanity are often portrayed as opposing forces. From *Metropolis* to *2001* to *Blade Runner* to *Total Recall*, most futuristic movies depict a techno-dystopia, where the tyranny of invasive machinery makes life inhumane and bleak. The lone exception may be *Star Trek*; its positive vision of times to come may account for its enduring appeal. Unfortunately, the *Star Trek* spaceship setting is enclosed. The issues of a larger society rarely intrude as the best, boldest, and brightest take part in a noble venture within a bubble. Maybe this is why it's among the very few future/technology-oriented films that have a positive vision for humanity.

Aspiring for a bright future is an integral part of our humanity. We are optimistic by nature. We build enduring structures like bridges that span generations. We have children and invest our assets. We want tomorrow to be better than today. We believe it will be. So why does the technology we lovingly embrace engender a vision of dystopia? What is the disconnect? How do our positive aspirations for the future and our affinity for shiny new devices add up to a pervasive vision of technical oppression? Perhaps because the wrong people, those with the grandest financial stake, seize control of technology and its experience. Maybe by doing what is possible, just because it can be done, we are diluting both our humanity and our technological ambitions. Wonder gives way to ennui and ennui becomes dread and oppressiveness.

This book is an attempt to re-synchronize humanity and technology. It briefly gives a background on how we found ourselves in this extraordinary nexus of culture and technology. It examines how these activities evolved and why they are running off course.

We can live with technology. Live well. Just as long as we remember that we ultimately must each exert our own personal control over it. Ultimately you are the judge, any time you want to be unhooked, just remember that you have the power to pull the plug...at least for now.

1.2

The Way-Back Machine

To understand how we got where we are, and why, we need to go back a bit. As with many world-changing technologies (airplanes for example), computing got its critical mass, or at least its big bucks, from the military. For computing, the objective was to calculate numeric tables to help soldiers know how to lob artillery shells accurately during World War II.

The eventual result was ENIAC, the first real digital computer. A collection of thousands of vacuum tubes and electrical relays, ENIAC performed differential calculations way faster than a human could. In war, as in life, timing matters. It was all about crunching numbers, *fast*.

With the post-war economic boom came a class of business managers who were all about "the numbers." It had become *au current*, and oh so 20th Century, to use "science" in the form of quantification and measurement as a business methodology. In the early 50s, therefore, the business computer came on to the scene to facilitate this number-crunching style of management.

In the popular imagination this "thinking machine" was full of blinking lights and whirling reels. Almost immediately people were concerned that the "electronic brains" would take over and displace humanity. It was a competition of unequals, because a computer is just a machine that can add, subtract, and multiply numbers very quickly. No "thinking" was involved. Still, the prevailing perception was that electronic brains were going to overrun or dehumanize us. It was "man" versus machine in an update of the John Henry folk tale. This fear is shown in movies like *Desk Set* with Tracy and Hepburn, which pretty well capture the public mood of the times.

So did dehumanization happen during this time frame? Well, yes it did. But the attempts to quantify human lives were more a reflection of the cookie-cutter culture of the 50s and early 60s, which was an outgrowth of paternal, hierarchical structures embraced by the WW II generation. After all, the GIs, along with their wives, elected the five-star general, Eisenhower, as president. It was a time of cascading authoritarianism and conformity.

This conformist culture of the 50s and early 60s had an electronic machine programmed for obedience and well-suited for promoting mass conformity: namely the "IBM machine" or, generically, the "computer." The computer culture of the time surrounded itself with a fortress of conformity personified by legions of blue-suited IBM salesmen and technicians functioning as interchangeable human drones to serve the machines. IBM's motto may have been "Think," but this was only in the Orwellian sense. "Big computing" became ominous. And people were right to be apprehensive — not about the machines, but rather the people who were using them as way to empower or enrich themselves.

As always, technology is a huge magnifier of a culture. In the larger mindset of the times, thus, we all became IBM punch cards. With computers in the hands of only the most powerful, they became numerically-driven dehumanizing machines. As a citizen and consumer, you became a number, all for the sake of "efficiency." If you were a school child at the time, you lived in fear of what would be recorded on your "permanent record." I wondered, at the time, what machine was recording all of this and where was it? (I was delighted when my friend Tommy, a proto-hacker, cracked the board of education's mainframe with a teletype machine and changed his grades without detection. In my opinion, if he was smart enough to do that, he deserved any grade he wanted to award himself.)

Little did those in charge know that there was a collision coming between this "command and control" authoritarian culture, and the emerging "do-your-own-thing" counterculture. The times they were a-changin', but it took a decade to get there.

Although I grew up as a child of science and the space age, I, like many of my peers, subsequently drifted toward being more of a flower child. My personal vision of humanity and technology began to intersect and collide. My solution was akin to Richard Brautigan's poem, *"Machines of Loving Grace."* I envisioned a world where computers and robots did the brutal dangerous work, while people could concentrate on craftsmanship and creativity. It was a lovely dream, and far from the reality of 1969.

By the mid-70s worlds were ready to collide. All the science kids of the 60s, myself included, who were pre-designated by the powers that be to fuel further adventures in space, instead discovered getting spaced out though the wonders of chemistry and some of botany's greatest "hits." In information-technology academia, white-shirted geeks were now sharing space with long-haired freaks. Rebelliously brilliant computer types dropped out of college, started hacking with the help of government surplus parts, and became the shock troops of the personal computing revolution. It is interesting to note that three giant computer companies of today — Apple, Microsoft and Dell — were the products of first-year college-dropout baby boomers. (This legacy of independent and idealistic genius continues today with Wikipedia and Mozilla, among other ventures.)

Micro or personal computers were wresting the power of computing away from the exclusive domain of accountants, managers, and actuaries. By the end of the 80s the big computer companies like Honeywell, RCA, and NCR had become the Philcos and Sylvanias of their generation. IBM survives, but only by having a huge pile of cash and sporting hipper attire.

Computing was put in the hands of a creative class, both among the entrepreneurs developing the applications and the users themselves. It radically changed the way music, movies, and even science was done. Creativity and intellectual property became the coin of the realm.

Things generally went the right way for a long while, but at some vague point near the turn of the millennium, the forces of control were aching to seize innovation and squeeze the independence out of technology. It was more subtle than before. While it seemed to be offering us personalization, it actually was becoming more authoritarian. The World Trade Center attack only accelerated this process.

The Net (The Internet) gave us all a wonderful window to look through but, like any window, it's a two-way arrangement. For the first time, we are in danger of sliding backward. As much as we love the Net, it has also become a conduit for the old forces to regain control and dehumanize us. Spyware, adware, NSA spying, datamining, supermarket discount cards, and RFID all are about the authoritative forces trying to seize control again. It is no coincidence that there was an ascendancy of authoritarianism in the executive branch of our government during that decade.

Scott McNealy, the former CEO of Sun Microsystems has said, "You have no privacy, get over it." When you are a billionaire with access to a private jet, private security services, private schools, and gated estates, it is probably pretty easy to get over it. For the rest of us it is a huge nasty issue. Our privacy belongs to us as an inalienable right. HP sells data security products for business, and yet its senior executives felt that they were within their rights to use false identities to invade the privacy of individuals deemed as enemies. How Nixonian. Even with the cute little euphemism of "pre-texting," it is a colossal invasion of privacy by a supposedly progressive corporation.

Currently, there are well-funded private companies that are buying up technology patents. Their goal is not to innovate, or make products, but rather to block others from innovating. It's nothing less than intellectual-property extortion and they've got the law on their side. Telecom companies are using their political clout to push for legislation creating a private toll-road system out of the public Internet. Add in our eagerness to adopt new gizmos that are changing our personal behaviors, and it all makes us a more pliable and passive populace less capable of challenging authority. Is our technology in our own image? Or does it look like the authority figures now shaping it? Who is being served? What are we willing to give up? What will we forget about? What Faustian bargains are we making? The questions are plentiful, but the discussions are not taking place.

The Way-Back Machine

It all matters because we have made digital technology so pervasive. Everyday activities of a generation ago that were tech-free are now are deeply embedded with digital tech. Traffic lights, your car, your insurance, your health care, the way you cook food, how you communicate and are entertained. You may not fully realize it yet, but digital magic is changing *you*.

Too Much Magic

Jason Benlevi

1.3

Monolog on Digital and Analog

Who Are We Fooling?

...Well, Us, Actually

Even though many have advocated the virtues of "being digital" there is a certain impossibility for a living, breathing creature to "be" digital. As biological beings we inhabit a physical world with infinite variations of colors, tones, and dimensions. We dwell in maybes, sort-ofs, and something-likes. The digital world on the other hand was built on absolutes: yes or no, zero or one. Bridging these two domains is a herculean task.

Just for clarity, in this context, "digital" is anything that uses a computer or microprocessor as a prime component. Digital technology adds "intelligence" to the basic functionality. Today's digital objects include cash registers, cell phones, pacemakers, washing machines, cameras, Tickle Me Elmo, Japanese toilets, your car, and iPods. While none of these is entirely new, each has been transformed by the digital element embedded within it.

Ironically, the term "digital" comes from digits, or fingers, which is why our number system became based on tens. It is just a random system based on our biology. Although we get excited about decades, centuries and millennia, 10 is just a random attribute of us humans. So even though the word "digital" is based on our biology, we really have nothing in common with digital technology. In fact, it's not even truly digital. It is binary, built on ones and zeroes.

While our human ancestors are complex squishy organisms of mysterious origins, your computer's ancestor is a light switch. Inside your computer's microprocessor are billions of switches, called "gates" or transistors. All switching is done at incredible speeds, making millions of yes/no decisions based on instructions that we generally call "programs." The on/off positions of these switches are the "bits" of computing. Since we created them, it's obvious that we know more about how computers work than we do about the functioning of our own human brains. We do know one thing extremely well about ourselves, however: we are remarkably adept at creating illusions…and believing them. That's a good thing for the most part, but it is subject to abuse.

In terms of communications and entertainment, since the time of Edison we have had an analog world –"analog" as in "analogy." It has been all about using technologies to create representations (analogies) of things from our "real" human life. We suspend disbelief and have accepted colored shadows moving on a screen (movies) as visual reality. We have accepted air moved by vibrating electro-magnetic driven paper cones (speakers) as familiar voices. Analog technologies gave us picture and sound anywhere. (Cave paintings were probably the first analog technology. They were hard to share… but talk about archival quality!)

Fortunately or unfortunately, it didn't take much to fool us; a flipbook of pictures or wax cylinder of recorded sound was enough to create some degree of illusion. This is the distortable mirror/analog to our reality and it has unleashed creativity and created shared human experiences. It worked because we are both flawed and amazing creatures. Our senses are fallible, yet our minds are agile and imaginative. We are gifted with a willing suspension of disbelief. We fill in the blanks with wonder.

For nearly a century technology focused on refining the fidelity of recorded images and sounds by improving analog technology (film, records, radio, tape). Over the years the goal has been to create increasingly "lifelike" illusions, taking analog further and further. We also made life experiences transportable by moving sound and images around through wires and over radio waves. As of this writing, we can't teleport our bodies, but we can beam up our senses and send them almost anywhere.

However, analog began to bump into limits in terms of fidelity and portability. That's when sound and picture recording crossed paths with computing, and digital media was born. Digital media promised to deliver more fidelity and reality through mathematically precise exactitude.

Our personal interfaces are still our eyes and ears. We can only understand analog. Everything in digital media needs to be converted back into analog so we can see and hear it. At least until someone puts a high-speed digital jack into our brain.

In a sense we are still making analog representations, such as photographs and recordings of our voices, but using digital means to create, transmit and store those analogs. Our lives are more complex than bits of yes/no decisions; trying to replicate aspects of our lives through bits is hard to do.

This is where things start to get lost in translation — either by omission or design. *Fidelity and veracity are no longer the same thing.* We can make reality vanish and portray fiction flawlessly even though it is entirely synthetic. The better we make these surface effects of digital video and digital audio appear, the more misled we may become. To paraphrase Bob Dylan, this is where "reality goes up on trial."

Although digital technology is an easy conveyance to bridge media types and facilitate communications, it is easily subject to abuse. Too many people are not aware of digital technology's power to distort — even obliterate — objective reality.

As always happens, we evolved the technology before we evolved the humanity. We have given ourselves more powerful tools, but we are lacking the social development to see these tools in the right perspective. Synchronizing our humanity and technology is an age-old issue. Technology creates social change, often with unintended circumstances. A tool for liberation can become a tool for subjugation. The cotton gin liberated people from the painful task of extracting seeds from raw cotton. At the same time, liberating cotton from its seeds created a massive demand for cotton and revived slavery in the American Southeast (when had been on its last legs.) Liberation and subjugation delivered by the same invention.

Or think about nuclear technology which is ideal for blowing up cities, and can also be used for boiling water to make steam for power plants. But is it sensible to use planet-destroying power just to boil water for generators? Plainly this is a stupid idea, especially since the waste products last up to 250,000 years. Just because it *can* be done doesn't mean it *should* be done. In our eagerness to adopt the next new thing we avoid circumspection and suffer from unexpected circumstances. That's how we wind up with plastics that don't break down in the environment, vaccines that carry unknown plaques, and a list of misguided science-induced disasters that goes on and on.

Yet, at the same time, the benefits that technologies bring are extraordinary and powerful. Certainly, in the early stages, each innovation seems magical, with limitless possibilities. Unfortunately, it's not always clear what the right path will be. If the *money* is going there, however, the chances are good that it's the wrong way. Despite current popular wisdom, crowds and markets are not wise, only selfish.

Devices and innovations are not good or evil. They have no souls. They are extensions of ourselves. Sometimes they have a positive effect, sometimes they don't. Often it's only after a long time has passed that we can see the effect. Let's use the automobile as an example. We have given ourselves 300 horsepower and 80 mph. But, because we still have 5 mph brains set for walking, we have not supplemented our ability to see, hear, or react any better or faster while driving. On the contrary, we are rapidly learning to ignore the few sensory inputs that we have as cars become laden with entertainment and communications toys. Consequently, inattention and sensory overload kill tens of thousands of us every year. The irony is that cars designed with computer-aided engineering (CAE) are becoming safer all the time, while drivers are becoming more dangerous due to computer-abetted distractions.

We all inherently know that technology can change behavior. For instance: think about how people behave once they are behind the wheel of a car. Here they sit inside a metal protective shell, seemingly insulated from all other humans in their own little world. At their command, hundreds of horsepower are available by simply pressing a pedal. Now, think about the way drivers behave toward other drivers. They engage in the worst possible behavior by cursing and rudely gesturing at each other. Even the nicest folks can become absolutely vile in the driver's seat. Can you imagine people behaving this way while walking on the sidewalk or pushing carts around in supermarkets?

Acquiring the insular shell of the car body makes us feel invincible, augmented. We have extended our personal power. Our whole mobile/ambulatory force, especially our speed, is amplified beyond the innate force of our own bodies. We become a sort of "borg," a hybrid of human and machine. The digital life similarly provides a protective shell and a powerful extension much as the car does. It changes behaviors in ways that we are just beginning to see.

People *creating* technologies are very smart — and generally hopeful and optimistic — but not necessarily socially aware. However, this is not always the case with those *purveying* these technologies: assorted digerati, intermediaries, marketeers, and fast-company venture capitalists. In the rush to the next big thing, no ethics are required. If there is money to be made, then technologies will be rolled out regardless of the impact on the public good. This is the chokepoint where the purveyors of digital magic seize control and dictate what technologies will be within our reach.

Typically, cautionary tales urge us to go slower in adopting technologies. Instead, we should be more concerned with direction rather than speed. We need to resist the urge to adopt every new thing no matter how appealing it is at first glance. Digital magic is powerfully attractive and we are easily dazzled.

In terms of user-centric design, our technology doesn't resemble us at all. We are not born to type; I'm living proof of that. It is not about technology *versus* humanity because, again, technology is an *extension of us*. And, too often, it is an extension of the power and influence of the *worst* among us. It's time to be critical and stop settling for bad technology just because we are told it's the Next Big Thing and therefore we *must* buy it!

Too Much Magic

Technology is and ever shall be a two-edged sword. It solves and dissolves. It destroys and creates. On the whole, it is always a matter of balance. Despite the hype, people are becoming so blasé about the ongoing flood of gadgetry pouring out of factories that we are losing our sense of wonder. When everything is possible, it all seems like "no big deal." Like the genie with infinite wishes to grant, the value of technologic gadgetry is diminished by its abundance. There's always another device available to save us or fulfill our whims.

We are all aware of the generational factor in technology. In schools, teachers and parents fret about kids learning "computers" while ignoring the fundamentals of the twentieth-century science that makes digital technology possible. Kids are only being trained as users with no sense of what happens inside the box. That is bad news because without understanding the building blocks there can be no basis for real invention. You don't change the world when, metaphorically speaking, you just learn to change the channels on your TV.

Even in the creative arts, digital tools mean content can be sampled and stolen from the original artists who actually took the time to learn the skills required to create images and play music. Simple digital tools have created musical groups in which no one plays an instrument other than a turntable. Working photographers with poor skills take bad pictures and are rescued by Photoshop, while Hollywood is so obsessed with digital effects that movies begin to resemble video games with infantile story development and a "shooter" mentality.

This borrowing and remixing culture brings us "mash-ups" and "re-mixes" rather than an original, skilled creative effort. Digital tools can unleash creativity but they also fill the market with mediocrity. We love how technology levels the playing field; unfortunately, digital tools also elevate the tide of mediocrity to a new level of technically proficient emptiness. Something is truly wrong with this picture, but don't worry — "we'll Photoshop it later" in this book.

Too Much Magic

Jason Benlevi

1.4

Not Made
In Our Image

Your computer is an idiot.

You have nothing in common with that little box you stare at. Computers are basically what used to be called "idiot savants." They can fundamentally do only one thing, albeit amazingly well: calculate numbers. Compute! That is why they were called "computers" instead of "really expensive office machines that remember stuff." Other than those extraordinarily fast math skills, a computer is deaf, dumb, and blind. Your computer doesn't understand a word you are typing, your digital camera doesn't capture anything but numbers and your MP3 player doesn't hear any difference between Mozart and the screeching of car brakes.

To a digital device everything is just numbers — specifically, ones and zeroes. Bits. It doesn't matter whether it is music, pictures, social networks, HDTV; they all are just long streams of bits. Bits are a super-low common denominator. (One goes into everything.) It makes it easy to move picture bits from your camera to your computer to your TV. Or take music bits and send them across the Net and park them in your iPod for playback. Inside the digital domain everything moves with fluidity. Bits are bits. This commonality and connectivity are the foundation of our digital life.

Commonality: It means that files on your laptop, voices on your cell phone, music on your player, sitcoms on your TV, and the colors in your photos are all made of the same mathematic stuff. Everything uses a common interchangeable language. It takes little, if any, work to have them recognize and exchange the same information. The bits on your computer, the government's computers, and corporate computers are all very much alike.

Connectivity: It means bits can go anyplace almost instantaneously. This is what the Internet is all about. Send your pictures, download music, talk with your friends, or buy a sofa. On the surface this anywhere, anytime model sounds pretty good. But is it? Maybe it depends upon which way this information is flowing, and for what purposes.

THIS IS A BIG DEAL! Converting the tangibles of our world into this digital process is the tricky part. Tangibles can mean pictures, music, bank credits, personal relationships, and so on. In fact, this translation is a mind-bending challenge. It requires teaching machines to capture a representation of things from our physical world and translate those representations into numbers so that your brilliantly dumb computer can do something with it.

Can everything be reduced, quantified, and described as a mathematic formula? Well, physicists postulate the mechanics of the universe with equations. Fractal geometry explains some of the randomness of nature in a tidy set of formulae. However, in these cases a human brain with all its wonderful intuitive randomness creates the formula. The real genius is creating the formula, not the act of calculating.

These formulae that computers compute are what are referred to as "algorithms." If that sounds like something from a math class you've avoided ever thinking about again, you'd be on the right track. It is the algebra of computing. An algorithm is the "word problem" of our organic and analog world turned into a numeric formula so a computer can compute it.

Once you come up with a formula, you can change the numeric values and everything still works. These "variable" values make it possible to change inputs and still have everything work. As an example, your digital camera has an algorithm to convert what comes in through the lens into numbers and numbers into an analog picture so you can see it. Vary the scenery coming into the lens, and the camera uses those fresh inputs to capture new image information exactly the same way the previous image was captured. Variables are the lifeblood of computer logic.

Jason Benlevi

Not Made in Our Image

Digital computers are extremely linear. They are procedural. One task follows another. They are about narrow streams of information moving very fast. We humans are about wide or multiple streams of information moving slowly. You can send the contents of an entire book to somebody online in a few seconds as bits. Try reading that book aloud to the same person on the phone and see how long it takes you.

Our brains are non-linear, random-idea fusion machines. We don't know where our best ideas come from. We don't know why music inspires us. We are a puzzle. Our best minds are those that can synthesize data from the real world in the most unexpected ways, such as seeing the lines of a newly plowed field, then realizing that moving images might be transmitted over the air by using a similar multilinear pattern. (It was, in fact, the hoed rows in an Idaho potato field that inspired Philo Farnsworth to invent television. This inspiration may have come full circle since he inadvertently invented the couch potato, too.)

Creating an algorithm is a work of human genius. It is a bridge between worlds. Next, the computer needs a set of instructions on how to perform the algorithms. These instruction sets are generally known as software. If the computer is analogous to the brain, then software is the mind.

The original digital computers required people to set instructions in an entirely mathematic formula. This made computers hard to use — and hard to program. Then someone invented a computer language to bridge the gap. It was called "Fortran," shortened from "Formula Translation." The guy who invented it did so because he said he was feeling lazy and didn't want to spend so much time entering the same information over again. Even the human trait of lassitude can inspire innovation.

For decades the trend toward more natural languages for computer programming (still not here) and for operating systems/user interfaces (much closer) has been the most important evolution in computing. It has made possible a huge workload transfer from the individual to the computer. The only way to make it simpler for people to use computers has always been to make the computers more powerful.

Oddly, despite the perception that spectacular innovation has taken place, the fundamental operations of a computer have not changed since the big IBM machines of the 50s. Just as with radios and TVs, what *has* changed is the industrial processes necessary to build computers. The parts, processor, memory, and storage are all smaller, faster, and cheaper, yet the basic logic is unchanged — they still perform functions identical to those of their larger antecedents. Either it was a terrific idea when it was designed, or perhaps there is technological neophobia. Is this a dead end? Does all the focus on binary digital computing close the door on radically new ideas that might yield a more human-centric form of computing?

For now, the machines are getting more dense, compact, and powerful, and the software is growing in complexity. It's always a tail-chasing game. Software itself has become a dangerous house of cards. (Think of how many system updates have been applied to your Windows or Mac OSX.) Yet we are dependent on this fragile stack of cryptic computer code to travel safely through the skies, run nuclear plants, and run life-support systems.

There is a world of invisible complexity growing as we convert more and more aspects of human life through digitization. That complexity and our dependence on those who supply the digital-magic "solutions" make us enormously vulnerable and undermine our independence as autonomous beings.

Jason Benlevi

1.5

The Cult of Tech

Dream or Dread?

The dream is *Star Trek*.
The dread is *Blade Runner*.
The reality is starting to look like *Network*.

The prophetic movie *Network*, released in 1976, is a vision of how a powerful multi-tentacled corporation and its amoral TV network management team caters to the worst of our human behaviors. (Imagine that!) Their goal is to boost ratings and please a board of directors, even if that means creating a broadcast circus of "reality" shows (including live assassinations) and treating the news of the day with game-show vapidity. The protagonist's populist rant became an enduring national catchphrase, "I'm mad as hell and I'm not going to take it anymore!" Then, cynically the phrase becomes a corporate marketing message. The objective is to sell advertising and promote big corporate business interests regardless of human costs. These are the network chairman's immutable "primal forces of nature."

Of course, it was all just…ahem…fiction.

The technology mavens and marketeers, whom we indentify as The Cult of Tech, were right when they called this the "Network Age." Though I'm not sure if they were aware of the irony. Are you mad you as hell? Will you keep taking it?

Are these three cinematic visions the only choices for the future? Of course not. We all have to decide for ourselves what mix of technologies will make our lives miserable or wonderful. But this decision needs to be informed by understanding the difference between what is technically possible and what is merely beneficial to tiny groups of investors. Like many decisions made in life, it is usually influenced by those who have money in the game.

What is different about this round of decision-making is the speed at which change is taking place. We have been a culture that has associated fast and easy with being good. Digital life scores high marks on fast and easy — so fast and easy that people are making dramatic choices about their personal future without even realizing they are doing it.

Ask yourself: Am I living in a "digital dream" or in "digital dread?" It depends upon who is defining it. For you, the "dream" might be about having freedom, choices, and a less onerous workload, allowing you to spend time with people you like and doing things that make you happy, while having less to worry about. Dread might be no privacy, no free time, always trying to keep up, and too much work for you to ever feel that you are finished. So which digital life are you living right now?

For the Cult of Tech, "digital dream" means yet more methods to invade your time and space urging you to buy stuff that you probably don't need. The accelerant for change is "synergy." Synergy, in this context, means that all the various types of media, both old-line and new, are "working together" to carry messages in a coordinated way, urging you to buy something or other. Digital media are the pervasive conduits for "marketing synergies" and "integrated marketing." You see them in the form of video screens, which are appearing almost everywhere: on your phone, above the gas pump — even over urinals. All of these electronic messages are screaming for your attention and often know who you are.

Is this the great "digital convergence" that we've been hearing about for a decade? Is it nothing more than the seamless connection of corporations, advertisers, and media empires that can target you anywhere at anytime? Where is the "off" switch when you are standing in line in the checkout or filling your tank? The ubiquitous LCD screen and its dazzling 3D graphics are everywhere.

It's oh so easy to be dazzled by digital, and that's exactly what technology marketeers are depending on. Give it enough flash; make it "cool," and whatever new gadget is flashed before you will wind up on your credit card bill. Technology can be like magic. In this case it is adept at making your money disappear. More seriously, it can make your rights disappear; we'll examine this in detail later.

Clearly we have a love/hate relationship with technology. We love to buy it, and hate it when it doesn't work. Admittedly, men have always been suckers for gadgets. They have been piling up stacks of blinking black boxes in home entertainment centers for decades. Now women are gadget happy as they covet and clutch the sleekest new mobile phone. We are seduced by the newness, adopt it like an adorable puppy, and then find out that it demands daily walks and perpetual poop scooping. Much time and money is spent just learning and maintaining technology. Not to mention that hamster-wheel cycle of upgrades that are mandated to stay "up-to-date." While you have been paying attention to the bright shiny objects, the real game is what is happening beyond the gadgets, well out of view. As they say in the business, it's all in the backend.

In reality, much of the "digital lifestyle" has become nothing more than commerce and marketing. The rise and fall and rise of the Dotcom Age is a good place to start understanding how the relationship between technology and money has evolved. In the late 1990s the intersection of technology and cash created a reality distortion field that we are still living through today. Fortunes were created without any underlying value being created. The word "tech" was applied to businesses in ways that were not appropriate.

Even now, financial news outlets report on the status of eBay and Amazon as if they are technology companies. They may be terrific services and successes, but they are not tech companies; they are merchants.

It's true that these companies were innovators around the edge by writing custom code to run on their computers, but at the end of the day they are merchants. They are not much different than Walmart or Target; they employ technology to run their operations, but invent little beyond business plans. These are storefronts that just happened to be placed in the digital universe and should not be confused with real technological innovation.

This is the story of most dotcoms, both living and deceased. Their only creations and inventions were business models, mostly bad.

Fortune smiled for a while on all, but grim reality soon weeded out those that were naïve and lame, which turned out to be the vast majority. Just ask the ex-marketing "whiz," who is now making you a latte at Starbucks. The people who really made out during the dotcom boom were the venture capitalists who, in a frenzy fed by both business and popular media, sold IPO stock to the unknowledgeable public eager to get in on the gold rush. Other big short-term winners were the "branding agencies." These are firms that help prospective companies create names, logos, taglines, and other communications that express their identity.

Now "brand" has become a product in itself. Coke and Nike are well-known brands, but they were products before they became "brands." People knew and liked the product, which established the brand in consumers' minds. In contemporary usage the word "brand" has even been extended to almost anything marketable, including felonious athletes, quasi-celebrities, and presidential candidates. I have even heard an army general on TV refer to a particular military offensive in Iraq as a "brand."

The era of dotcoms was the first time in history that "brand" preceded product. The whole idea was to plant a flag with a catchy name and website. Many companies tried to create "brands" without engaging in the tedious task of actually creating a product in the first place. Pure marketeering. All package, no contents. So it should have come as no surprise when the whole brood, including Pets.com and Petopia were sent to the cyber kennel in the sky.

As we move through Web 2.0, which is often tagged as the "social networking" web, we actually have some content on the page. In this case, the users of the websites are doing the work of creating the content. The blogs, viral video, and personal profiles cost the website owners nothing. Whether it is YouTube, Facebook, MySpace, Yelp, Twitter, or some other new flavor doesn't really matter. All that is required to start a billion-dollar company is an incongruously compounded name, a 22-year-old CEO and a few lines of computer programming code. Not much innovation there, but the appeal to users and investors seems irresistible.

The Cult of Tech

Why are these companies, which have scarcely come into existence, reaching multibillion-dollar valuations overnight when they don't make, invent, or create anything? It is all about advertising. Capturing eyeballs.

There is no purpose for these sites being created as businesses other than to attract advertising dollars. Social networking sites may have started out just for fun, but certainly no investors are funding and buying these companies to altruistically help teens chat with their pals. It's all about the ads.

Even Google, which provides a great service, is entirely financed by selling ad space. All of this Silicon Valley talent and brainpower is concentrated on placing ads more effectively. It seems like an awful waste of intelligence when we have so many difficult problems in our world that the power of technology could help solve. Merely "not doing evil" is not as beneficial as doing "good."

Contrast this with the early days of personal computing where the 22-year-old college dropout took what had been the rare and exclusive power of computing and put it in the hands of every person to do art, write, or start a business. The point was empowerment of the individual, not to create another conduit for advertising and selling fizzy sugar water.

There is a huge shift going on here. Technology has changed from being a tool to give power to the individual to just another way for the powerful to manipulate and extract cash from the less powerful. As we move more of our lives into the digital realm, we alter both the way our society operates and our own behavior. This is especially true with the youngest amongst us. They are arriving in an on-demand world. What levels of expectation will be set?

Certainly social networking/Web 2.0 is changing the way people interact with each other. It is a huge social change when teenagers and younger people are converting real lives into digital lives. It is a seduction that is irresistible. People, especially young people, need social interaction. They need to feel autonomous and powerful. Here, through the web, on their computers, in their rooms, in the safety of their shell they are reaching out for companionship and community (gossip, too.) It is a compelling proposition. They are drawn to the experience, and marketeers are drawn to them as targets for advertising. Digital life is seductive and deceptive.

Your Faustian Deal

The core properties of commonality and connectivity that make digital life seem so appealing are exactly the same ones that make it so destructive, invasive, and subject to abuse.

- You can buy whatever you want from anywhere in the world. You learn amazing facts. At the same time, digital magic has made it possible to outsource service jobs on massive scale. Because of the digital network, customer-service phone calls are routed to low-wage workers anywhere in the world.

- You love GPS to help find your way. But did you know that your car has a secret recording device that can tattle about your driving to carmakers, insurance companies, and law enforcement — without your knowledge.

- Dial an 800 number and they instantly know who you are. That's nice. Except for the fact that your phone number is linked to a database with a massive volume of personal information about you, that you yourself are not allowed to access, examine, or correct.

- Your TV is watching you. Every time you TIVO or use a DVR service, that information about you and your family's viewing habits is sent back to a database and tracked.

- You can search the web for vast and useful information while search engines keep records of what you were searching for. Anything known anywhere about you, in any database, is easily sent as a stream of bits to anywhere else without your knowledge or permission.

• Every door you look through on the Net opens another door for a persistent 24-hour salesman to wedge his metaphorical foot in your door. Digital life becomes a mall or infomercial instead of a town square or university.

Who is forcing us into these arrangements? Who is making it appear as if these are our only options? Who is writing the script for this vision of the future? Who has their hands on the controls directing this digital juggernaut?

Meet The Cult of Tech

There are at least five main classes that comprise the Cult of Tech. Each group has its own band of interest and influence. The categories are not mutually exclusive. In the digital world of convergence, nothing is entirely discrete. These are the decision-makers of digital life.

The Cast of Players:

The Drs. Faust — *PhDeluded*
The Digerati — *Kool-Aid Kids*
The Fast-Company Few — *Devils in the Deal*
The Intermediators — *Taking Their Toll*
The Marketeers — *Warring for Eyeballs*

THE DRS. FAUST — PhDeluded

The first of the Cultists are the ones who are actually responsible for inventing things. For the most part they are found at places like MIT's Media Lab, and deep-thinking parts of IBM or other organizations both commercial and academic. They are scientists, engineers, and other technologists — the real magicians.

These magicians are out to realize their sci-fi dreams; the problem is, like all creators, they need money to do research, explore, and invent. Science costs money. Consequently there are a multitude of "Dr. Fausts" in great universities and Silicon Valley. These are brilliant innovators, people with the best intentions. However, just as Nobel (and presumably noble) physicists of the 1940s unleashed the nuclear war machine to "save humanity" during WWII, today's well-meaning scientists are eagerly delivering technologies that fuel the digital-marketeering juggernaut. Technologists have always had a difficult time considering the social impact of what they have developed, and genies are notoriously difficult to put back in the bottle.

What is disturbing is that the demarcation between universities, especially state schools, and private industries is being muddled. Often we see corporations funding university research that solely benefits them, not the world at large. Also, many talented scientists are enticed into private industry by generous offers, taking with them the knowledge they developed at the learning institution, knowledge that should be shared, as it was in years past. Many of the significant digital-age companies including Cisco, Sun, Google, and Yahoo are direct offshoots of universities.

THE DIGERATI – Kool-Aid Kids

The self-named "digerati" are academics, pundits, journalists, and impresarios of digital culture who look at the digital life as a cultural revolution. They share a deep belief that technology can overcome all boundaries. A hearty round of Kool-Aid is in order for them.

Raised on a rich diet of sci-fi and gadgetry, most digerati think the idea of fusing with a machine is "kinda cool." The digerati presume that digital life is a panacea. And it is — at least for their tech-stock holdings, consulting fees, and book sales. They breathlessly applaud each new gadget and emerging business model and rapidly drop whatever was "last week" like a mall-shopping Valley girl going through outfits. There is an almost weekly coinage of lingo such as "crowdsourcing" or "The Cloud," which are as easily dismissed and forgotten as fashion dictates.

These digital fashionistas have also presumed that it is their unique prerogative to declare what is "Wired," "Tired," or "Expired" for the rest of us. Given their credentials (or media-friendly appearance) they exert a huge influence and easily intimidate the mere mortals of mainstream and business media who fear being left behind.

All it takes is a look at the advertising in a publication such as *Wired* Magazine to grasp that the real agenda is object lust. Have a problem? Here's a device you can buy that will solve the problem. Count the pages of ads for tech offerings in *Wired* and make your own judgment about their objectivity. Overall, much of this mindset is a "boys with toys" mentality.

In the end, the digerati are all gas and no brakes. Do we want to turn the steering wheel of our digital lives over to them?

THE FAST-COMPANY FEW — *Devils in the Deal*

Fast money in, fast money out. Fast Companies with short lifespans. The fast crowd of venture capitalists, type "A" sociopaths, accidental billionaires, old-money scions, championship raconteurs, egoists, frat boys, and some actual technologists who lucked out with the right idea at the right time and have a huge pile of cash to invest, usually unwisely. What matters in this social milieu isn't just winning — it's total domination. For these folks, an appealing new product idea might be discussed in such terms as an "iPhone Killer," or "a Google Killer," or a "Twitter Killer."

No set of entrepreneurs has ever made so much money so fast. Yet they always want more than the other guy. They are extremely small in number, yet their wealth powers huge changes in society at large. Many appear to have a peculiar lack of empathy, which is evident in their management styles and laissez-faire politics. It is all about *them*.

The business objective is to find an innocent genius with a great idea, finance getting the idea off the ground, and then issuing shares in the new company at the first possible moment though initial public offerings (IPOs) of stock in the new company. Soon, they cash in their millions in stock and bail on the new company. Unlike the companies of capitalists in past generations like Ford or Edison, these are not businesses built to last. Many of them burn out fast. There is a long list — Netscape, Excite, Silicon Graphics, AOL, etc. Fast money in, fast money out. Fast companies.

There was a bumper sticker a few years back, often seen in Silicon Valley:

The One Who Dies with the Most Toys Wins

Are these the people you want driving your future?

THE INTERMEDIATORS – Taking Their Toll

We like to think of the Net as a free and open entity. Although the Internet was initially funded by your tax dollars and mine, it has become a huge for-profit business. It has gatekeepers and toll-takers at every juncture. You can't log onto the web without a service provider. These SPs are big media and telecommunications companies that are increasingly being merged. Intermediators may also be providers of key services or applications, such as Facebook or Microsoft. It doesn't matter whether you are connected by wireless, satellite, telephone wire, or cable, you can't get there without someone letting you in. Intermediators may seem to be neutral parties, but they have the potential to put a chokehold on your life choices and freedoms.

It is well within the capabilities of service providers to let you see only what they want you to see. As an example, they can provide fast access to websites and media with which they have a business arrangement and, conversely, they can lock you out of anything they don't want you to view. They can push your business to one particular company or keep you from shopping online with another. Worse than that, they have the potential to control the political dialogue by filtering out what doesn't fit their agenda. This political-content filtering is common in totalitarian nations such as China and in the Persian Gulf region. The sneaky part is you may never know what is missing if you are inside the walls.

A service provider with a political agenda can influence your view of the world. It's sobering to realize that somebody like Rupert Murdoch can run around snatching up media outlets (including MySpace) at will. It brings a queasy feeling to know that anyone at this choke point has the digital power to sway opinions and lock out dissent. There are no laws to stop this from happening. The "free" market is really a private roadway.

Your freedom to blog is always subject to a service provider's innate ability to filter content and monitor activity. Basically, you are only as free as they will allow you to be.

Intermediators are the drug dealers of the digital life, and they are out to hook you. They even have multiyear contracts to bind you. That should tell you something about the relationship they'd like to have with you. The simple fact is that it is easier to add devices to your life, such as a car or cell phone, than to give one up. Once you adopt a technology, you become dependent on it. As you become dependent on it, you cede control to the entity that supplies the technology or service, whether that is oil or bandwidth.

Above all else, intermediators are all about "privatization." Thirty years ago people watched TV for free with antennas; now people pay for cable or satellite. Water was out of the tap on municipal systems for free or nearly free. Now bottled water sells at prices that ounce-for-ounce exceed that of Saudi crude. Gated communities spring up around the country using public money for their roads.

The thing about privatization is that now they are trying to sell you things that you already own, such as "privacy" and "democracy." The curious thing is that the proponents of privatization use all the tools of government to enforce their privatization of public functions. They believe in free markets unless you want to buy your medicines from Canada.

Look at how our democracy itself is getting privatized. For 200 years a name on a piece of paper with an "x" marked on it was the foundation of American democracy. Now democracy has been turned over to the lowest bidder with electronic voting machines operating with secret proprietary processes.

Digital technology is insinuating itself into every aspect of our lives with amazing speed and pervasiveness. Even areas of our lives in which we were served well for generations with conventional methods are being digitized. Why? Because it is possible and it is profitable.

THE MARKETEERS — *Warring for Eyeballs*

They are everywhere. They interject product messages into every medium known to humanity and dig around in your private life to find the trigger that will get you to buy whatever they are selling, including more technology so they'll have even more channels to inundate all of your waking time with their messaging. They are the Marketeers.

These folks march under the banner of "creativity," but their creativity is a gun for hire as they infuse messages beyond the point of saturation, striving to find the one extra bit of magic that does the trick. Marketeers compel you to have more and more intermediated experiences to replace what you are able to accomplish on your own.

Almost every aspect of the digital transformation has been packaged and sold as desirable and inevitable. Resisters are painted as out-of-touch, or just not bright enough to "get it." There is a synergistic relationship among the digerati, fast-company types, intermediators, and marketeers. Each promotes the interests of the other. Your only role, in their view, is for you to be a consumer, selecting your flavor of "brand experience."

Your privacy itself has also become a "brand" as marketeers emerge to "protect" you against identity theft. In reality, information about you is for sale and proliferating around the world at an alarming pace, and you have no control over it.

Should the decisions about your digital life be in the hands of private companies who only have their profit as a motive? Who is more fit to make these decisions? That's where we meet the most important player of all.

YOU — *Yeah You!!!*

There is only one player that can overrule all of the above. You are the ultimate decider of what digital technology you will allow in your life. You need to set the rules. But first you have to learn what is possible, both negative and positive, in the digital life. That's what this book is all about. Together we will have to act individually and in concert to pull the plug on the Cult of Tech to prevent them from being the dictators of digital life.

Too Much Magic

Jason Benlevi

Section Two

SCENES FROM A DIGITAL LIFE

Jason Benlevi

2.0

Pushing Your Own Buttons Feels Good

This section examines various aspects of our digital life that have evolved over many years. There are reasons, which predate the technology, why it looks the way it does. You'll now see how these ideas emerged and where they are going.

It is important to restate that this book isn't about devices, gizmos, faster performance, particular services, or what product to buy. This book is about how digital technology is changing the way we behave, who will benefit from this transformation, and how it is more driven by financial concerns than by scientific advancement. Developing technology takes money. Wealthy investors have the cash and, as history reveals, what is good for capital is often at odds with what is good for humanity in general.

Fortunately, you can choose between living in a digital dream or digital dread by understanding what is taking place behind the hype and spin. Above all, remember this: For the time being, at least, you are in control; almost everything has an off switch or a plug you can pull — don't be afraid to pull it if you don't like what you see.

Too Much Magic

2.1

The Entertainment Invasion

The Dark Side of Fun

With so much of our news coverage and web traffic devoted to even the most minor celebrities and their dust-ups, you might get the impression that this is pretty important stuff. Admittedly, such puffery can provide a refreshing break from some of the harsher realities of the world. At the same time, the entertainment industry provides an opportunity for the few fortunate and truly creative souls among us to emerge and express themselves. Yet there is a problem of balance. How much of our time and treasure will we pour into keeping ourselves amused by watching other people do things?

Modern mass entertainment renders people into passengers rather than active participants. They are required to create nothing and do nothing except watch, buy and watch some more. With digital technology, the entertainment business has the tools to deliver entertainment pervasively, invasively, and without the limits of time and space. Has the point come where there is just too much? When does amusement become constant distraction? Is it even a diversion when it is available all the time? Is anyone having any fun here? Or are we just filling personal voids and media-company coffers? What is the role of entertainment in the first place?

Out of the Darkness

The need for entertainment is primal in humans. To avoid being eaten by beasts, our ancestors sat around the nightly fire, watching the smoke rise and taking in the persistent glimmer of the stars above them. All of that empty darkness allowed imaginations to soar in a limitless world of creativity. They began filling the time by telling stories. They entertained themselves by recalling the heroic drama of the hunt, telling tales of ancestral times, or inventing entirely fictitious yarns. Often these stories involved unseen spirits and forces the ancients believed ruled their world. So the story of entertainment starts in the primordial darkness of night and relates directly to the natural rhythms and divisions between day and night, work and entertainment.

Our ancestors began to project characters from their minds onto the random formations of stars. The resultant tribal mythologies were just as rational or valid as anything that people worship today. There are story elements common to every human group, including the members of today's mass religions. There was the creation, the product of the heavens, potent invisible forces, and the requisite battle between good and evil. Little has changed except the names of the deities/characters as civilizations matured.

There was a thin wall between godly tales and storytelling for entertainment. Even the relatively modern Greeks had gods as prominent characters in their plays. When the playwright wrote himself into a narrative corner, he could always invoke a *deus ex machina* and the gods would descend to resolve his final story conflict with some improbable solution beyond the realm of human activity. It was the CG (computer graphics) approach of the age, providing impossible solutions to irresolvable storytelling problems. The wall between entertainment and faith remains permeable, in both directions, judging from the profits of televangelists, "Jesus rock" bands, and the theatrics of megachurches. The entertainment and religion businesses may use different venues, proscenium-arched theatres versus vaulted churches, but ultimately they are places people come to hear stories that they have agreed to believe. Entertainment and faith require a suspension of disbelief. Both have the same primal origins and share one idea: It's all about the story.

Leave It to the Pros

We all have our own stories populating our minds. Many of us share these stories. Sometimes they are true, sometimes not. You may not think of yourself as a storyteller, yet your dreams betray remarkable fictions within you, even if you may not have the skills to communicate or share them. (Movies themselves are really just mass dreams shared through the technical means of cameras and projectors.)

Everyone starts out in life as a storyteller. When we first learn to put a few words together, innocently leaking the crazy stuff that is traveling around in our minds, we begin the practice without training or fear. Just listen to young children as they synthesize the particles of knowledge they have and then begin to weave amazing tales that fill in the gaps, just as the ancients did. When my daughter was a toddler she ascribed the powers of gravity to a group of invisible "baby giants" who sat on her shoulders so she would not fly away out of her seat. Children are human time machines helping us to understand our primal-to-present-day story-making evolution.

In the process of maturing, as individuals or civilizations, the storytelling dynamic begins to change. It becomes clear that some people are obviously better storytellers. It is the same with music. While we all have the capacity for making music, some are more natural practitioners. Where it is okay to beat a drum out of time when we are primitive (either in personal age or culturally), pretty soon our maturing ears demand a bit more order. It becomes time for the music and storytelling specialists to take over, which is a mixed blessing.

A lucky (and sometimes talented) few become entertainment professionals as writers, actors, musicians, and singers. The creative class discovered early on that it was a better than working the fields or pounding on hot iron. There is a certain pressure to be good at your craft or you run the risk of having rotten tomatoes landing on you, maybe worse in primitive times before they had sewers.

The rest of us, intimidated by our peers, stop making our own "original music" by the time we are in first grade. We start becoming more "audience" and less "performer." Most of us become consumers of stories, rather than originators – watchers and listeners. We leave it to the pros and buy our entertainment experiences rather than creating our own. In the modern era we have turned our children's imaginations over to Disney and organized religion to be blanched and homogenized.

The Balance Between Work and Entertainment

There has always been a ratio between our working hours and our entertainment hours. Waves of technology over the past century have incrementally unglued us from the ratio that nature imposed. It used to be that day and night gave us a system of balancing entertainment and work. The sun rose: it was time to work. The sun set: work stopped and the entertainment began.

In the electric age of the 20th century, we began to alter that natural balance. There were electric lights, which meant people could work later. Entertainment choices expanded as they were now sharable over time and distance through records, radio, movies, and TV. A performance was captured or broadcast once and shared by millions. The age of mass media was born, as well as an amazing business model — more about this later.

There were physical limitations to mass media. For example, you didn't have a TV at work. It was at home in the living room. In the tradition of the campfire, the nuclear family gathered around in the gray flickering glow of the television. It also followed the tradition of entertainment being primarily a nighttime experience. In the early days, TV stations were only on from 6 to 12 p.m.

Music media were subject to the limitations of time, place and choice. You generally could not strap on a record player and go for a run. You could, however, listen to music on radios that were becoming increasingly portable. You couldn't pick the songs, but you could pick a station that tended to play the music you liked.

You had no control over what they played, and maybe that was a good thing. DJ's, who were pretty smart about music, exposed you to new things that you had never heard before. It was random and expansive to your experience if you had a good DJ. Even if the DJs often were persuaded by gifts of cash or substances by record companies to air new selections (product), new music was always being introduced and cycled.

Music, unlike watching TV, is the entertainment of which you could partake while still doing work. There were even studies that showed that it enhanced work and study. On the other hand, TV was completely distracting and it wasn't portable anyway.

For both music and TV, therefore, your consumption was limited; you couldn't have anything, anytime you wanted. The test pattern meant, for even the most TV-addicted, that it was time to go to bed. That was then. Now the late-night 500-channel zone has become the home of "informercials" for weight-reduction gadgets and "real estate for no money down." You may lose sleep, but you'll be able to purchase a "new body" and earn millions of dollars in a just few minutes a day "without any cash investment at all!"

Infomercials are a genetic mutation of TV created by an incremental sell-off of public airwaves to private interests. When Ronald Reagan removed rules about the balance of time between TV entertainment programming (such as it was) and advertising in the 80s, the infomercial business was born. The "info" part is misleading since these programs are nothing more than feature-length commercials whose "information" is purely pitching a product. They are all wrapper and no candy bar, the perfect creature of marketeering. (Ironically, there is a building in San Francisco's North Beach where Philo Farnsworth invented television in the 1920s. In the 1990s that same building was occupied by what became the leading company producing infomercials. Since infomercials represent the ultimate devolution of television — the commercial without the show — the building, for a time, housed the complete life cycle of TV from birth to its sad death. What would Philo have thought?)

Getting Unstuck in Time

With the advent of videocassette recorders (VCRs) in the late 70s, people were finally freed from the dictates of network TV programmers. VCRs conquered the time barrier because you could see TV shows on your own schedule. What was called "time shifting."

In reality, not too many people watched TV shows on their own schedule since the timers on VCRs were a textbook case of user unfriendliness. Instead, the VCR became a home movie theater using prerecorded tapes. Viewing time was not a barrier — pop in a cassette and you were at the movies. Rentals from dedicated video stores were the business model. The tape was a physical thing that required two trips to the store: one to rent and the other to return. It took a bit of planning, or personal programming, as to what you would be watching, and when. Tape rental turned out to be a great business because people often didn't (or couldn't) watch their movies within the prescribed time limit and incurred "late fees." At the peak of the tape-rental business, up to 40% of a typical video store's revenue was generated by late charges.

VCRs, and a decade later, DVDs, meant viewers had the capability to control the content and schedule of what they wanted to watch. However, they were still limited by place. TVs and VCRs were not terribly portable. It was not a combo you took with you in the car or the train to watch on the way to work. Watching at work would probably be a firing offense for most people anyway. So the world of TV watching generally stopped at your front door.

For most people, then, watching movies on their VCR or DVD player was still a nighttime activity subject to physical limits. There was still a balance between entertainment time and work time. The content choices were better, but the ratio of entertainment to work was not substantially changed.

However, there were some rather odd cultural changes percolating among the kids of the 80s and 90s. The world's first "any-time-you-want-to-watch" generation started indulging in an unhealthy habit.

They would watch the same movies or prerecorded shows on their VCR or DVD players over and over and over again. These kids had collections of movies. Personal collections. It used to be that kids could only see a movie at the theater and then maybe again at some later time, interrupted by commercials, on TV. These new children now had Disney and Snoopy at their beck and call, and would watch their videos over and over again.

I don't quite understand why these tots would want to do that. Perhaps it was linked to a child's natural neophobia, like wanting macaroni and cheese for every meal or not having foods touch each other on the plate. Generally, parents were glad to have their children glued down to one place for an hour and not watching commercial TV. I consider myself among the guilty on this count. Was this only a quirky behavior of the childhood psyche or was there something more fundamental changing in the way a generation thought about media? Were we about to see an epidemic of self-administering media addicts?

The Rise of Generation E

Now these same digital children are in their 20s. They are the first digital generation: "Generation E." The Net made "E" a common prefix. Originally it stood for "electronic." Now, given the pervasiveness of video and music content on the Net, and the amount bandwidth it is consuming, we might want to make the "E" stand for "entertainment."

The current millennial generation has been completely swaddled in entertainment and is the most pervasively entertained since the indulgent royals of centuries past. They are truly "Generation E."

Earlier generations have always been emotionally tied to "their" music. It was a cultural communications system apart from the mainstream media that fueled social revolution. Each generation owned its own music and outraged the previous generation who had "their" music. Generation E is different; for one thing "their" music is every music. They can choose from everything ever recorded and download it in a few seconds along with decades' worth of films that are also available online as well as on DVDs.

On the positive side, this emerging generation has the potential for an amazing cultural literacy. On the negative side, there are only so many hours in the day; if you spend a lot of time watching, you are probably spending less time creating and being productive. They are the music and video-on-demand generation. Their gateways to digital entertainment are their computers and phones. Ostensibly bought for doing schoolwork, they are complete with music and DVD players. Students no longer need a TV or stereo at all. They download music and clips from their favorite TV shows, or whatever video pops up on the viral shared-video sites. Full movie downloading is increasingly part of the picture, as is trading and ripping DVDs.

Where going to college once meant getting together with friends for an on-campus movie screening in some lecture hall or going to a funky revival/art movie house with a date, entertainment now involves sitting around in your dorm room. Chances are there is abundant junk food to go along with the lack of physical activity.

It breaks down into different entertainment modes between the sexes. The guys are busy working their thumbs on video games and drinking "energy" drinks; the girls cluster in small groups watching chick flicks over and over again while eating sugary junk food. With a DVD-capable laptop and a net connection, the college dorm room has become an extension of the multiplex theater. The main difference is that entertainment can occur on a 24/7 basis.

Among the general population as well, work and entertainment is getting out of balance in this digital magic age. The time of day and your location are no longer barriers to having the entertainment you want. If there is a LCD screen on your computer, phone, gas pump, and supermarket checkout line, you've got a viewing surface that can host entertainment.

In the workplace, which could use some levity, viral video watching and music downloads are hogging business bandwidth to the point that computer-system managers are adding devices that prioritize network traffic to filter out the music and video content. In terms of the work-to-entertainment ratio on corporate networks, entertainment is swamping business usage. Network technology marketeers are selling businesses pricey new hardware to control these network traffic jams. The same company can sell both the problem and the solution. It's like doctors peddling you an illness so they can sell you the cure later on.

Entertainment is Good Business

What does any entertainment, anytime, anyplace mean?
It means M-O-N-E-Y – LOTS OF IT!

Entertainment was the very first modern intermediated business and created the economic model for the computer software industry that followed it. For the entertainment "industry," the emergence of an always-on environment is like getting a license to print money. Movies made 50 years ago collect $3.99 a pop for being viewed on a cell phone. These are films whose production costs were amortized decades ago, when movie tickets were 50 cents. Intellectual properties such as movies and music can live forever in the digital realm and deliver cash long after everyone involved in creating the work has been dead for decades. The 24-hour marketplace of downloads and streams creates increased time to sell more media experiences without having to share the revenue with retailers. Even the most inept and self-absorbed studio executives can't screw this one up. Perhaps the most famous financial disaster in movie history, *Heaven's Gate*, will wind up breaking even in the digital world. The biggest turkeys in Hollywood can eventually find a profitable cult market, even if it takes decades. Anything is possible.

Movies and music are good business. In spite of management regimes facing brutal turnovers, a colossal new-product failure rate, and cluelessness when it comes to understanding technology, there is no way they can fail, given the unique creative assets they possess.

If you browse the business news, you'll notice that moguls are always eager to invest in the entertainment business. Although some of it might be about finding their way onto the red carpet with some glamorous cinematic deity, it's mainly because of the particular economics of the entertainment media.

It is an economic model that defies common sense. Mass-media technology makes it possible to manufacture something, sell it, and still have it to sell all over again. Compare this to making a car. To sell a car, you need to make a car. To sell another car, you would need to make another car, incurring the requisite costs. You make money on the margins as you create and ship physical objects. To make more money you have to make more cars. The economics of mass media defies common sense. Basically you can have your cake, eat it infinite times and paradoxically, still have it!

(A Brief Chauvinistic Aside)

In certain respects, we in the U.S. should be delighted that the entertainment business is so amazingly vital. Movies, music, and games are among the few products made in the U.S. that actually deliver a trade surplus to the economy. We are the overwhelming champions at producing entertainment. Our media crosses all borders and is welcomed all over the world.

Entertainment is our greatest export because of our greatest import - people. Americans have come from all over the world to form a fusion culture unlike any other nation. The world enters our cultural kitchen and creates endless new flavors of entertainment. It is our cultural diversity that is our greatest strength in creating engaging entertainment. Other advanced nations — France and Japan, for instance — just don't have the same ability to become truly global because they are proudly and stubbornly monocultural at their core.

Ours is a common human experience infused from all the world's peoples, which is why our creative media resonates so well in the world. When it comes to entertainment, we are definitely the world power (even if we still harbor some sense of cultural inferiority toward the mothership of the UK.) It also helps that we have invented most of the core hardware of mass media, as well: TV, radio programs, phonographs, sound on film, satellite TV, video tape recording, the personal computer, and the web all are products of our culture.

Make It Once, Sell It Over and Over... Forever!

Media purveyors early on, hit on an amazing formula. They just needed to make one movie or one recording, and then sell it an infinite amount of times. No matter how many times it's played, 20th Century Fox still owns *Star Wars*. No matter how many pressings are generated, Epic (now Sony) still owns *Thriller*.

This is the formula that makes media moguls and a select circle of entertainers exceedingly rich. The early moviemakers learned quickly that all those nickels added up to much more than the few thousand dollars it took to make and distribute a movie. It is economics like this that made Charlie Chaplin — who was a businessman as well as an artist — a millionaire back in the 1910s. As an example, The Tramp was made on a few sunny days in 1914, then seen by a hundred million people, yielding amazing returns. Even at one cent a viewing that would equal a million dollars. Films such as these continue earning money up to this day.

Today, the cost of copying films or pressing discs is relatively small, compared to the profit stream generated thereby. With digital delivery, even those manufacturing costs are eliminated, and there's no need to share revenue with the retailers — in this case, the movie theatres and record stores. (Whatever happened to record stores anyway?)

Music and movies made 70 years ago are still delivering revenues to entertainment companies, though not to their creators, who have long since passed from the scene. Selling 1940 media at 2010 prices is a pretty nifty proposition, especially if the cost of production was paid in 1940 dollars. All you need to do is make DVD copies, or put it on a video server for a few cents and collect another $19.95. The production costs have Gone with the Wind but the revenues from DVD, downloads, and cable are still streaming in.

Late in the last century we saw the emergence of a similar model in the software business. Bill Gates and his band of mirthless coders needed only to make one somewhat functional version of Windows and then go out and sell it hundreds of millions of times. The math is obvious. That's how you get $80 billion in just 15 years.

So here we have entertainment/mass media companies that are constantly merging, each owning 60, 70, 80 years' worth of entertainment content: huge libraries of movies and music that basically cost them nothing. Even as they blunder blindly through executives and technology, they wind up sitting on their imperishable assets. And now they have more channels through which they can sell their wares than they're probably capable of imagining.

Instead of one weekend trip to the movies, you can have a movie or two every night. Why limit it to the night? You can take your entertainment on the plane or the train, to work or to class. The goal for modern media empires is to keep the money flowing by filling as many of your finite 24 hours as possible with their virtually infinite resources. At least, that is the dream of the big media intermediators and marketeers.

So, Is Everyone Happy?

With so much entertainment available we must have a citizenry that is deliriously happy — or seriously distracted. With only 24 hours in the day, and more of that time spent on "entertainment," what is it that we will be giving up? What activities are put out of balance or surrendered completely?

There are at least four areas where there are obvious deficiencies:

1. Not interacting enough with others
2. Consuming instead of creating
3. Not experiencing "the here and now"
4. Excluding randomness and ambience

Not Interacting with Others

Originally, entertainment took place in a shared environment. It was as much about people gathering together in one place as it was about the show itself. It was a common experience to sing, laugh, or be scared together. Going to the movies or to a concert is still appealing because a shared experience carries a huge emotional impact. A funny movie seems funnier in a room full of people laughing than it is when you are watching it on your phone. A concert, whether at the symphony or at a stadium, is a hugely interactive experience: You can respond to performers in real time, then have a drink and chat with your fellow concertgoers in the lobby.

With the advent of the Walkman and lightweight headphones, people started to become islands of personal entertainment. They became more cut off from the people around them. Certainly having a conversation with someone wearing headphones is frustrating and annoying for both parties, though for different reasons.

When commuting on a train, it's comforting to have your own personal sonic island to either excite or soothe you. However, when you are listening to music, you are partly removed from the physical environment in which you find yourself. If you have five senses, at least 20% — and probably more, given the importance of hearing — of your consciousness will be missing.

You become socially removed since you are no longer verbally interacting with other passengers. A conversation with a seat partner is out of the question. That could be good or bad. If your seatmate is like John Candy's character in *Trains, Planes & Automobiles*, it may not be readily apparent whether that was bad or good. What would be unfortunate is missing out on the random human experience of speaking with a total stranger and learning something completely new, or being able to tell the other person about the things you feel passionate about. (Just avoid using the phrase "criss cross" on a train while talking to strangers.)

Your time crossing paths with another person can be serendipitous and valuable — emotionally, intellectually, and for many people, financially — if you have shared interests. Yet if you are off in a trance of tunes or video clips you will never know what opportunities you have missed. To this day, I have friends and memories of others that I met on public transit systems. If I were ensconced — sonically cocooned, as it were — I never would have met these people.

So maybe random conversations with strangers are not your cup of joe. What about interactions with those who are a little closer to home — say your own family?

A Pod of One's Own

The most ubiquitous devices of our decade are probably cell phones, iPods, and "smart" phones. For teens, these devices mean personal music without records, tapes, and CDs to clutter up their room, not to mention (especially to legal authorities!) a way to share music.

There are people who have grown from teenagers to twenty-somethings with iPod ear buds firmly in place. Some of them are now parents of young children. I'm aware that one generation of parents tends to criticize the next generation of parents as a matter of course. This is usually born from a combination of envy and some sense of our own failures as their parents. That being said, "What's the matter with parents these days?"

One disturbing trend concerns young mothers and their babies. Lately, I am seeing these mothers strolling their babies and toddlers on city streets and in supermarkets with the telltale white iPod earbuds stuck in their young parental ears.

This is problematic on two counts. The first is that this audio input reduces awareness about the environment through which these young families are moving. Their impairment reduces awareness of auditory threats and hazards. It seems counter-intuitive to buy a hypersafe over-engineered Euro-stroller while moving your child around in public with one of your key senses diminished.

The second, and possibly more important, concern is that children learn to speak by hearing a constant stream of language from their parents. We speak to them in simple sweet chatter. For a while it is like talking to the dog. However, unlike the dog, pretty soon they start learning to use the language they are hearing. Children learn language by hearing a constant stream of language from parents. When they are babies we talk to them, even though we know they are not going to talk back. (That comes somewhat later, in spades.)

Is it really more important to be entertained than to have this most critical interaction with your child? You'll only have one chance to engage in these primal and bonding parent/child interactions. The music you are listening to will be around forever. The long-term effects should also be considered: Having Daddy or Mommy preoccupied with Lady Gaga while you're gurgling your very first words may cost somebody therapy bills down the road.

Back-Seat Strangers

They are sheer torture. They are joyous memories. Road trips. The ultimate shared parent/child experience. The road trip is not just about getting from point A to point B. It, like most of life, it is about the journey itself. Looking out the window onto an unfamiliar world. Seeing life other than the one you live in every day — and seeing it all unfiltered and unedited. No special effects. The boring and the exciting coexisting for young minds to tolerate and interpret, remember and forget. This is the true widescreen of life. Compare that to the narrow field of experience your child receives through a video or computer screen. In the universe of human experiences, TV is a black hole where no life escapes. If you were going to use technology to create a better life for your children, your first thought would probably not be "Ya know, my kid just doesn't get to watch enough TV. Gotta fix that."

So why on earth are we putting back-seat video systems in cars? This may be one of the stupidest ideas ever conceived. It wasn't an issue back a few years ago when picture tubes were implosive and not exactly what you'd want in front of your kids' faces while driving on the interstate. With the arrival of the cheap LCD screen, the physical hazard disappeared, but the mental hazard has only grown.

Too Much Magic

TV and video have always been considered electronic babysitters. Do you really need that babysitter when your kids are actually with you? Kids will squirm and complain on long car trips. So what? Adults do, too. What kids actually crave is engagement, not pacification. Gluing their eyes to a video screen and plugging their little heads with earbuds is exactly the wrong thing for them. All you are doing is extending their addiction to entertainment and cutting them off from the critical interactions they need to engage in. They become even more hooked on prepackaged entertainment products and disengaged from the cause and effect of the real world.

Kids need to learn that not every aspect of life is "fun" or intended solely for their entertainment. They need some time and space to figure out how to engage their own minds. Are all the games that kids have played in the back seat for generations — including the eternal "Out-of-State License Plate" and "Punch Buggy" — doomed to extinction? They need to prepare themselves for a journey, not plug in and vanish from their surroundings into a Hollywood video confection.

A road trip is one of the few opportunities when the nucleus of the family is in one place at one time, interacting with each other, physically unified, and headed in a common direction. It is both metaphor and reality. You are creating lifetime memories as you share a journey of discovery. All the giving, taking, arguing, and negotiating are inescapable; there is no exit to another room to be swaddled in distraction and self-indulgence. A road trip is an indelible life experience.

Even the daily drive to school is a great time to chat, play the radio, sing together, explain the news or have a good private talk. Both of you need this interaction. You need this time to learn about each other. Life is short and time with your kids is even shorter. If your kids have to choose between talking with you and watching video, you're going to lose. In the long run, you both will lose. So tell the car salesman to put those LCD screens up *his* back seat.

Jason Benlevi

The Invasion That Went Unreported

The Roswell Incident, the purported UFO crash in the New Mexico desert, fired the imagination of post-WW II moviemakers. Not content merely to exploit the McCarthyite "Red Threat" emanating from the war-hobbled Soviet Union, the American film industry unleashed paranoia from above with new enemies from outer space. We were visited by Invaders from Mars and other denizens intent on destroying our "American Way of Life."

The best of these movies, one which actually broke the mold, was a film called *The Day the Earth Stood Still*. Yes, it had the usual elements: the sleek saucer descending in Washington, the befuddled world leaders, and the macho, but clueless military lobbing firepower at alien, robot, and spaceship to no avail. In what turned out to be a prophetic scene, an extended family sits in near-darkness, illuminated only by the glow of a TV set. Then the alien, played by the dashing Michael Rennie, appears out of the shadows. What terrible presence has invaded that room, spreading fear and interrupting family life? Here's a clue. It wasn't the guy from another planet. It was that other new arrival in the room. The TV.

The postwar period was a time when we faced great invasions both real and imagined. Among imagined threats there was the four-letter variety (U-S-S-R) and the three-letter variety (U-F-O). However, the real invasion was identified by only two letters: T-V. This culprit in our living rooms hindered family members from talking to each other and dominated dinner with its unblinking eye. What we got in return was a false intimacy with Uncle Milty, Uncle Walter, and leagues of white-coated men who recommended cigarettes as a boon for our health and social desirability.

A few years later, when I was a teen, watching broadcast TV was an act of desperation. Something to do when you were so utterly bored or lonesome that sitting in front of the idiot box was the only option available. What you saw was other people having enviable adventures and getting into fun/trouble. As a baby boomer stranded

75

in the suburbs, your TV was a periscope telling you that there was a larger world out there — unfortunately, its representation was mostly fictional. In the suburban cocoon, it was either watch TV, with at most a half-dozen channels available, or get high. Or get high and watch TV, which somehow transformed old movies like Busby Berkley musicals into something almost incomprehensibly brilliant (at least to my teenaged mind).

Paradoxically, the first TV generation held its social revolution by tuning out of TV entirely. The "turned on" generation turned off the TV because the social revolution was not being televised. In the parlance of the day, only the "co-opted" version of hip culture showed up on the tube, usually clad in wacky tie-die attire with actors using the word "man" as both punctuation and pronoun. For the most part, we boomers were out doing stuff. Social change — and socializing — took place on the street, in the parks, on campus and in shared dwellings. It was about dancing and moving around. The "movement" was indeed imbued with movement. At any rate, the TV was definitely not "where it was at," nor were the kids sitting in front of it, either separately or together.

Co-Watching: TV as Unsocial Medium

We now come to a crucial question: Is watching TV a fundamentally social or unsocial experience?

It must be said that TV can be useful for people who are confined to their homes by physical circumstances as a reasonable proxy for experiencing the world community. Although local news shows and their "if it bleeds, it leads" editorial approach can make the world seem like a more dangerous place than it actually is, still there is programming that can truly open their world.

If, however, you are normally active and not sidelined by age or health issues, it is hard to imagine what social benefit there is to being parked for hours in front of a TV. Yet this is exactly where most of us are sitting, for longer and longer stretches.

We've already examined TV's babysitter function. What happens later? Between the ages of 14 and 24, you are consumed by your social life. You pick TV shows according to what your peers watch. It is the raw research material you need to be part of the social dialogue at school. You need to know what happened in the last episode of whatever au courant series depicts precociously sexual teens and their soap-opera lives. What's baffling is that this age group has turned watching TV together into a social activity. Instead of going out and hanging out, many are opting for just watching. And what are they watching? Reality shows! Yes. They are watching someone else's "real life" instead of having one.

Who are the top models? Idols? Bachelors? Decorators? Rock stars? Who's the winner and who's the pathetic loser? Young viewers are eager to pass judgment, and it's ridiculously easy to make derisive comments about contestants from the safety of the couch. Yet even the "losers" on these shows are comparative winners; at least they got off the couch and got out there, striving, taking chances. Contrast these folks to their stridently opinionated — and thoroughly passive — audience vegetating on a comfortable sofa with remote and cell phone at hand. Talk about "American Idle."

The sad fact is that TV has been invited to the party and it is not a good guest. It dominates the conversation. It has the loudest voice and it cannot listen and interact. When TV becomes the center of social interaction, chances are that the TV is the funniest one in the room, the one with the most memorable lines, and the one that commands the most attention.

This "co-watching" model is social life built around watching rather than doing. There is an important difference here. Doing creates your own memories. Watching creates no memories of your own life. You were not there. When you are sharing a memory of a show you've watched together, rather than what you've done together, it seems a bit pathetic. Where are you in the picture? It's like buying a new wallet and keeping the generic photos that are included as your own.

As if the prevalence of shared viewing weren't bad enough, there is a new trend: co-watching in the same place but with different media. Everyone is sitting around together watching their own show. Laughter comes in asynchronous waves. For once, TV is not the culprit. Laptops and mobile phones have enabled this dubious practice.

Lately, I've seen couples sitting in cafes, mainly twenty-somethings, each wearing a set of earbuds, each using the café's Wi-Fi connection to watch their own selection of YouTube clips or video streams.

The best thing that can be said about this co-watching experience is that these viewers are not talking to each other at a movie theater. It is a small blessing for the rest of us.

Even More of the Same Sameness

Around the prehistoric campfire, the ratio of creators to consumers was rather modest — one or two storytellers among a few dozen spectators. Today, the ratio has exploded to become one author, one singer, or one movie star known to hundreds of millions of people. It is this scale that has made entertainers stratospherically rich. All it takes is one recorded performance; there are hundreds of millions of consumers eager to part with their cash to get an eye or earful. With aging stars reprising action roles well into their social security years, and endless sequels, new faces and new material are not a requirement. In fact, they're sometimes disadvantageous, as people around the world prefer the known entertainer playing his/her branded role to anything new and unusual, regardless of merit.

With originality undervalued, the "Disney Version" becomes the pervasive model. For years, Disney has taken stories from our common folk heritage and converted them into "brands" that saturate movie screens, airtime, toy stores, and fast-food joints. With the exception of the Pixar films, Disney animation "events" generally take stories that are in the public domain and create a "marketeer-friendly" version perfectly formulated for endless merchandising.

Disney's forte was and is cultural claim-jumping, exploiting stories that are already part of folklore. You can look at this two ways: The folks at Disney are universal storytellers disseminating tales that everyone can relate to; or, alternatively, they have created high-volume homogenized versions that blast the originals and all their subtleties out of sight and mind. My view is the latter.

The Entertainment Invasion

These Disney Versions appear everywhere in the world. They crowd out other storytelling and drown out other voices. It's not that Disney stories are any better told (most of them have an identical formulaic story arch and set of character archetypes); it is simply that their marketing is so overwhelming that everything else recedes to the background. Every now and then someone lucks out with a *Harry Potter*, but, generally, Disney reigns supreme.

Along these same lines, the sequel has run amok as branded entertainment. Not to mention dreary remakes of decades-old TV shows. It's a sad state of affairs for what should be a creative business.

Mass entertainment is like fast food. Just as McDonald's, Lays, and Budweiser wiped out food regionalism — huge mega media is destroying storytelling on a global scale.

It's not just a global problem; it's a problem as local as your kid's bedroom. Think about what your kids know. What stories are they familiar with? What toys are they playing with? They are actively discouraged from being storytellers in their own right by the steamroller of big media. My daughter is a prime example. As I mentioned earlier, when she was little she had her own explanation for the natural forces at work in the world. But after exposure to Disney and McDonalds, her fanciful imaginings began to fade into imitations of the Little Mermaid, Aladdin, Pongo, and Perdita.

Then, as the child grows and schoolwork starts to mount, there occurs a final departure from making up songs, writing stories, and drawing pictures. Ridicule for wasting time on such trivialities rains down from peers. We move on to buying our entertainment — the legitimate name-brand stuff, that is. Although we seem to have agreed early in our evolution that, for the most part, professionals would specialize in creating entertainment, it's evident that people would be happier if they were granted some license to be creative instead of just consuming.

In our society we deride those who strive to be artists; they are only "would-be" writers, "aspiring" actors, and "amateur" musicians until they are branded as successes. Artists are the crazy people whose urge to create supersedes the prohibitions of authority. These were the class clowns, the daydreamers, egoists, and people who just couldn't live any other way. It is not a path for the timid — or even the particularly sane — because success has no direct relationship to talent.

Given the global digital entertainment marketplace, the top of the pyramid is a narrow place, and it's hard to dislodge the top financial performers. So we have ancient Rolling Stones and Eagles filling arenas well past the point when they are creative, culturally relevant, or even particularly entertaining.

The relationship between brand and success is hard to prove absolutely. Are Spielberg movies big hits because he is a better filmmaker, or are they hits because his name is attached to them? Now with multinationals as masters of all media — print, web, and screen — it will be harder to find out, since so much money is vested in the success of big-name talent. Formula is clearly running the big casino of the entertainment business.

There is, however, some hope. One of the truly positive things about the digital age is that suddenly people have the tools to create their own entertainment again. They can become original storytellers. HD cams, desktop recording, and editing are all relatively inexpensive and don't have a prohibitively steep learning curve. This means more people can create, and it may be possible for new voices and visions to emerge — at least for now. Unfortunately, it also means that there is way more to watch and listen to, and there are only so many hours in the day. The problem remains that a huge part of our population will find more distractions and excuses to do nothing in the real world.

Experiencing the Here and Now (Being a First Person Again)

We like entertainment because it gives us an escape: an hour or two of being transported elsewhere, walking in someone else's shoes. When we watch a movie we suspend disbelief and enter a hypnotic trance where we believe that we are in another space and time, experiencing a life other than our own. Unfortunately, we have no impact on the experience.

The Entertainment Invasion

Most modern forms of entertainment are vicarious. Your real life is a first-person experience. It is about being here, now. It is about doing tangible things, moving through space, and using all your senses.

Although some escape can be welcome, the problem is excessive time stolen from your first-person life. If your own existence is troubled, sitting in front of the TV isn't going to make your situation any better. The top part of your life's hourglass is trickling away; that time would be better spent in your first-person world enjoying your own experiences.

Entertainment is no substitute for living. A movie or TV show doesn't care about you; it exists without and beyond you. Yet you surrender your limited time on the planet to it. How much of your life is wasted sitting in front of a TV, watching shows or movies where you could predict every plot twist and line of dialogue? Ross and Rachel are not your friends, they are a re-run.

In reality, we have our highest level of pleasure when we are "in the moment," engaging our whole being with all of our senses: playing sports; having sex; sightseeing; parachute jumping; cooking and tasting great food. The good times you have watching movies or TV are actually all borrowed: You watch someone else doing something while you just sit there. It's true that you can get a glimpse of things outside your normal life and that great movies can be inspiring and exciting, but in the end it is a highly inter-mediated experience.

It's striking to watch a sporting event on the tube among beer-guzzling fans who scream "we won" when the local team is victorious, as if they themselves made the plays, took the hits, or participated in the process. It's worse yet to hear the same overfed observers castigate players for not hustling when they haven't seen their own toes for a decade. In these instances, when the team scores, they haven't done anything. They've won nothing. Touched nothing. Moved nothing. Accomplished nothing. They are completely outside of having any impact on the experience. They are along for the ride. They might get a vicarious thrill, but all they did, really, is sit there.

In general, entertainment requires too much watching and too little participation to be a truly satisfying experience. It feeds the eyes and ears but the rest of our body and senses are left behind. That may be why snacking in front of the TV, at a sports event, or at the movies is such a huge part of the experience. (The modern multiplex could be regarded as nothing more than a fast-food restaurant with screens.) Our senses are screaming for something to do while we sit there as motionless experiential passengers. As we move inexorably toward always-on entertainment, we could easily become even more passive, sensation deprived, and intermediated out of the real world.

There is now some evidence that this change may already be taking place. Contrast the antiwar activities of the 60s with Generation E's approach. Students today share clever anti-war videos on YouTube, but there is little action in the real world. The streets were on fire in the 60s. Now they are silent. America's longest war is steadily consuming the bodies of Generation E's own, yet the response is little more than creating and sharing entertainment experiences. That seems an inadequate and detached response. The powers that be are undoubtedly satisfied to see dissenting opposition occurring in a box that can be switched off remotely, happy with this generation of Chauncey Gardners who "just like to watch."

One thing that seems to be a constant in both eastern and western philosophies is the idea of happiness resulting from being in the moment and experiencing life with all your senses.

Think about the joyous moments of your own life: wandering in a new place; trying new foods; meeting and talking with new people; walking into a forest and hearing the sounds emerge from the silence; the wind and sun on your face when you ride a bike; someone's gentle touch on your body; the subtle scents wafting from the ocean, a potential paramour, or a bakery. Even the sound and smell of terror while you wait at the dentist's is different when you are there, in that moment.

Compare watching fireworks on TV versus being there. On a screen you miss the percussive feeling in your chest, the scale of the sky's void filled with fiery color, the crowd's "oohs" and "aahs," the smoky scent in the air. You just need to be there.

So what will you remember in your life? Will the most memorable scenes be what you saw on TV or will they be from your own life?

What will you be doing with the rest of your senses while you are slumped in a couch watching TV? Judging from current trends, the chances are good you'll be eating junk food — stuff that people barely taste or experience outside of the movement of their jaws against some sort of crunchy texture. Munching is becoming the only interactivity connected to the viewing experience.

Even powered by hundreds of watts, big screens, and 7.1 sound, watching TV creates a sense of memory not unlike those generic portraits in your new wallet. There is no evidence of your interaction with the world. You have affected nothing. You don't exist. On the other hand, try doing nothing and you might be amazed at how interesting the experience can actually become.

The Joy of Randomness

Randomness is a good thing. It is the opposite of "on-demand" culture that the Cult of Tech is promoting. On-demand is a way to bring you a "top-of-mind" product so you can consume it. And the only reason it's top-of-mind is that some marketeer made it so. On-demand gives people control, but narrows their scope and exposure to what they already know. If the only flavor ice cream you know about is vanilla, you will demand vanilla. Cherry Garcia would not be top of mind. You don't know what you don't know.

Randomness, on the other hand, presents you what you may not know or think about — a surprise. Welcome to the delight of serendipity. From all indications, existence itself is a product of serendipity, a happy accident. It's this same random creative force that makes life interesting, unpredictable, and ever changing.

Apple made a clever move when they introduced the iPod Shuffle. Creating a display and control for a player that tiny was not a practical solution. Their response uses randomness as a selling point. As they said "Life is Random." Last I checked, I think they sold a few iPod Shuffles.

There's a tradition in the great restaurants of Europe whereby you do not order, but rather put yourself in the hands of the chef, to let him surprise and delight you. Roasted drunken little birds may not be to your taste, but how would you know if you never got the opportunity to try the dish. The idea of discovery is based on not knowing what you are looking for. If Columbus had India-on-demand, we'd all still be living on other continents. Many of us owe our good health to some random mold invading a science experiment to yield penicillin.

Randomness can bring inspiration. In Bob Dylan's book, *Chronicles*, he writes about his parents moving into a house where the previous owners had left behind a record player that he quickly claimed. When he opened it, he found a folk-music record, a style completely unknown to him as a teenager in Minnesota. It was an unexpected and serendipitous gift. Suddenly he was exposed to something new. It showed him a new world, one that eventually led him to open other new worlds to millions. Artists and other creative people hunger for inspiration and have developed the sensibilities to treasure randomness as source material.

It is actually a good thing that we will have access to much more variety in the digital world. Unfortunately, the other side of the coin is that many people, when confronted with a multiplicity of choices, will seek what they are already familiar and comfortable with.

Perhaps this is the difference between two personality types: those who seek comfort and familiarity and those who seek novelty and inspiration. The digital realm becomes an amplifier of both tendencies.

Seeking Balance

The fundamental question as digital technology extends the reach of entertainment is how to keep it in balance. If our eyes and ears are too busy with screens and headphones, we are going to miss out on the life around us. We will never have the quiet time to let our own thoughts emerge and develop.

There is a truism that people do their best thinking in the shower. There is a reason for that. It's just you, literally stripped bare, warmed by the water and immersed in the white noise of the flowing stream. There your mind is free to wander, randomly, undistracted. It is primal, like those ancients looking up at the sky in the night.

Contrast that with the noise that comes at you on a daily basis, the sounds and sights that invade your time and space, specifically focused on trying to get you to buy things that you probably don't need. We need more time in the figurative shower and less in front of the literal TV.

2.2

InCELLated:
The Mobility Bubble

Disruptive Technology Is Calling

Among the Cult of Tech there is always talk about "disruptive technologies." They use the term positively to describe developments that create massive changes to the status quo and, therefore, business opportunities for them. However, if you have been in a restaurant or movie theater where cell phones are buzzing away, you know technology can be a disrupter in another sense. And it's not only obtrusive noise; people are now staring into the palm of their hands for the latest word on their "smart" phones as they move blindly through public spaces. So it's obvious how someone else's device can disturb you, but have you ever thought about the disruption your own mobile phone might bring into your life?

Mobile communications have triggered huge changes in our behavior. Even the most technically challenged can master the cell phone without much difficulty. The handsets themselves are on the steepest upgrade trajectory we've ever witnessed in technology product. With faster product cycles, the hottest model becomes the down-market version in just a year or two, and garbage a year after that. It has become more like buying fashion accessories or cheap sunglasses than buying a TV or a computer. Mobile phones are the most personal digital technology ever; always at hand, they are worn close to the body and often custom outfitted. Indeed, for some people, especially teens, cell phones have become a huge statement about self.

With near-universal connectivity, we are experiencing the emerging dichotomy of instant connection with people at distant locations, while simultaneously becoming less connected with our immediate physical location. Talking on the phone is the earliest form of telepresence. However, you cannot truly be "present" in multiple locations. Beyond the obvious physics problem, the governing human factor is that we have a finite amount of attention.

Although our attention is easily divided by technology, no technology can augment our attention capacity. As we try to do more things at the same time, we do them less well. Meaningful conversation takes an enormous amount of attention. A phone conversation requires even more focus, since you are not looking at the person to whom you are speaking, and reading visual cues and expressions. Other tasks during phone conversations either become secondary or performed by reflex.

Consider that stage magicians use live subjects in tricks and depend on their conversation in order to divert the audience's attention and hide the process of the trick, even though they are situated in full view of the proceedings. Distraction is powerful.

When there were only wire-line phones it didn't matter that you were distracted since you weren't going anywhere. You were cocooned at home or at work. It is a different matter when you are free to roam and to attempt to do other tasks at the same time. Now you carry your conversational cocoon around with you, and that becomes problematic.

Now Entering the State of *InCellation*

Being inCellated is the paradoxical state of being in touch with someone at a distance while being totally out-of-touch with your immediate surroundings. It is a digital cocoon.

A cell phone creates a radically different state of mind than a wired telephone. You carry it around, wear it, customize the ring tone, have it to recognize your voice. You share it with no one. Your cell phone is your phone. It is an extension of you. (Ask any teenager.) No matter where you are, or what you are doing, you have everything you want, at your beck and...call. Order pizza. Get movie tickets. Reach a friend. Have telesex. In contrast, you never personalized a ringtone for your phone at home. Think of the product names marketeers use — MyVerizon, iPhone, MobileMe, Personal Communicator — and it's clear they know how to pull your emotional triggers. "Me-Mine-My-I." This egocentric model engenders insularity, putting the user in a state of inCellation.

While users are inCellated, they are connecting with someone at a distance and unwittingly experiencing a diminished capacity in the space where they are physically present. It can be expressed as mechanical incapacity or social dysfunction like bad driving or extreme rudeness in public spaces. There are myriad studies attesting the inattentiveness of the mobile-telephonically engaged. But you don't need studies to know this. You have witnessed it, perhaps been frustrated by it — even been guilty of it.

For example, there's the chatty driver who seems to have forgotten he's maneuvering three tons of steel against the red light among unarmored urban pedestrians. Or the egocentric loudmouths in restaurants and cafes who spiel away on their handsets, while everyone around them is rendered invisible or incidental because the caller is inCellated in their cocoon of "personal communications." What about those people walking by your house straining their vocal chords and your nerves as they "cell yell" obliviously? Do you pray for open manhole cover to appear beneath their feet?

For mobile callers, people around them virtually cease to exist. A local barista I know refuses to serve customers while they are talking on their cell phones. He says it makes him feel "like a vending machine" since these folks are not personally engaged with him. And, because they aren't paying attention, they also aggravate the other customers by slowing down the line.

Despite the current belief that we can "multitask," we have to remember that the term itself came from the computing world, and that it was insanely hard to get computers to do multitasking. It's even more challenging for humans, despite our modicum of built-in ability to walk and chew gum at the same time. We actually have fairly strict limits on our capacity to do simultaneous conscious tasks. This is called the "attention budget" and it is finite. Again, we only have so much attention to share among tasks. Unlike computers, we are not going to be updated with a faster processor and more memory any time soon.

Middle-aged folks think that kids can multitask better. In reality they do more tasks faster with less attention and with compromised results. They are still subject to the same cognitive rules. If you are under the impression that teens are cognitively superior, just take a look at teen car-accident statistics.

Driving, of course, is the most obvious activity for demonstrating our failure to multitask. Studies show that cellular-communications activity while driving puts drivers' skills on a par with 80-year-olds and drunks. States are passing "hands-free laws" that mandate speakerphones or headsets while driving, but that doesn't really address the issue. The impairment isn't because hands aren't on the wheels, but rather because minds are not on roads. We all suspect this from our own experience; now numerous studies have proven it. These include a 2005 Insurance Institute of Highway Safety study that found drivers who talked on the phone had a 400% higher incidence of injurious accidents – and that was before mobile texting and web browsing had even reached the mainstream.

Is all of this talking and texting necessary, or can it just wait? Is the new normal to ping and buzz each other habitually? Habits often grow into addictions. For some, being "in touch" delivers a sense of power. Others gain comfort. Yet it also sacrifices time with our own thoughts or compromises in-person time with our friends and family.

Is there such a thing as being too much "in touch?" Does it undermine our self-reliance? Remember that all telecommunications are intermediated experiences and entirely reliant on the telecom server. So what happens to this "connected life" when the intermediator fails? Events in the news give some insight.

The Great Black(berry)Out

The Blackberry is a mobile communicator that is highly text-centric, with an easy-to-use keyboard. It has been a favorite of business, political, and media movers and shakers. The addictive power of the Blackberry is well known, as evidenced by its nickname,

"Crackberry." Admittedly, being in touch easily, with just a few taps on the ergonomic keyboard, is appealing. It's so simple: just push a few buttons, get a quick fix. Soon you can't get enough. Messages start to ping-pong. The ball returns to your court and you must volley. Get the last word in. Add one final zinger.

With the alleged security provided by Blackberry's parent company, RIM, government officials move all manner of secrets around among the knowing and powerful. President Obama would not give his up Blackberry, even after his election. In D.C. or Hollywood, surrendering a Blackberry would, like Charlton Heston surrendering his pistol, require cold dead hands.

There are myriad stories of post-coital situations with both partners still glowing and sweaty, yet yearning to get back to their respective Blackberrys. An adult with a Blackberry can be a like a tweener with a Gameboy. It becomes a preoccupation, an addiction from which withdrawal is painful.

This pain became apparent on February 11, 2008 — a dark day indeed for those in the habit of gazing into their palms to divine all that is important in the world. Although it had nothing to do with palmistry, the unfortunates did discover that their lifelines had suddenly vanished. Without warning, the uberconnected elite were suddenly among the disconnected class, flung onto the wrong side of the digital divide. All was lost: Their Blackberrys were dead.

It was the great Blackberry Blackout of 2008. What we learned in those hours would tell us a great deal about text and mobile communications. On that day, with a just few lines of erroneous computer code in their network, the Blackberry World had ended without a bang (but with plenty of whimpers — from customers). Blackberry was out of service, not just for few minutes but for many hours. That's like a year in Blackberry time.

In the end, the technical reasons for the blackout were irrelevant. Whether the code malfunction was the result of bad software or rats chewing through a power cord doesn't really matter. The interesting part was observing the most-connected, self-important people on the planet suddenly disconnected. Switched off. Unwired and unplugged.

Too Much Magic

The great 1965 New York City blackout taught us how the mass of people behave when technology fails on a grand scale. The birth rate soared nine months after the city went dark, proving that folks still remembered how to entertain themselves without staring at a TV tube. With technology in failure, people may pull apart or pull together, though not always as literally as this NY example.

The Blackberry Blackout, however, could be considered a cruel experiment on a limited set of powerful and privileged guinea pigs: self-proclaimed leaders and pundits, along with their retinue of cheerleaders and followers. This circle of players contained the earliest adopters of communications tech-pagers, cellphones, and wireless laptops. The high price of these services was a statement about one's self-importance as much as it was about utility. As these toys move downstream, and become commonplace, the status evaporates, but, unfortunately the problems, as foreshadowed by the blackout, remain.

Nobody died as a direct result of the blackout, but certainly there were high dramatics in high places — especially when money was involved. We know that thousands of Wall Street workers, bankers, and lawyers were left clueless, flying blind. One high roller was in the middle of a $1.3 billion deal. He was quoted in the paper as saying that it was "a real ball ache." (Just because you get to play with big money doesn't mean you're particularly eloquent.) A real-estate consultant from Atlanta, who was traveling on business at the time, said, "My blood ran cold! I was offline!" A national political reporter proclaimed, "It was like being underwater without an oxygen tank. It felt like every minute was an hour." One New York-based investment banker cried, "It's a total debacle. We can't send or receive e-mails, we can't browse the web. It's an absolute crisis." Obviously this person has never had a gun poked in his face, been homeless, or had his family swept away by a tsunami.

One positive result of the outage was that George W. Bush's advisors were rendered incommunicado. At least that was a few hours when they could do no further damage.

One blogger proclaimed, "Men with beards and sandals will be very interested to learn that Western civilization can be brought to its

Jason Benlevi

knees because those who run it are too stupid to pick up the phone or walk down the corridor." Indeed, wired phones, cell phones, and the normal email channels were still available and functioning. Just not that personal strap-on communicator called "Blackberry." So, ultimately, business deals were still made, news still found its way to the media, and lovers conducted rendezvous and quarrels through more traditional means, as they always have.

While for some the Great Black(berry)out was a curse, for others it was a delightful time(out). On Parliament Hill in Ottawa (capital of the country whence the Blackberry comes), instead of panic, the Liberal Party spokesman said "Things seemed very relaxed for a while." Oh yes. Relaxed. Remember that? Back before things were buzzing all the time. Back before "callus interruptus" became the common bane of social interaction.

Although they were initially thrown into disarray, Blackberry users soon found themselves freed from the endless ping-pong chatter and the "tag-you're-it" mode of conversation. They were no longer compelled to check. No longer compelled to compose, nothing was beeping for attention. People looked into each other's eyes at lunch instead of starring into their palms for enlightenment. Many who found themselves without service said they felt "liberated." For several hours, they were free from the digital monkey on their backs. It was as if some giant noisy fan was turned off, and everyone could hear the sound of the breeze moving around them again.

It was clear that this always-on communication model carries a certain burden. You get a message, you must respond. There is a social and perhaps a professional burden on you to reply promptly. The question is how much of this communication is as vital as we think it is? Once again, we come to the question that technology always poses. Just because we can, does that mean that we should?

How and why did mobile phones get so pervasive and invasive?

Was it a necessity, or was there an external force that drove the super-saturation of cell phones buzzing all around us?

Talk Got Cheap

The simple answer is that talk got cheap and very profitable. Yet again, it was digital magic. Then, as usual, the technology got ahead of the sociology, but those who were selling mobile communications services didn't really care.

People started out with cell phones as something to use in an "emergency." For some, it was truly an instrument of security, but for many more it was just a new toy.

In its infancy, long-distance telephony was expensive and used only for high-value calls. Likewise, the cell phone, at first, was just for important stuff, since phones and airtime were expensive. That's because the technology was analog and required lots of bandwidth. Only a few phones could be on the air at the same time within a "cell" (the area served by a small local ground station).

The cell phone market only took off when it went from analog to digital. Digital phones meant that it was possible to multiplex calls. Thousands of calls were able to be transmitted in the same few radio channels where, previously, only dozens could. Multiplexing meant that many phones could subdivide those scarce radio channels through cleverly sharing/dividing the time they were on the air, or by breaking up a channel into thousands of sub-channels. The sound of cell phones dramatically improved as well, because users were no longer listening to static and dead airtime.

Using the same network of radio towers, mobile phone service providers could serve many times more customers and leverage the infrastructure investment. It was all about economy of scale. Digital allowed rapid scaling up. To really make money, though, they needed a lot of users. Therefore, packages of cheap minutes and cheap phones were offered nationwide to individuals and families.

Early cell-phone company investors sold their start-ups to the major telecom companies, and cashed in big time. One bought a personal island, while another bought himself a seat in the U.S. Senate.

InCellated: The Mobility Bubble

As minutes of airtime continually got cheaper (almost free) the spigot was opened to talking all the time. It wasn't just about emergencies and business anymore. It was "do you think he likes me?" and "aren't these shoes cute?" and "whatup dude?" and...well, you get the idea.

In the beginning, parents bought their kids cell phones as a security device. Soon, however, kids and teens adopted it as the engine of their social lives, free (they think) from parental monitoring. Throw in long distance that was cheaper than "land-line" calling, and soon there were no barriers to talking to anyone, anywhere, anytime — regardless of the caller's social and financial circumstances. I've even witnessed homeless guys on the street chatting with one hand and begging with the other.

Walk around a supermarket where people talk while shopping and listen to the nature of the conversations. Clearly much of this chatter can wait. Is it eavesdropping when you can hear half the conversation two aisles away? No, because half the conversation has been put in the public ear. Frankly I'm amazed at what I hear people talking about in public. They are clearly unaware they're being overheard.

Then there is the silliness of guys with their Bluetooth earpiece indulging their Star Trek fantasies. From the look of these guys, they are all dressed up with no one to talk to. Sometimes I think they are talking to themselves and just need cover.

Finally, there remain some vestigial aspects from the "old days" of cell phones: the "look-at-me" self-importance, bluster, or urgency of the callers. Conversations that probably could — or should — wait to be made in private are freely conducted in public spaces.

What rapid progress has been made: we have an endless array of users that can't talk and drive, can't watch a movie without texting, and continue to cell yell in cozy restaurants. Cell phones themselves are brilliant things. It's unfortunate that many users aren't.

As socially dysfunctional as it appears, all is actually going according to plan. Telecom intermediators have created a huge mass market and have grown their customer base from a small elite to hundreds of millions of users who consider it a "necessity of life" and spend far in excess of what they were ever willing to pay for their land-line services. Mobile calling is now something that no one would be willing to be without. Try to think of anyone you know who, once having a cell phone, gave it up.

So Let's Make It Even Worse

Even though people have barely learned how to function with cell-phone calls in a public context, the units have morphed into mobile computers with email and web applications. The attention challenge grows. Instead of just talking, people are trying to do more complex tasks that require an even greater share of their finite attention, all while being mobile or in public situations. They move through space impaired, like zombies driving on Ambien.

To the growing army of insensitive public callers, add some new battalions: annoying self-absorbed gamers playing noisy phone-based shooter games on the bus; folks reading their text messages as they drive on winding country roads; and automotive texters hurtling down the freeway, unaware that their eyes cannot refocus fast enough from 18 inches to 50 feet ahead to avoid running over an errant deer, dog, child, or grandparent.

The inCellated society is an analog to the car-culture suburban society of the 20th century. Automobiles are capsules, designed to be autonomous and insular. Mobile communications devices create a similar metaphoric capsule for the user. Cars and mobile digital devices allow people to cross distances, while maintaining that comfy insular cocoon for the journey. People feel individually empowered, but physically encapsulated — until they literally run into someone.

In car-centric cities like L.A., people go from their home to their workplace and back home without ever coming face to face with another human being. Their experience excludes human ambience, environmental experiences, and chance encounters — unless you count fast-food drive-up windows. Your car is highly personalized. You carry your entertainment with you. You have things your way.

Contrast this to taking public transit or walking, where there are ambient and random encounters. You are moving at a pace that allows you to interact with the environment. You can pause to look in a shop window, strike up a conversation with a stranger, observe behaviors, and maybe even eavesdrop. If you are either plugged into your personal Bluetooth or hermetically sealed in your car, you experience none of this richness of life. You've got it your way and everyone else be damned. "Don't tell me I can't double park here!" "Don't tell me I can't talk on my phone in the movies!"

The trade off for communicating with anyone, anytime without regard for distance means less contact with immediate surroundings – being less in touch with where you are, insulated and cocooned.

Smart Phones: This Time, They've Got Your Number

Most new mobile phones (or so-called smart phones) include media features, such as cameras, music, and movie-playing software. They are becoming pocket entertainment devices and mobile-phone service providers are trying to position themselves as gatekeepers for the content. They are able to sell more airtime and/or sell the media itself. With a shrinking number of wireless providers, this emerging form of media is falling into the hands of fewer, and bigger, intermediators and marketeers.

As if you weren't already distracted enough, you can now fill every free second of your day with the same dreary formulaic entertainment found on the big screen or your flat panel at home. You can pay a ridiculous amount to see it on your thumb-sized screen. When your mobile phone becomes yet another entertainment conduit, it will also become an ideal way for marketeers to beam you messages. But wait! There is the promise of "free" entertainment as well.

For a moment let's suspend the idea that people are too distracted and don't need wall-to-wall entertainment. For argument's sake let's assume it's just fine to be entertained every spare waking moment. Let's focus on the nature of "free" entertainment. Free always has a price. It's called "advertising." As previously established in the broadcast TV business model, you aren't buying the entertainment; the advertiser is buying you as a potential viewer/consumer.

Sometimes, like in modern movie theaters, you are now stuck with paying and watching ads.

Ads on your cell phone? You might be outraged and think, "I won't pay for cell-phone service to watch commercials." A survey shows that 2/3 of the public rejects the idea of advertising on their cell phones. However, marketeers are forging ahead. They know that people will get used to almost anything once they are glued to a moving picture on a screen.

Okay. So what? You've already got commercials on TV. You're free to ignore or zap them. You have commercials in the movies. You can arrive late and, during the film, decide not to notice what brand of beer Matthew McConaughey is drinking. Those supermarket screen and gas pump ads? Just close your eyes and hum. You get spam in your email? Just filter it out. So what's the big deal with ads on your cell phone?

Here's the difference. Most other forms of advertising are rather general and anonymous. Marketeers broadcast messages widely and find out what sticks when they see results at the cash register. No one really knows what you are watching. (The exception is TiVo, where the capability exists to register exactly what you are watching. TiVo is finally the TV that watches you. They claim they don't, but….)

Up until recently, to target and place ads, advertising agencies used demographic assumptions about who might be watching a given show from services like A.C. Nielson, but it was basically just an educated guess, extrapolated from a few thousand viewers into hundreds of millions. TV ratings are just generalizations about type and demographics. You are not actually being counted. With mobile media it is radically different. Why? Because they literally have got your number!

They know who you have called. With GPS, they know where you are going and where you've been. They know your credit history. They know how fast you are going, and who you are going with. Two people with their GPS phones active in the same car or moving together are very revealing. Your associations can be mapped all day long to create a portrait of you and what you are likely to be interested in buying.

Where spam is random and telemarketer calls at home are a nuisance that can easily be ignored, ads targeted to your mobile media phone are just for you. You are tagged, tracked, and micro-targeted. There's a buffet of personal data for marketeers to feast upon while they follow you home or wherever else you wind up.

If they want to know even more about you, they can just activate your camera and microphone. Well, remember: you have a microphone and camera on your phone, and service providers can control them remotely. You really don't know if they're on, do you? There is no switch that turns them off, is there? We already know about spyware parked in the laptops of unwitting users. There is a case in Florida in which a repair shop remotely activated a customer's web cam and posted nude photos of her on the Net that were captured as the PC sat on her desk in her bedroom.

The Privatization of Spying

There is always paranoia about government snooping, and with good reason: Wiretapping has been with us as long as we've had phones. There have been times when the executive branch, the FBI or both have targeted enemies by abusing this system — with impunity.

When the Bush administration decided to monitor the entire nation's email and Internet traffic, they circumvented the Democratic Congress, and just went directly to the phone companies. Then, when the government was late in paying the bill, the telecom companies simply cut off the wiretaps. So much for urgent national security interests. I wonder if the U.S. Treasury, like the average consumer, had to pay some sort of "reconnect fee."

The chances are good that you, like 99.99% of our citizenry, present no threat to the government. You just want to have a comfortable life and buy things — that's what really makes you worth watching. Remember, the patriotic sacrifice required of you after the destruction of the World Trade Center was to "go shopping" for presumably Chinese-made goods with borrowed Saudi bank funds. The business of America is shopping.

Too Much Magic

With virtually no effort, and some smart software, your lifestyle and shopping affinities are automatically watched, sorted, and sold to advertisers who receive access to reams of information about you. This data is easily sorted and analyzed without any human intervention.

There are already companies dedicated to weaving advertising into mobile media. The most attractive approach is to give you free minutes or other stuff if you watch the ads. The freebies could amount to nothing more that extra "free" entertainment. After all, it has been a proven model with TV and radio broadcasters for nearly a century. Watch the ads, get the entertainment for free. Although it is just starting up, the estimates are that mobile advertising is already a multibillion-dollar business with some projecting that it will near $15 billion in 2011.

Google floated a plan for their mobile Android phone that would be based entirely on an advertising model. You buy the phone, and the service is free, just like radio or TV broadcasting. The rub is that the phone is just a conduit for targeted advertising, based on surveillance of your web searches and calls (including voice conversations!). This is a more efficient and economical model for advertisers than traditional network TV.

There are applications incorporating GPS with social networking that broadcast where you are and what you're doing to your circle of friends. They could know if you are close by, or even track you. Do you really want to share this information? What will you gain from it? How will having your relationships, movements, purchases, and dining habits known by an intermediator affect you? Think of what they will they gain from this. If incorporating these technologies into life becomes the new norm, you are giving away far more than you are getting in return.

YouMedia for NewsMedia

Just a decade ago, the world was blown away by reporters using a satellite broadcasting system that was contained within a single suitcase. It was a revolution. Now the average 12-year-old girl has the same capability with a $99 media phone. While making amateur videos has been easy for years, it's now just as simple to disseminate them. Every 11-year-old has a distribution deal with YouTube.

The prevalence and capabilities of YouTube and mobile phones are now changing the news business. CNN and other networks have encouraged viewers to send in footage from events they have witnessed and captured on their media phones. This has created a vast network well beyond what would be possible by a news crew. Virtually any event can now be captured and instantly uploaded to a media outlet. The timing is fortuitous for corporate news organizations, since they are cutting correspondents and closing bureaus to improve the bottom line. The border between traditional news-gathering and amateur reportage is beginning to vanish, in much the same way as political bloggers have nearly replaced syndicated columnists on newspaper opinion pages.

With hundreds of millions of mobile media phones online, the world is being watched — and it is quite revealing. In the U.S. the impact on political campaigns is already apparent. Time and time again, an amateur has captured what a politician has said outside of the glare of TV lights and made that video available instantly to friends, bloggers, or YouTube.

Previously, politicians and their handlers would often play hardball with media outlets to essentially "burn the tape" and make inconvenient comments go away. Certainly anything offensive or off-color would be filtered out by a reporter or news producer and never reach the air. A long-standing tactic used by political handlers to manipulate press coverage was to control access to the candidate. If a newsperson crossed the politician, they would no longer be given the access they needed to do their job; the reporter would then be reassigned or fired. Not playing ball with the politician you were covering was a bad career move.

The new digital/amateur state of affairs made itself known during the 2006 off-year election with the now-famous "Macaca Moment." George Allen, who was then the junior senator from Virginia, was considered a shoe-in for re-election. Virginia is a state in transition from the old Southern culture of white supremacy to what we've come to call a "post-racial" environment.

With the boon in technology companies that once surrounded AOL, the Old Dominion is being repopulated with fresh, well-educated immigrants and their diverse cultures. Senator Allen, who was widely believed to be the next George Bush (with a meaner streak), was considered a leading Republican presidential nominee for 2008 — at least until some Virginians got a better look at George.

This George, like the other one, was fortunate enough to have a famous father, a well-respected football coach with decades of wins. Popular with the old-boy D.C. press corps, he was welcome on the Sunday shows and talking-head circuit. He never faced much scrutiny and pretty much had a free ride. Reporters wanted to be George's pal.

There were stories about him having a noose and Confederate flags in his office, and making racist comments, but these weren't generally reported in the mainstream media. Strangely, George had these predilections even though he was not a Southerner, unless someone from Southern California qualifies. Like George Bush, the phony cowboy from Connecticut, George Allen was a self-styled Southern sheriff from L.A. Yet the media never did their job vetting his past behaviors or attitudes, especially concerning race. They were more interested in hearing about his dad's football war stories. Scrutiny was simply not on their agenda.

Fortunately, a Virginia student named S. R. Sidarth decided to follow Senator Allen around to good-ole-boy backcountry gatherings to get a true picture of him. And did he ever! After about a week of tracking Allen, Sidarth had captured the infamous "Macaca Moment."

Allen had recognized Sidarth from previous appearances that week as the student was capturing his campaign speeches. For some reason, Allen decided to call attention to Sidarth at the beginning of a speech in front of a small group of prospective voters at Breaks Interstate Park. Pointing a finger to Sidarth he said "I want you all to say hello to a Macaca who has been following me around. Welcome to America, Macaca." Sidarth, who is of South Asian ancestry, is a natural-born citizen of the U.S.

InCellated: The Mobility Bubble

Sidarth passed the video recording to a member of Allen's opponent's campaign, who put the clip up on YouTube and posted it as an email attachment to reporters. Overnight, the clip had 48,000 hits on YouTube and eventually found its way into the national media. The question was, why did Allen call Sidarth "Macaca?" Allen made the rounds of the talking-head shows trying to explain that it was a term of endearment, but the true etymology of the word emerged as North African slang for monkey, an ethnic slur aimed at dark-skinned people such as those from South Asia. Once this video opened the door for reporters to talk about Allen's racial attitude, more questions were asked, and soon — specifically on Election Day — Allen was political toast.

Having informal media in places where it didn't exist before, beyond the Beltway filtering process, had a huge impact. Certainly, this kind of reporting is good for openness and democracy. With the ubiquity of mobile media phones, we can expect to see more candid exposure of the powerful.

That's the good news. Here's where it gets more troubling. The network is not always a conveyance of verified truths. Spam, phishing, identity theft show that it can be a land of bandits, thieves and outlaws with policing agencies that are always a few steps behind.

Conspiracy theorists, hate groups and corporate PR shills can make their web sites look just as much like legitimate news sites as the N.Y. Times. Combine this lack of verification with the easy digital manipulation of video and audio, and soon there's a potent system for the rapid dissemination of untruths and distortions. Digital media "truth" is inherently malleable.

Truth and objectivity are not gating factors for authoritarian conservatives. As Karl Rove said, "We are making our own reality." And Henry Kissinger has said "the perception of reality is more powerful than objective reality itself." Pictures are powerful and in the digital world they are elastic and irresistibly distortable.

Truth is already being taken for a joy ride by right-wing practitioners of pseudo-journalism by fringe groups that get airtime on Fox News. Much like the Hannity and O'Reilly shows, these segments are dressed up to look like something out of Murrow or

Cronkite. Elder members of our society do not perceive a difference between Cronkite and O'Reilly. It looks the same; a middle-aged white guy in front of the camera in a studio with some graphics appearing behind him.

Although we now know there were CIA programs that infiltrated our media by putting certain reporters on the payroll, journalists mostly had some sense of social responsibility. They viewed themselves as public servants rather than entertainers. If they never revealed the truth about JFK's infidelity, J. Edgar Hoover's frocks, or Nixon's criminality before Watergate, at least it was a matter of purposeful omission rather than brazen lies to promote their own political agendas. With the new breed of faux news, faux viral video, and faux blogs, truth is harder for most people to discern. Digital manipulation and a virtual wildfire of viral distribution is a combustible mix.

I Just Like to Watch

Cameras are rolling everywhere; whether mobile or fixed, they are recording modern life. Police departments are deploying cameras in patrol cars and on certain streets. Citizens are watching the police, too. It's a sort of standoff. Ironically, in some states, police are abusing the privacy laws to arrest and prosecute citizen/witnesses who record the actions of police in the process of making arrests or beating suspects. The police disingenuously claim to be enforcing these laws "to protect the privacy of the suspect." The laws' intent was to protect citizens from the police, not the police from the citizens.

It is increasingly common to have nanny-cams in homes and in daycare centers so that working parents can view their kids on the web during the working day on their smart phones. It could provide some protection from child abuse, but a clever abuser could use it to create a smokescreen of comfort to avoid scrutiny. It would be hard to know whether you were watching a recording or a live webcast.

What we know for sure is that cameras are everywhere, all the time. Sending those images to the public over the Net is going to be part of life from now on because there are hundreds of millions of mobile media phones operating everywhere. It is part of the Generation E lifestyle.

For Generation E there has been a mingling of fictional and "reality" TV series, the latter including shows based on police car chases and spycams. There is a predisposition among Generation E in particular to be "watchers," so accustomed to seeing reality and fiction comingled that when they are confronted by the real world, by a threat from authority, that they remain in passive-audience mode rather than fully engaged participants.

Let's look at two incidents where college students were confronted with authority figures while "armed" with mobile media phones.

"Don't Tase Me, Bro"

It was September 17, 2007, and Massachusetts Senator John Kerry was addressing a Constitution Day forum at the University of Florida. A 21-year-old communications student named Andrew Meyer was anxious to ask a question about why Senator Kerry was not more forceful in challenging the purportedly manipulated results of the 2004 presidential election in Ohio. Since Ohio Secretary of State John (Ken) Blackwell, the man responsible for counting the votes, was also working as the state chairman of Bush's reelection committee, the question deserved to be asked. There is some debate about Meyer's belligerent tone, but the senator didn't seem to mind and was, in fact, answering the question.

At that point, one campus police officer, and then another, began manhandling Meyer. Soon a whole squadron of uniforms were surrounding him and dragging him away from the microphone. We can hear him loudly pleading, "What have I done?" Still screaming, Meyer is dragged to the back of the auditorium with officers piling on this young fellow armed only with Greg Palast's book, *Armed Madhouse*, and some moxie. In the video, we can see him rendered totally helpless by the police. Then he shouted out the now famous "Don't tase me, bro!" as they administered thousands of volts to the immobile student. We hear his screams of pain.

We know what happened in that room because of the abundance of phone cameras trained on the event. Beside the police deciding that asking questions of a willing respondent in an academic environment was somehow a crime, or that being "annoying" was illegal, there is something else troubling about this incident. It is clear that among the thousands of witnesses, not one person intervened on behalf of the student, or even challenged the authority of the police. In short, no one came to his aid. Video reveals students gathering around him, but rather than interacting with the officers, they are just standing around and recording images of the event.

Maybe it's because I grew up in the confrontational 60s that I was particularly disturbed by the inaction of these young people as a fellow student was assaulted for trying to engage in a reasonable academic dialogue. But there's something more: while there were lots of phone cams capturing the episode, the users were simply observers, detached, not interacting, as if this were just another reality show unfolding before them.

Coast-to-Coast Passivity

So now let's jump across the country to a calm library at UCLA. It was after 11 p.m. on November 14, 2006. According to university authorities, community safety officers routinely check the IDs of students who are in the library at that hour. One particular student, 23 year-old Mostafa Tabatabainejad, an American citizen of Iranian descent, was among the students studying. The officers demanded to see Mostafa's ID card, which he thought was somewhat odd, since they hadn't seemed to ask anyone else. Mostafa felt that he was being unfairly racially profiled. He was a student doing his work and not disturbing anyone. The officers told him if he didn't show them his ID he'd have to leave. He refused and went back to his studies. The officers then summoned the campus police (UCPD), who appeared in force and in full riot gear. We know what happens next from the video that a fellow student recorded with a mobile media phone.

Tabatabainejad is first heard (though not seen) repeatedly shouting "Don't touch me!" to the officers. Over the course of the video, he is tasered multiple times, while officers repeatedly order him to stand up and stop fighting, and threaten to administer further stuns. Tabatabainejad repeatedly states that he is not fighting and that he will leave the premises. He shouts that he has a medical condition.

Witnesses say that when it was clear none of the other students were going to help him, Tabatabainejad said, "Am I the only martyr?" By the way, Mostafa is a member of the Bahai Faith, not a Muslim, despite that all too easy assumption. According to one witness, "He was no possible danger to any of the police. He was getting shocked and tasered as he was handcuffed."

At one point, the officers told the crowd to stand back and threatened to tase anyone who approached too closely. A female student said that the officers threatened to tase her when she asked an officer for his name and badge number. According to an ACLU attorney, a threat of force in response to a badge number request constitutes a crime.

A press release issued by the UCPD claims that the officers "asked Tabatabainejad to leave the premises multiple times," and that he refused to leave. Witnesses dispute this account, saying that Tabatabainejad had begun to walk toward the door with his backpack when an officer approached him and grabbed his arm, whereupon Tabatabainejad told the officer several times to let go. The release also states that Tabatabainejad "encouraged library patrons to join his resistance." At this point, the officers "deemed it necessary to use the taser in a 'drive stun' capacity."

A small silver lining in this gloomy tale is that the UCLA students did better than those at the University of Florida; at least they confronted the authorities abusing power. Now, while we are in the world of higher education in California, let's make a quick trip north to Stanford University in Palo Alto to see what's going on at the campus at ground zero in Silicon Valley.

Pervasive Persuasion: "Captology?"

Ever heard of "captology?" Don't bother looking it up. It will not be in your dictionary and there is only a scant paragraph about it in Wikipedia. Don't even think about decoding the Latin root since it doesn't have one. Like most words originating in Silicon Valley, it is actually an acronym. Computers As Persuasive TechnOLOGies. It is the product of Stanford's Persuasive Technology Lab. "Persuasive Technologies" — that should give you a chill right there. Do we really need any more technologies for persuasion?

Like many academics, the lab has accepted a Faustian deal. On the face of it, their goals sound noble. "Persuasive technologies to bring world peace in 30 years." We already know from 100 years of applied technology that when someone needs to persuade someone else by technical means, he probably doesn't have anything beneficial to offer the target audience. So they resort to a rationalization fit for a beauty pageant, "It will bring world peace."

This reminds me of the promises made during the development of dynamite and the atom bomb that these "weapons are so terrible that no one would dare use them." Like so much of technological research, one can bet that the funding comes, if only indirectly, from companies that would utilize the results for their own gain.

Currently the lab's focus is exactly the same as the technology and media businesses': mobility. As they now say about themselves "We Specialize in Mobile Persuasion." Yikes!

The Too Much Magic Bus

Mobile connections are no longer just personal and cellular. Wi-Fi has moved out of cafes and found its way onto public transit systems. For commuter trains and buses it is a mix of benefits and distractions. Downtime is converted into extended work time, online shopping, and yet more time to watch videos. However, with newspapers disappearing, it may become the only way to keep on

top of current events, with more depth and less bluster than is found on cable news outlets.

Who else is riding on the digital magic bus and what are they doing? In Arizona, a school district has put Wi-Fi onboard a yellow bus filled with rambunctious teenagers for the long trek to school. School officials got the idea when they themselves were carpooling with a wireless broadband laptop and thought it would be great for their students to do the same and "be productive." These rocket scientists were obviously clueless about how middle school kids spend their time online. They will be on social sites, watching videos, and playing games. And even if there is any school or homework being done, the question is why wasn't it done at school or at home?

To these administrators, a more appealing benefit than "being productive" is pacifying a bunch of "rowdy" teenagers. Given that these are suburban kids, the "rowdy" behavior is mainly being normally loud teenagers, and any fisticuffs are not exactly bar fights. Sure, the bus is suddenly quieter, but what's missing is the social education. A typical school bus is a hive of interpersonal social interaction free from undue authority. It's a learning laboratory where kids learn to get along with each other, tease each other, defend each other, and develop the social skills they'll need for life. Giving them more time to stare at screens will make them even more insulated and isolated — connected to the Net and disconnected from kid in the next seat.

Too Much in Touch?

This just in: You're too busy. Some of it is mere survival in ever more challenging economic and social environments. And some of it is your own damn fault. Everyone is doing a lot of multitasking. Despite having only 24 hours per day, the average individual performs the equivalent of 43 hours of activity on a daily basis, according to a study conducted for Yahoo, if you double the count when doing more than one thing at a time like watching TV, eating, using the Net, commuting, listening to the radio, working, and sleeping.

Too Much Magic

Although you have bought into mobile communications as a solution to help you manage your busy life, it is, nonetheless, a safe bet you are still too busy. It's just that now "being busy" includes answering your phone, reading your email, and checking blogs in the moments that used to be your free time.

These days, because we can do more, more is expected of us — including your boss calling with "one last thing" as you trudge through traffic to finally get home at a reasonable hour; including your kids asking you for something at the exact moment that particular desire is aroused by a marketing campaign. All of this sucks up your time to be reflective and to just plain old relax. Remember "relaxing?" It was the state that existed before non-computer geeks, normal humans, started using terms like "multitasking."

Communication is good. We all want to communicate. It is our natural tendency. Solitary confinement in prison is harsh because it is tortuous for people to be deprived of communication. But people need time for themselves, to dwell in their own thoughts rather than becoming Pavlovian slaves to their ringtone of choice.

Nothing that is being said today via mobile communications is any more important than what was being said fifteen years ago, before you had that phone in your pocket. In the beginning of this chapter, we described how the Blackberry meltdown may have incited drama among the users, but really had no significant impact on realities. Powerful users were merely "de-mobilized" and life went on. Do you really need to know the sports scores while you are working? Do you need to check out eBay while playing with your kids at the park? Chances are all of it can wait.

Tired of Wired and Unwired Too

One might think that a professor of robotics and the founder of the Webby awards would be gung ho into continuous connections. However, among early adopters, there is a growing awareness of the invasiveness of mobile communications.

Tiffany Shlain, the founder of the Webby Awards said recently, "I feel very strongly that people need to set boundaries with technology."

Jason Benlevi

InCellated: The Mobility Bubble

The Webby Awards honor the world's best web sites and Schlain was at ground zero of the dotcom boom. "I think we've become a society where access is 24/7, and you still need to create a space for your own thoughts and for having lunch with a friend."

Her husband, Ken Goldberg, a professor of robotics at UC Berkeley, had plans for his iPhone: "I'm turning off the email function." Cell phones are valuable, Shlain continued, but "when you're at lunch with someone, and they take a call on their cell phone or answer an email, I think it's very rude. It should be like 'Guns on the table.' You sit down with friends, and everyone should put their cell phones on the table and turn them off."

The mobile phone is a life-changing idea. It can be a way to communicate with a child if you are a working parent. It is huge public safety asset. For the Israelis who had to deal with daily terror-bombing episodes, mobile phones are a way to keep in touch with the family through the day, perhaps providing one last human contact or a comforting reassurance. Certainly the emotional impact of doomed victims calling their families during the destruction of the World Trade Centers towers will forever leave an impression on us all.

But that same mobile phone, arguably a tool of necessity or comfort, has been transmuted into an all-invasive conduit for commerce and distraction. The intermediators are intent on using this convenience to directly hook into your mind. If they had access to a Bluetooth-enabled brain implant that directly influenced your purchasing decisions, the marketeers would be only too delighted.

There is a wonderful movie that was made in the 1960s called *The President's Analyst.* James Coburn, famous as *Our Man Flint*, played a semi-hip New York psychiatrist who is secretly assigned to treat the President of the United States. Along the way he falls into a comical spy vs. spy plot that shows a CIA agent and KGB agent as collaborative pals battling a more pervasive but less obvious superpower. It was not a nation nor a political ideology. It was instead the globally ubiquitous "Telephone Company," which had envisioned global domination by injecting a small wireless communicator into every human being's cranium at birth. It was called the "CC" or "Cerebral Communicator."

The Phone Company even had a slick corporate "vision video" to sell the concept. (I've always wanted a client of mine to introduce such a product so I could recycle that video.) The idea is that from day one everyone is linked in their network.

Again, what was intended as parody is only a day away from reality as younger and younger children are imbedded into cellular mobile life, and its dependencies. The sad part is that in reality it required no global plot, nor implanting hardwire in our brains; we are willingly buying into the dependency without resistance. Hundreds of millions are voluntarily doing the job. Although Apple has created a great product, there is no gap between the "i" and the "Phone" The phone is me and I am the phone, indivisible. Don't leave home without it.

As an adult who grew up without a mobile phone, I know that it is possible to live without one. For people 20 and under, mobile phones have always been there. They can't seem to get through a day without checking in by text or photo with their friends about buying clothes, love relationships or what they are eating. As the messy world of social networks fuses with smartphones expect dependency to grow and independence to erode.

Will it be possible to make a decision without constant consultation and mutual affirmation from their circle? When these young people get together will there be any news left to share? Maybe that's why they spend their time watching videos, because they have little left to say to each other after hours of chatter and creatively spelled sentence fragments.

So what is the impact? A 2006 survey by the Pew Internet and American Life Project survey showed that while 85 percent of American adults used the Internet or a cell phone to communicate, 18 percent of that population felt "teched-out" and suffered from "tech-gadget remorse." This percentage adds up to a huge number! Tens of millions of people feel this way, and those are just the ones who admit it!

People spend all day stuck to a screen, at home, at work, and school — and now they've got a screen in their pocket or purse. The strange thing is, despite the plethora of devices, our actual communications are shrinking. Text messaging in wacky shorthand carries less information, and voice-mails allow you to avoid live contact with the person you are calling. Actual face-to-face communication seems in decline at the moment. The visual cues and body language of a live conversation tell us a great deal. Tech marketeers, of course, know this very well and are selling expensive video conferencing/telepresence systems with extremely high fidelity.

Ironically, one of the few places where you have been assured some level of downtime these days is on an airliner. (Hopefully, not that kind of downtime.) But now this Eight Mile High sanctuary may be in real danger of digital encroachment. With wireless connectivity finally having some success on airlines, people are about to find out that the metal body of a jetliner will no longer prevent radio waves from reaching them in their cramped and uncomfortable seats. The meals have been downgraded to peanuts, you have to pay to have them transport your luggage and soon you will have no excuse for hiding out from work for a few precious hours.

Balancing Act

The advance of mobile technologies unleashes expectations that are both negative and positive. As much as people might carp about their mobile-phone company and dropped calls, cellular communications are just short of miraculous. The core idea of sharing airtime with short-distance radios that automatically switch as you travel between geographic "cells" was extraordinarily brilliant.

In just over a decade, engineers have managed to shrink the components, extend talk time, improve fidelity, find ever more complex methods to squeeze information into a narrow bit of radio spectrum — and deliver the handheld miracle for under a hundred bucks. Now the mobile-phone business virtually supports the money-losing and shrinking land-line phone businesses. It was a smart bet and the cell-phone pioneers were well compensated when they sold their stakes to the big telecom companies. Once again, however, we have gone from dozens of companies to a concentration of a few intermediators that have a legal lock on the airwaves. On the surface, there are huge pluses and some minuses in terms of public safety, especially when it comes to notifying rescue services after car accidents, which are off-set by the accidents that could be attributed to talking-while-driving.

Mobile communications are excellent for tracking absent children but, at the same time, granting them a phone starts an addiction to all-the-time messaging — and those tracking technologies are not limited to your children. Everyone is trackable by anyone, even those with ill intent. Still, there is the reassurance that dear ones are safely on the way to their destination. It is a comfort to know someone has safely made it through a violent storm or a natural or man-made disaster. There are those final moments of human contact from soldiers in Iraq or the victims of the WTC attack. In a deeper study we would probably find that mobile communications were key in planning those attacks and we know that they were a key part of the decision of United 93's passengers to attack their attackers. Mobile communications have changed history and will continue to do so.

Like most technologies, there is always a balance, which tips on a moment-by-moment, incident-by-incident basis. There is, however, a fundamental shift taking place. There is a growing sense of expectation — even entitlement — that accompanies mobile-media culture. It is expected that people will have phones, carry phones, answer when called, and talk anyplace and anytime they feel like it, no matter what social environment they are in.

There are expectations upon you as well. Your boss can always reach you, and you are always expected to instantly answer questions and respond to demands that are often trivial (though cloaked in immediate importance). There is little latitude for solo time. You will own less and less of the minutes of your day. In fact, time itself erodes as a moderating factor for your life. The line between your work time and playtime is evaporated. You are already seeing that happening as you are being required to multitask. They call it "productivity." Instead time and attention are divided and challenged.

The reason cell phones are eating up our time and attention

is that they have turned our mobile communicators into mass-communication receivers for music and TV programming, as high-value conduits for marketeers who've got your number. If you don't think these folks are smarter than you, then why do you spend $2 to download a 10-second ringtone while you pay $1 to download a whole song?

You are becoming increasingly dependent on an intermediator, the Cult of Tech, to conduct your life. Often in younger people you will see that there is no "Plan B" to conduct their lives without constant mobile communications. Life can be very ad hoc when you are in contact. Without that instant contact, more planning is required, as is the ability to independently take actions. If someone can't decide what blouse to buy without messaging a photo to a friend, how well can they learn to act independently on more weighty matters?

Lastly, there is privacy. This is perhaps an antiquated notion when we are so dependent on intermediators that disregard or violate the law and then receive retroactive immunity. We have already learned that they will disregard your privacy with impunity no matter what agreement they offer or promise they make you.

So before you continue to voice dial and download the mobile magic, you need to start making some informed choices. These are your choices. You are under no obligation to spend your day in constant contact with others. You are under no obligation to "upgrade" your phone. You may covet a newer phone with more features, but most likely you will just increase your dependency on those features and the service-providing intermediator.

There was a 120-year gap between the original Bell phone and your smart phone, and much was accomplished without mobile communications. If you tossed your phone right now into a local body of water, your life would not significantly change for the worse. The technology remains dazzling; however, the sociology has become utterly miserable. It's up to you to make the rules that work for your life. It's also time for us to stigmatize the abusers who are living in a state of inCellation. It's time to urge people to leave their cocoons and spread their wings in the moment and place where they stand.

Jason Benlevi

2.3

The Games of Death: Are Wii Having Fun Yet?

Play Is Serious Business

All children have an instinct to play. Whether playtime is social or solo, it's serious business. If you look at what they are playing, it will give you a clue as to why playing is so developmentally critical. Structured, unstructured, social or solo, play is simulation, practice and essential skill training for life. Most play is an analog for what children will encounter in their life as adults. It is how problem solving and social skills are learned, and the experience is imprinted.

Nor is play exclusive to humans. Look at a cluster of kittens and you can see how they practice being predators, taking turns attacking siblings. Even as adults, dogs scuffle in fun for practice. Play, in the end, is not just play, though it may still be fun.

Certain human play instincts appear to be primal and hardwired in the brain. Even in a house with no toy guns or instruments of destruction, boys inevitably will find something from which to fabricate a pretend weapon; virtually any object soon becomes re-imagined as a sword or a gun. As a parent, it doesn't matter what your politics are — the impulse seems to be built in. Regrettable as it is, boys start splitting the world into allies and enemies and seek instruments to enforce that order.

Girls inevitably have an extreme affinity to cuddle with small furry or miniaturized creatures: dolls, stuffed animals, and real puppies and kittens. Excavations of ancient sites often reveal primitive dolls. Girls also delight in play that creates a social order— especially if they can be the princess — or learning to accept a different role when the princess spot is not readily yielded.

Miniatures of almost anything will fascinate children: toy cars, dolls, animals, houses, and human figures. With a floor full of miniature items they can create scenarios informed by the world as they perceive it. Kids run though situation after situation in their minds, acting them out by using their hands to move the tiny objects in their "world." The play includes voices and sound effects, even if they are playing alone and there is no one listening.

Both genders enjoy playing with blocks and other objects when they are babies and toddlers. Filling cups and buckets with sand or water, connecting and unconnecting pieces, piling blocks into towers and other physical objects teaches children about the physics of the world. They learn to estimate volume and grasp the power of gravity and balance. (This, by the way, is where robots often fail to grasp the physical world.) Clumsily knocking objects around, toddlers are doing more calculations and "writing to memory" than a supercomputer. It looks like a mess on the living room floor, but it is a miniature MIT right there on your rug.

Let the Games Begin

Then, there are games. All cultures of the world have games. Game play is the most simulative of activities. Games have rules and, more often than not, multiple players. Though they begin in childhood, games of chance and sports continue into adulthood.

Chess is the regal simulation game that is a direct analog to war; American football resembles a combative battlefield; and poker simulates business — deal with the cards you got or trade them, then bluff to your advantage. It could be said that Bill Gates' real skill was not as a Harvard-trained technologist (he dropped out), but rather a Harvard-dorm-trained poker player. Gates mastered the game theory of poker with bluffs and bets, and then went to play for higher stakes at Microsoft, humiliating the much-respected high-roller IBM along the way.

Video, computer, and electronic gaming is the same as any other game play, providing simulation as entertainment. It is, however, radically different in depth of experience, delivering rich and powerful immersion through realistic vision and sound. As electronic games evolved and attained a greater "fidelity of illusion," they provided more realism, more intensity, and increasingly visceral experiences. This simulative experience has continuously accelerated, along with the raw power of computers, specifically driven by 3D graphics processing chips.

These rich simulations are now akin to movies; in fact, they are often created using the same computer-graphics systems. The difference between films and games is that games grant the viewer a set of controls for their experience. That's the interactive element. For decades there have been prognostications of interactive movies. They haven't yet arrived on the big screen, but they have arrived on TV screens, computer monitors, and smart phones as electronic games.

Electronic games deliver illusions of experiences that are both familiar (such as driving) or beyond our experience (battling dragons and alien invaders). Users get a visceral reaction from the games. They physiologically experience the game in a simulation of reality. For many, the virtual experience of a game vastly exceeds the excitement they encounter in their daily lives. It can be a useful catharsis, a useless distraction, or just an addiction.

The Black Hole

Simulation, like all technologies, has a tendency to offer both an upside and a downside. As always, technology is the enabler and amplifier of our best and worst behaviors.

I'd guess that many people have learned to fly a plane encouraged by low-cost, low-risk options, such as flight-simulator games. Then again, others used these devices to learn to crash planes into buildings, killing thousands of living, breathing human beings.

Some teens fine-tune their hand-eye coordination by firing away in arcades, while others use the practice as preparation for arriving at their high school with both a bad attitude and a fully loaded assault weapon. Kids in the 'burbs now get to learn the "urban" skills of running drugs, stealing cars, and beating up "hos" in the comfort of their bedrooms while scarfing salty snacks and sugary drinks. If these "training exercises" were not bad enough, there is another issue beyond enabling those who have ill intent.

Where once play was practice and simulation for activity in the real world, now simulation has become an end in itself. For many players, electronic gaming has become an all-consuming pastime and distraction. Electronic gaming and its culture becomes a magical black hole into which time and ambition to pursue real skills and human interactions simply vanish. Demographically, gaming has also moved from being a transitory experience of frustrated preteen boys into a life spanning pursuit. Unlike child's play, participants are not growing up and growing out of the experience. In fact electronic game play for adults is expanding every day. So what's driving this change?

The Change They Seek Is Yours

As with most technologies that arrive in our living room in a glossy package, there is a lot of money involved. The video-game business was an outgrowth of the arcade pinball business. Although all those quarters did add up, the limited clientele of arcades also limited the business opportunity. Arcade business was nothing compared to the opportunity to reach into hundreds of millions of living rooms.

One of the strange things about the video-game business is that Sony, Nintendo, and Xbox lose money on every game console they sell. You might say, "That's crazy, why would they do that?" The answer can be found in the famous marketing mantra "We'll get 'em on the blades." This refers to the razor business where the manufacturers give away free shavers. The catch is the shavers only happen to accept the blades their "generous" suppliers make. The game-console makers earn nothing on the consoles, but, instead, take a slice of every game that is sold for their machine. The more games that become available and sold, the more money the console makers receive in licensing fees from game developers. The more players out there, the greater the return on the investment.

Unlike PCs, game-console makers do not introduce new machines every few months. They reach for the most advanced technology available for their platforms in the hopes of being able to sustain the longest viability in the marketplace; that way, game developers have a consistent target for developing games. These companies spend colossal amounts of money developing game consoles that contain mind boggling computing technology when it comes to graphics and sound. I don't believe, even now, that sales of the X-box units themselves have returned a profit for its maker, Microsoft.

No matter: The revenue for games is just enormous. Sony at one point was deriving 30% of its global income from its license fees from developers making games for PlayStation. Consider the size, scope, and innovation of Sony globally and you realize how huge this business has become. In the last few years, the sales of video-game "titles" have exceeded the revenues for the movie industry. Once again, digital economics kicks in. All you need to generate more income is to make another copy of the software. That's a few cents for a DVD and almost nothing for a downloaded game.

My Life in Game

My experiences with video gaming start at the very beginning. As a college student, I worked in a record store. One day, a mysterious truck backed up to the store. The driver unloaded a huge wooden box and wheeled it into the store. It was as tall as a person, but only about two feet wide and painted nondescriptly. The front side of the box featured two knobs that looked like volume controls. At eye level there was a big TV screen. When switched on, the only picture on the screen was a few white lines and a squarish white dot that seemed to float around the screen, until it hit one of the short white lines at either side of the screen. When it hit a line the dot would ping off the line like a bouncing ball.

This unlabeled box was an early version of the ping-pong simulation game that became known as Pong. It was a prototype that had neither a coin slot nor any name brand on the box other than the word "Pong."

For us, it was a fun break from stacking and pricing records on the sales floor. Even our boss soon succumbed to non-productivity. Needless to say, it was addictive. Just what the generation growing up in the 1970s needed: One more addiction.

Atari, the company that made the box — and thus started the video-game business — placed some of the prototypes in bars with slots for quarters (fortunately ours was free). There are stories about the early days of these new boxes. One involved an annoyed bar owner who wanted the machine taken out of his establishment because it wasn't working anymore. When the Atari tech came by the bar to check it, he opened the machine and found that it was so full of quarters that it had just jammed up. Ka-ching.

Pong became a hit. Atari's business grew, starting in arcades and bars, then later when home games were attached to TVs. (A Pong-like game by Magnavox for the home succeeded at first, but since it only featured one or two games, interest soon faded.) Atari exploded in growth when Sears ordered in excess of 100,000 machines for the 1975 holiday season.

Arcade-game makers, purveyors of the classic pinball machines, were rapidly introducing new video games to arcades. The graphics were simple white lines on dark screens, but the action was fast and fun. I went through dozens of quarters at a time, back when a quarter bought you a bus fare across town in San Francisco or New York. The great early games were *Space Invaders, Asteroids, Battle Zone,* and *Tempest.* I frequented early video-game parlors such as the legendary Westworld in L.A. and the one in San Francisco's North Beach near the seminal punk-rock nightclub, Mabuhay Gardens.

Not long after this, I saved up for two big purchases: an electronic chess game and a Sinclair computer. For the computer, I wrote my own baseball simulator game, which was entirely text based. I was also buying up old game machines in garage sales. My biggest tech challenge was that I didn't have a TV that worked (at least without banging on it) to use as a display. I was always ready to waste a few quarters in an arcade. Well, more than a few. Especially if the game was a personal favorite, Burgertime, in which the object was to make and eat the food before it could eat you.

Eventually Atari introduced a game machine that allowed home users to plug in different cartridges and play more games than just Pong and created a revenue stream of new "titles" to be bought. At the time, games were relatively easy to design and program. Costing only tens of thousands of dollars, they generated sales many times that. Time Warner bought control of Atari as part of its media empire. For a while this was a hit, until mismanagement of Atari crashed and burned the home-gaming business in the U.S.

Arcades were still going strong. In Japan, two game makers were poised to bring the video game home: Sega and Nintendo. Sega (Service Games) was actually an American maker of pinball and arcade games for military bases. It had a hit game in the 1960s that was a submarine simulator. In the late 1980s, Sega and Nintendo were pursuing arcade- and home-gaming systems. Nintendo was a maker of playing cards that also invested in other, disconnected businesses, such as a chain of "love hotels," instant rice, and, eventually, electronic toys. Nintendo finally found success in making the arcade game Donkey Kong. This was followed in 1980 by a handheld game machine that was the predecessor to the uber-successful GameBoy.

By 1985, Nintendo had introduced the Famicom system, known in the U.S. as the Nintendo Entertainment System or NES. Sales were powered by the hit game Super Mario Brothers. As the name indicated, Famicom's game console was intended as a family-entertainment device. The games themselves were simple, cartoonish scrolling and puzzle games. With the advent of GameBoy, Nintendo became the ruler of the electronic gaming market. Meanwhile, Sega got busy developing its own game console to catch some of the wave Nintendo had created.

Welcome to the Next Level

That's when I became directly involved in the video game business, not just a player. I was already developing media and messaging for a wide array of Silicon Valley companies when I was invited to participate in helping Sega of America introduce their breakthrough game console, Sega Genesis, at the Consumer Electronic Show (CES) in Las Vegas. CES is where gadget makers and retailers get together to see and discuss the latest consumer tech products.

At the time, Nintendo completely ruled the game market. Their target was 10-year-old boys who would naturally move on to other interests — mainly girls and rock music — as they got older. So even though Nintendo dominated that current generation, the market was poised to completely flip within two to three years and the kids coming up needed to be secured. Other people inside the gaming business knew this as well, and that success would be about demographics and aspiration. While Nintendo was cute and cartoonish, Sega was seeking a different product and market. We positioned Sega with a more aggressive attitude exemplified by my tagline, "Welcome to the Next Level." I thought the differentiator should not be technological (although I felt Sega was superior in that regard) but cultural. I made the analogy that Nintendo was a nice, safe family-oriented Disney cartoon, while Sega was more like Ren & Stimpy.

We aimed for a cooler audience than Nintendo: not 10–12-year-olds, but rather grunge-rock loving 14–16-year olds who would come to think Nintendo was for little kids. Sega had the advantage of being CD-based, which meant customers could also play their music right on the box. The box itself was sleek and black, while Nintendo's was pale and bland enough to meld into living-room décor. The game titles themselves were more aggressive. Fighting and sports games, shunned or toned down by Nintendo, were big for Sega. In Sega there would be blood.

The media and advertising Sega had adopted up to that point was standard Japanese corporate fare, what we called "BIV" (Boring Industrial Video). Our team took Sega in a more MTV direction — which in those days (unlike now), was actually a bit edgy — and steered them to an ad agency that amplified the outrageous cyberpunk identity we had created for them.

Sega had the good fortune of developing a killer game called *Sonic the Hedgehog* which really showed off their system. Sonic was a speedy blue hedgehog with a mohawk who evaded an evil scientist who wanted to turn him into a robot. It was essentially a scrolling puzzle game. The difference was that it was fast and graphically brilliant. Nothing had ever looked so good on a home system. Even the audio quality was great. Sonic was dazzling and had attitude.

Unlike the bitsy looking games of Nintendo's Mario, Sega Genesis was delivering interactive animation. You controlled what appeared to be a cartoon character. My two-year-old daughter, who watched me play, became as engrossed in the little hedgehog's adventures as she would in those of animated characters on TV. There were frequent warnings from her to the little hedgehog, "Watch out Sonic!" For her, watching was an entertainment experience.

Almost overnight, Sega became the leader in video games at home and in the arcade. They were working on VR systems and innovative ways to control gameplay with your whole body. With our media for Sega showing up on ABC's Nightline and the cover of Newsweek, it was clear that games were no longer just kid's stuff. No kid wanted the NES. It was "last generation" and ready for the garage sale.

Where Are the Girls?

One aspect of video game success exposed something that, in retrospect, should have been glaringly obvious. No matter what, girls didn't want to play video games. Sure, there were occasional exceptions, but overall the audience was overwhelmingly male. The demographic targets were pubescent males who needed an outlet for their pre-sexual aggression. 12–16-year-olds were the core audience, with younger boys aspiring to want what the older guys were playing. Video games are inherently male-oriented. They have goals, levels, and points — just like in sports. (I remember a friend of mine, the father of two pre-teen boys, awarding points to his sons when they completed various household tasks and chores. The numbers were random and never tabulated in any way, but the idea of "scoring points" was irresistible.) Even the terminology of sexual success for young males is "scoring." The process of teen-age sexual conquest itself is categorized by what "base" you reach. Then, of course, there is that whole "joystick" thing.

As we noted earlier, guys start to outgrow gaming by the time they get to be 16, because that's about when most of them can actually get their hands on real girls. Therefore, the life expectancy of a game system was rather short. Every three years or so, there was a new crop of young teenage boys who wanted the newest system, and this coincided with the product development cycles of Atari, Sega, Nintendo, and eventually Sony and Microsoft.

With Sega's video-game sales surging and generating amazing profits, Nintendo knew it had been bested and sought a technology partner for its next system. They selected Sony. But by the time the Japanese electronics giant publicly announced the decision, the executives at Nintendo had changed their minds. Sony was left at the altar.

A Sony, Spurned, Gets into the Game

Sony, although spurned, realized they now had an opportunity to develop a game system under its own flag and raided the Sega team for talent. Sony, which had missed the boat by not owning content when it launched Betamax, had learned the positive financial benefits of royalties and licensing with the CD and floppy disk. That's why Sony was willing to pay any price necessary to own a movie studio (Columbia Pictures) and then eagerly bought Columbia Records from CBS. Software and intellectual property tied together with hardware is a winning combination.

At one point in the 90s, Sega, Nintendo, and Sony were all spending enormous sums of money building new gaming systems. The E3 (Electronic Entertainment Expo) event in Los Angeles that year featured huge tradeshow exhibits for each company with dozens of games and booth babes to attract the crowds. It was also the loudest place on earth for three days.

The game console business, like many other business categories, consistently has one leader at a time, a moderately successful second banana, and a third-placer that has not fared particularly well. It's Coke, Pepsi, and…well…somebody else.

This next level was a huge leap. Nintendo made the decision to go with a cartridge-based system instead of using the CD, which was a fatal mistake. Console makers, just like computer makers, are dependent on third-party companies to make software (games). The hardware for a game cartridge can cost several dollars to make. A CD only costs a few cents. Yet, the price for the game had to be consistent across game systems. For game developers, Nintendo-based games would be intrinsically more expensive and, therefore, less profitable. Nintendo had already lost against Sega. Meanwhile a very determined Sony was extremely supportive of game developers and even bought a few of them outright to ensure exclusive product.

I personally became involved with the launch of the PlayStation well before it was introduced. It was clear that this was a stellar product. No pun intended, it was a game changer. Where the previous generation of games (NES and Genesis) was basically 2D, the PlayStation was a 3D system. At its core was what is called a "geometry engine," which is a graphics processor that generates shapes embellished with color and texture. Creating solid-looking objects in three dimensions, the simulations were rich and almost movie-like. I remember seeing a helicopter-simulation-game prototype that was mind-bogglingly realistic. Only a few years earlier, I was working on a video for a company called Link Systems, which built military flight simulators that cost millions of dollars. This $300 PlayStation blew away the "out-the-window" view of the pricey military simulator.

The name of the PlayStation product had its origins in the vernacular of the day for high-performance desktop computers, which were called "workstations." Sony was delivering a high-performance computing system focused on game play, hence "PlayStation."

The much-anticipated Sony marketing onslaught did not disappoint. Neither did the games or performance of the console itself. Though the initial price was more than previous game consoles, that didn't deter customers one bit. PlayStation was an international hit. Sega and Nintendo were left in the dust. (Eventually, the original Sony PlayStation sold over 100 million units. The Nintendo 64 and Sega Saturn that were introduced in the same time frame shipped mere fractions of that.)

Too Much Magic

With a longer game plan and a bigger investment, companies started to strategize how to get more out of the opportunity. They could no longer afford for the game to be over by having the target market grow up. The games became decidedly less juvenile and perhaps even adult. Suddenly, 16 year-old guys were not trading in consoles for girlfriends. Scoring on the PlayStation was even beating out "scoring" in the backseat of a car for many high school and college-age students.

Putting Away Our Childish Things?

PlayStation was reaching a wider market. It wasn't just parents buying them for kids. It was also young adults buying the consoles for themselves. Guys who were well past the late-teen cutoff age were standing in line to get the hot box on release day. These were Nintendo kids who grew up but did not put away their childish things. They were spending their own starting-wage job dollars for the nearly $400 game system.

The nature of the game business was changing for economic reasons. A target market of mid-teenagers was simply not large enough for the business that was imagined. Game consoles morphed from being a "toy" to a becoming a form of mainstream home entertainment. Sony, as a major movie and TV studio proprietor, was looking for synergies between movies that they owned and new games titles. Spiderman the Movie plus Spiderman the Game gave marketeers two for the price of one. Media worked together to sell more of everything.

Adults were getting into gaming on a different path. In the mid-90s, the PC world was seeing a gaming revolution. Graphics on home computers were rapidly advancing as add-on 3D cards became available for PCs. Each new generation of PCs was distinguished by faster graphics, rendering images in greater depth, detail, and velocity. In the 80s businesses required the fastest PCs for work; in the 90s most high-performance PCs were destined for homes. What started as simple, flatly rendered games, such as solitaire, were becoming more action-oriented. Even chess became 3D and used character-based pieces that engaged in battle. The same 3D-graphics technology found in advanced workstations and the PlayStation were becoming ever more mainstream for high-end home computers.

There were plenty of children's "learning games" to rationalize a family's computer-buying decision. But the real drivers were adult men seeking adult and action titles that would have made Nintendo blush. Video gaming was rapidly becoming a "grown-up" playground. Just as porn drove the rapid adoption of VCRs into homes, gory action games were driving the market for PCs. While parents were alarmed about sexual content, they seemed to be less alarmed about the rising level of violence that was appearing in PC games and on the PlayStation. The improving graphics systems were making violence much more, well, "graphic."

This period of time was synchronous with the explosion of Internet growth. People were making the leap from the training wheels of AOL accounts to actual Internet connections. 3D Graphics and Internet connections left no child, or adult, behind in the explosively growing business of electronic gaming.

Big Game Hunting

Technology dictates what games are possible. Human beings decide what games are popular. The combination of more realistic graphics and Internet connectivity combined to enable two major interrelated trends in gaming with massive appeal:

- *FPS: First-Person Shooters*
- *MMORPG: Massive Multiuser Online Role-Playing Games*

FPS — First-Person Shooters

"Shooter" games traditionally had you controlling some sort of armed character who was committing mayhem with a gun or sword while you watched on screen. First-person-shooter games, however, were a radical departure: *You* became the character, through your own point of view. In some ways, it harkened back to the old days of shooting galleries. In front of you was your weapon, aiming outward as you advanced. Ahead of you was a mazelike environment to navigate through, populated with enemies for you to blast with your magnum weapon.

These new games were specifically designed as "network games" that would allow multiple users to shoot it out with each other. These FPSs were the most obvious example of the increasingly violent nature of video games. If it moved, shoot it before it shot you. There wasn't much back story or subtlety.

DOOM was the first FPS to excite the popular imagination. The programmers enabled rapid navigation and gunfire. The premise was as infantile as any in the paranoiac sci-fi films from the 50s. The task was to blast your enemies, then get rewarded with more lethal and destructive weapons for your efforts. The fidelity of the game experience was getting better, which made it more compelling to play. The games were less abstract, which made the compulsion to shoot it up more disturbing. It is hard not to get a visceral response when playing *DOOM*. You must kill or be killed — fast.

In 1995, it was speculated that *DOOM* was on more computers than the current release of Windows. The marketeers of the software proudly proclaimed their product "the number-one cause of decreased productivity in businesses around the world." It did not, however, decrease the productivity of profits for its inventor, id Software.

As noted earlier, play is practice and simulation to perform acts in real life. In 1999, we saw the results of *DOOM* simulation when two students in a Colorado suburb arrived at Columbine High expertly trained from their game-playing experience for a shooting spree. One of the killers said their "adventure" would be "like fucking *DOOM*." It was.

MMORPG — Massive Multiplayer Online Role-Playing Games

Role-Playing Games (RPGs) seem to have evolved in tandem with the sci-fi/fantasy sub-culture. *Dungeons and Dragons* was among the first branded role-playing fantasy games, though among sci-fi fans it seems like there were always RPGs of some sort. When computer-based chat first began in the text-only days, RPGs were already popular among computer nerds. They already inhabited cyberspace even though they used only words and imagination. With graphical computers or game consoles that had an Internet connection, the ability to interact in a fantasy world became more fully realized.

As the PlayStation grew more dominant, the Internet was working its way into more homes. Sony built a network connection into its gaming strategy. Called *Everquest*, it's a beautifully rendered fantasy world of wizards, warriors, beasts, and buxom babes. Users inhabit characters and move through a world that only exists on a bank of servers run by Sony. And, just like Disneyland, everyone is welcome — so long as you pony up the price of admission.

Some people have called *Everquest* "chat with weapons." Others have named it "NeverRest" or "EverCrack," because of its addictive quality. For the user, it is a pay-as-you-play fantasy. For marketeers, it is a dream come true, a fake location customers are eager to pay lots of real money to visit. Just like any addictive substance, the marketeer gives you the first hit for free. Once the needle has gone in and the junk flows into your veins, you must pay to regain the altered state — a feeling to which, before you know it, you've become hooked. Why are games like this so addictive? It's pretty simple: For many people, things look better in there than in the mundanity of daily life. They feel powerful, beautiful, and in control.

Everquest and RPGs are an alternative reality, just like drugs or watching movies. When you consider all the time spent by players within this realm, you realize these precious hours could be spent improving social skills, getting in shape, or learning to *do* something that might make them more powerful, more attractive, and more in control of their lives.

There are myriad stories of lives that have crashed and burned by traveling in the *Everquest* escape vehicle. There are tragedies of estrangements, divorces, and even suicides. Like drugs, you can't blame the substances themselves since they are self-administered. While we have hundreds of thousands of people in jail for using drugs, addictive immersive gaming is just "play." Like most addictions, what starts off as fun can soon become a burden — another job. For heroin addicts, it's an all-day experience: funding, finding, fixing. But *Everquest* is just a password and credit card away.

Creating a parallel life in *Everquest* requires a huge investment of personal time, yet the game goes on whether you are there or not. Persistent play is rewarded. It moves from being a pastime to becoming a black hole where time in real life disappears. You can buy more game time, but real time is finite. You can't buy more of it.

Then there are the MMORPG interest groups who organize boycotts and protests about changes in rules or features of various games. With all the worldly problems in need of attention and resolution, one might think that these individuals could choose something other than the rules of a pastime to protest. Equally foolish are government agencies that seek to prohibit gameplay, as occurred in a province of Brazil. With the grinding real social and environmental issues of that country, it's obvious they must have more important matters for their legislative activities.

What Will the Children Play?

In the 90s, as teenage males started ruling the electronic gaming space, and expensive PCs and game consoles were becoming mass-market entertainment devices, what were the younger children doing? Certainly there was no real prohibition against their playing violent games. On the Net, no one knows how old you are, and in all likelihood, most parents weren't monitoring the games their preteens were engaged in.

What electronic toys could children exclusively call their own? Basically anything that would fit in a school backpack or be unobtrusive in the back seat of a car. Something that Mom, or more likely Dad, would not want to commandeer or easily restrict access.

Robotoys

There were early robotic toys such as Tickle Me Elmo. Even if children got tired of the actions of Elmo, they at least had a friendly stuffed toy to cuddle. Furby, a plump talking robo-bird, represented a possibly more sophisticated approach. These toys were so successful during the 1996 Christmas rush that parents were resorting to physical violence in retail aisles to get their hands on them.

Probably the most miserable idea was encoding TV shows and videos with invisible instructions in the picture that would activate them. This style of digital magic may have impressed adults, but what kid wants a toy that plays with itself while they just sit around and watch? The box it came in was probably a more compelling toy for these children.

GameBoy

Nintendo's GameBoy has been an enduring success. The magic is its simplicity. Though GameBoy has become smaller and more colorful, it is still a just a box with simple controls that retains the addictive properties intrinsic to all electronic gaming. The games themselves are a throwback to the early days: The motions are simple, the graphics are spare, and the colors are garish. Yet the action is just as riveting. It successfully makes time disappear, reduces social interaction, and insulates the user from the ambience of the world — just like big, expensive game consoles. Easily portable and concealable, GameBoy has the ability to enter a small person's life without parents realizing just how invasive it truly is.

Tamagotchi

A digital pet? No, your dog doesn't have designs on becoming WiFi-enabled. Over the years there have been multiple attempts at digital pets (not counting "Rags the Dog" in Woody Allen's *Sleeper*). Some were simply animated characters for computer screens that mimicked the behavior of creatures like dogs, cats, or fish. They were cute, but useless. However, one digital pet designed as an inexpensive toy for pre-teens was amazingly successful. The gadget was called "Tamagotchi." Introduced in 1997, this fits-in-your-palm plastic oval, similar to a digital watch, had a matchbook-sized screen with three simple buttons. It was named after the Japanese word "tamago" (which means "egg") partly because of the oval shape of its case, and partly because that's how its vitual life begins.

After eagerly shredding the package that Tamagotchi comes in, the child is greeted by a small egg on the screen that hatches to reveal a chirpy, cute animal-like creature. Using the three buttons, the child is charged with caring for the creature from that point forward. That means feeding it, playing with it, keeping it clean, and, in return, watching it grow.

As a parent, you might think you're getting this toy to help your kid learn what you have been doing for the past several years. If the creature is not cared for, it grows unhappy, unhealthy, and dies. The difference is, should it die, you just press the "reset" button and it lives again. That's where the simulation hits an obvious snag. The toy tends to either educate or program your kids. Some children accept the experience with great responsibility. Others are more inclined to hit the reset on a regular basis as they forget to take care of the "pet."

One difficultly is that the little creatures need care every four hours or so. So what happens when the kids are in school? Educators rightly considered the toy to be distractive and urged parents to keep the little plastic eggs at home. For the conscientious child, that meant returning to a dying pet, which created terrible anxiety. For other children it was no big deal; they just hit "reset" and started again.

As a parent, you see either your compassionate child suffering with anxiety or your less empathetic offspring merely pushing the reset button to be absolved of irresponsibility. You could, of course, take care of the pet while your child is at school, but that isn't what you've signed up for. So your choices are to encourage your child toward compulsive behavior and anxiety, cover for her to keep it alive, or teach her that there is always the reset button.

Compare this to having your child take care of a real pet. Animals have random unpredictable behaviors. They can't be switched off or restarted. Kids learn a lot of perception and caring skills. Tease the cat or dog and you'll pay a price. Learn to please them and you get rewarded with affection. If they are supposed to feed the cat, and forget, there are real world repercussions. Live pets teach an important lesson: Life has no reset button.

Hitting the Pause Button

By the late 90s, the game business was exploding in both senses of the word. There was exponential growth as the market expanded beyond pre-teen boys to men who hadn't quite grown up but had a mature disposable income. More pent-up frustration was evident in the games' growing violence and bloodshed. Something was going on here with your adult-male population. It was evident in what they listened to on the radio. Though they were political opposites, Rush Limbaugh and Howard Stern shared an attitude that lacked empathy. Meanwhile, *Beavis and Butthead* and *South Park* carried some of that same attitude to basic cable TV.

Even driving-simulation games, which had been a somewhat benign first-person experience about honing automotive skills, were suddenly becoming games of road rage and destruction. *Road Rage* was both a specific game title and an acceptable state of mind. Cars actually became weapons in games like *Carmagedon* and drivers were awarded points for running over pedestrians. This four-wheeled mayhem was arriving on the scene just as budget-strapped schools were cutting real driver-training programs. *Carmagedon's* box cover actually depicts a car an instant before running over a seated race official.

Non-technical adults were dazzled and awed by the "magic" they were seeing on the screen. And many tech-savvy parents probably coveted the toys for their own personal use. In either case, adults bought into gaming systems; after all, what kind of parents would they be if they denied their child the latest technology?

The late 90s were prosperous times and gaming invaded more living rooms and stole time from more kids and teens. Anxious schools and parents were pushing computers in front of students at ever younger ages; kids were spending too much time in front of screens, getting used to controlling their own little worlds; and parents looked on in awe, fright, or pride. The era of the "screen-ager" was upon us. The marketeers had clearly scored a victory. Academics were lauding "growing up digital."

For me, it represented a noisy invasion of family life, a total distraction neatly packaged, and a potent marketing strategy, all enabled by both tech-fearing and tech-loving parents. Some adults would argue that their children needed these "skills." Others would say it was better than TV because it was "interactive." The marketeers had indeed done their job.

Consider this electronic gaming in the larger context of a child's finite waking hours. Video games and TV were filling the time with what the legal profession calls "attractive nuisances." Factor in the mandatory soccer teams, music lessons, and the need to do well in school, and it was clear that there was almost no free playtime — exactly the kind of time that is necessary to foster creativity and self-reflection.

The electronic gaming business was creating an increasingly ugly and violent culture that was now bleeding into the larger pop culture. I wondered: Where was the fun? It seemed like a lot of shooting and blowing things up. If play is simulation, is this the world for which we're helping prepare our children?

Although most of my income was derived from companies selling these products, my conclusion was to remove as many digital toys and games as possible from our home. I even removed every game from my own computers, realizing their addictive power. After this realization, I withdrew my family and myself from the gaming world.

Reset While I Was Not Playing

During my absence, multiple generations of gaming systems cycled through the marketplace, each an engineering and marketing marvel. Sony PlayStation became PSP, PS2, and PlayStation 3. Cumulatively, nearly 300 million PlayStations were unleashed on the world.

After two failed attempts to keep up with Sony and outlast Nintendo, Sega tried one more time with its well-named Dreamscape console system before shrinking into a software-only company. Nintendo tried once again with GameCube but faltered, saved only by the powerhouse of GameBoy, which was now available in a variety of colors and had tweener girls playing them as well as tweener boys. Nintendo still had games; it was small, but mighty.

Microsoft, which ruled the PC world of gaming, was the only major-league challenger to Sony with their Xbox. Microsoft was the only company that could afford to lose money for years to build a franchise. Their success at losing money on things other than Windows and Office was without peer. (Remember *Bob*, *WebTV*, or *Zune* anyone?) Microsoft could afford to lose for many years and still be in the game because of the Windows/Office monopoly.

The most dramatic change in my absence from video gaming activities was just how much older the demographic had skewed. The kids whom we were selling to more than a decade ago were still playing, only now they were adults. Game titles were being advertised along with beer and phone-sex services on late night TV chat shows.

The target demographic before was sexually-frustrated pubescent boys. Now, the market was socially-inept and sexually-frustrated guys in their twenties and thirties. Rather than move on with life, they just grew increasingly stunted and twitchy fingered. Was the draw of the game console more compelling than the opposite sex? Had they grown so used to the artifice and control they experienced in the gaming world that they were incapable of interacting beyond that realm?

In preparing for this book, I put a toe back into gaming culture to learn what new games had emerged. Although there was vastly improved graphics power, I was shocked at how little the games themselves had changed. Then I realized that since the beginning of electronic gaming decades ago, there have only ever been a few types of games. Sure, they would get dressed up differently, but underneath all the marketing and among thousands of titles, there was nothing new at all. From the dawn of video gaming to today, almost every game ever created falls into one of these categories.

- Fighting/Martial Arts
- Shooter/First-Person Shooter
- Puzzle/Maze
- Role Playing
- Sports Simulation
- Warfare/Strategy
- Vehicle Simulation (driving; flying)
- Bio Simulation
- Construction Simulation
- Music/Rhythm Games
- Learning
- Action/Adventure (may include other genres combined)

It has been said that Hollywood only has a few story lines that have been recycled for decades. One might expect a younger business to be more innovative. Sadly, just as in Hollywood, financial concerns dictate the creative.

The Hollywood Trap

Electronic video games are stuck in the loop of non-innovation. Although there are incremental improvements in graphics in each new version, many best-selling game titles are just extensions of games that existed 15 years ago. Scanning a 2009 list of popular games reveals product extensions of long-lived titles.

Final Fantasy XII (started in 1987)
Dragon Quest IX (started in 1982)
Halo 3 (started in 2001)
Prince of Persia (started in 1989)
Resident Evil 5 (started in 1996)
Grand Theft Auto IV (started in 1997)
Super Mario (started in 1981)
Tony Hawk (started in 1999)
Gran Turismo 5 (started in 1997)
Half Life (started in 2004)

Legend of Zelda (started in 1986)

The gaming business has fallen into Hollywood's trap. Complex graphics in games cost considerably more to develop than a simply realized game, so developers go back to the proven franchises and keep making sequels of existing successful titles to avoid risk. Games become brands with "extensions" and peripheral merchandising. Like James Bond, these franchises can go on for generations. Zzzzzz.

The cost of developing games has risen from tens of thousands of dollars in the Sega Genesis days, to tens of millions of dollars today. Given these numbers, the game business depends on a few megahits to cover overhead. The process is a mirror image of producing a heavily computer-generated (CG)-based motion picture (itself often a sequel) and even uses the exact same software tools for production. The game business has also resorted to the movies' little production-budget helpers, embedded advertising and "product placement," as methods to raise capital. With online games, these ads can be updated on a regular basis. In the end, there is no breakaway innovation. The gaming cycle is vicious in both senses of the word.

The games have become clichéd, with some sort of alien or evil overlord against whom our lead character must defend civilization, using elephantine weaponry that never seems to jam or need cleaning. The characters dwell in a sci-fi realm, a quasi-medieval fantasy, a hostile contemporary urban environment, or some incongruous combination of all these modalities. Dystopia is a persistent theme, no matter what era is selected. These are not happy worlds that gamers inhabit.

Six-Pack Heroes

What about the typical hero in these games? The character archetypes really tell us more about the players, or at least about their fantasies and alter egos.

Physically, the male characters are buffed out, armored, and helmeted or visored in a way that renders them faceless. While the on-screen heroes have well defined six packs, the game players' six packs generally have pull tabs. They do share a taste in gaudy clothing inspired by the NFL. The characters are distant. There is no empathy,nor any consequence from all the violence that is wrought. The player simply presses "reset" to resuscitate himself.

Years ago, critics had an estimate for how many killings a child would see on TV by the age of 18. It was a staggering number. It would be interesting to know how many killings the typical gamer has himself committed by the time he reaches 25. There is no doubt a strong case to be made that this type of play fosters a detached response to violence. It shows up in the way a generation drives and conducts itself in public situations. If play is simulation for life, what might their idealized life look like?

Grand Theft Auto

Perhaps we can judge the attitude of gamers by seeing which was the biggest, fastest-selling game ever, *Grand Theft Auto IV*, or *GTA IV*. In 2008, in the midst of the most serious economic meltdown in 80 years, gamers turned out in force to buy *GTA IV*. In just one week, gamers bought $500,000,000 worth of its well-rendered criminal intent. That comes close to beating the domestic box-office gross of any *Star Wars* movie for its entire run! The best-selling game before that was the Xbox first-person shooter *Halo 3*, which pulled in $360,000.000. What they both have in common is a lot of shooting.

Even before this sales blowout, the previous *GTA* games sold over 70 million copies. What does the player of this game get for his 60 bucks? In short, they get permission to engage in abundant and abundantly violent felonies with impunity. For those of you unfamiliar with the game, *GTA* follows the exploits of an aspiring criminal who, under direction of organized crime bosses, takes on various felonious "missions" such as assassination, pimping, street racing, and, of course, automobile theft. The game can have a linear storyline, or be played in a "sandbox" mode where the player selects his own activities in an urban environment filled with opportunities for crime. The game player's task is to pilot his character successfully though the criminal missions and climb the crime ladder. *GTA III* made a leap to greater realism by moving into a fully rendered 3D environment. In essence, *GTA* is an adventure game that combines driving simulation (in which pedestrians can be run over) and a "shooter" that includes assault rifles and flamethrowers — just your average big city adventure. The game has been widely criticized for "secret scenes" that show our hero getting down with a prostitute and for its level of violence. So if games are simulations, what is being learned here? Is this, in essence, sociopathic training neatly shrink-wrapped for sale at Walmart?

Is playing the game a safety valve for the indulgence of evil male fantasies in a safe environment, or does it portend actions that may become reality with some unbalanced individuals? For it to bring in half a billion dollars from eager players who could be doing other things with their time is a possible measurement of the irrational male rage that circles around right-wing media pundits such as Glenn Beck and Rush Limbaugh.

The line between what is real and what is imagined on screen is a very fine line. With Beck and Limbaugh both "recovering" drug addicts, there is a connection to the game play. It is about instant gratification; expressing rage, escape into an altered reality, and immortality. It's the indulgence of the child/man who feels powerless. But the real trouble comes when this behavior becomes sanctioned and the skills it generates become sought by more powerful forces.

The Drone Wars

The goal of industrial designers is to create a fusion between machine and human for efficiency and a compelling user experience. However, the fusion can go both ways, with people winding up as accessories of the machines. Operating a car allows people to behave in antisocial ways that would never occur if the drivers were sitting together in a room. It is part of the insulated/distanced/amplified experience that I have touched upon before. Likewise, using a weapon that kills at a distance is an entirely different experience than killing with, say, a bayonet at close range. The perception of the threat and the possibility of harm are much more immediate.

Too Much Magic

For years, a goal of U.S. military industrial designers has been to create maximum distance between our combatants and their opponents. One reason is to keep the fighter out of harm's way. Another is to dehumanize the enemy and depersonalize the kill. And a third objective is to prevent stressed soldiers from "fragging," or killing their own officers, as happened in Vietnam. Combat design today is about using targeting devices so that a soldier is not looking into the eyes of another human whose life he is about to extinguish.

During the course of Bush Gulf War I, the press admired the precision bombing of "smart bombs" and the excellent TV pictures that they provided for the newscasts. Clean, on-target explosions. No messy body parts or ambiguity that would complicate the stories. Some clever reporter called it "The Nintendo War." He probably didn't realize how spot-on he was.

Remember: this was the first generation of warriors who grew up playing video games and, though later many experienced PTSD, in the beginning they likely saw themselves as "players" who were bombing "aliens." Flying their stealthy airplanes they were reenacting a familiar experience, one that started with a game controller in hand. As in the gaming world, they were merely running up scores with faceless "enemies." The Nintendo War could have been the inspiration for an extraordinarily prophetic movie by Barry Levinson called *Toys*. Starring Robin Williams, the wildly imaginative film tells the story of how a privately owned toy company is slowly taken over by a washed-up ex-military member of the family. Though the official policy is not to make war toys, the interloper secretly develops remote-controlled weapons that appear to the users as common video games. He populates the war command center with gamer-aged children who, as they adeptly control these game-cum-war machines, rack up points for kills. The movie is a visual wonder with amazing non-digital art direction and special effects. Despite the participation of actor Williams and director Levinson, the movie did not ignite the box office. It did, however, predict the future.

Jump ahead ten years, as the wars in Afghanistan and Iraq drag on, and the cost of military aircraft climbs to a hundred million per plane. The U.S. Air Force has taken a lesson from the Israelis by using remote-controlled planes to monitor guerilla activity. U.S. military contractors upped the ante by creating remote UAVs (unmanned aerial vehicles), or "drones," that fire Hellfire missiles to easily obliterate targets (even if those targets frequently turn out be civilian tents or wedding parties). While the Air Force previously has had stand-off fighting capabilities and stealth planes to keep pilots out of harm's way, UAV drone planes completely remove the pilot from the theater of war. Using satellite communications and TV cameras, the planes are actually controlled from half a world away.

The Nellis Air Force base, in North Las Vegas, is the real home of the air war in Afghanistan and Pakistan. This command center doesn't have much in common with the front lines except for the dry climate. The missile-firing Predator UAVs take off from airbases in Nevada, Arizona, and Southern California and fly 8,000 miles to the shooting war. The airplanes often fly in shifts, since they are capable of fulfilling missions for up to 24 hours, day and night.

In 2001, there were only a few hundred drones in U.S. arsenals; now there are over 5,000 operating around the world. Therefore the demand for drone "pilots" is increasing. The Army and the Air Force have vastly different criteria in seeking these personnel. The USAF trains the drone operators to have the same skill sets as a "real" pilot. They are even dressed in flight suits as they command their planes from air-conditioned rooms or trailers. The Army, on the other hand, has its own drone program, and an appropriate candidate, according to one general, can be any grunt with PlayStation experience.

Rather than design the drone controls after those of a real airplane, with a yoke of pedals, levers and a joystick, the decision was made to model the controller on the one found in standard video games to leverage the training these candidates already have — ten or more years' experience on a PlayStation. This is the ultimate video game. The shrink-wrapped variety may promise a realistic experience, but actual live bombs and actual dead foreigners are hard to beat as they are televised back to the command center.

Some of the drone "pilots" are into the game, enjoying the sound of fire captured on remote mics and watching human targets being taken out. They get the thrill of being a warrior along with the convenience of a Big Gulp near at hand — but without spattering blood, and the loss of buddies, limbs, eyesight, and other personal body parts.

Civilians and military analysts have concerns about the cavalier nature of warfare with so little at risk for the warrior. Certainly the number of civilian deaths would seem to raise a red flag in these new asymmetrical wars. The U.S. military knows that they have a ready pool of drone-operating candidates. By his own admission, the target recruit has been in training from the instant he first holds a game controller in his hand. These guys will have already inflicted thousands of "kills" without personal consequence. It is not uncommon for drone pilots to fill downtime with more action on a PlayStation 3 and Xbox back in the barracks.

In Vietnam, the first "television war," we were able to see it all. In the decades since, the military has sought to isolate the toll of warfare from the general population. The American public has a low tolerance for seeing its young people blown to pieces. What's more, we are an empathetic people who generally exhibit kindness and generosity to our vanquished enemies. We like the idea of punishing the foreigners until we see their suffering faces and hear their stories. Then we reach for our national checkbook. In wars since Vietnam, therefore, the Pentagon has either banned the media (Panama and Grenada) or subjected them to limited access by "embedding" reporters among fighting groups.

With digital magic, the military is now separating the combatants from the front, making the mess, stench, and risk of warfare disappear. Civilian military analysts have real concerns about the cavalier nature of this type of combat, one with so little at risk for the warrior. Certainly the number of civilian deaths should raise a red flag in these new asymmetrical wars. There's little comfort in knowing that many remote operators are suffering from some of the same stresses that real pilots do. More worrisome still are the drone "pilots" who show no signs of remorse or emotional distress at being remote-control killers.

And now the Army is developing a ground "game" with roving robots for recon, along with a brand-new model, cleverly called

MARS, that totes a machine gun and is operated by a game control pad.

An Army of ONlinE

Vietnam has been called "the rock music war." It was the dominant pop culture of the time, powerfully expressing the rebelliousness of a generation. The square, crew-cut military recruiters with shiny shoes who showed up at schools in the 60s and early 70s, therefore, didn't manage to make many connections with the students of the day. There was no cultural affinity whatsoever, but it really didn't matter since they had a draft to snag the young men who wouldn't sign up on their own.

With today's all-volunteer military, recruiters have become as slick as marketeers, using all the tools of the times and going anywhere potential recruits hang out: not just the suburban malls and the small towns of the nation, but online as well. Instead of a rickety card table covered with glossy brochures showing globe-trekking soldiers commanding local respect, the Army has put gaming to work.

In Philadelphia, the shabby downtown recruiting center has been upgraded to the "*U.S. Army Experience Center.*" This theme park of gruntness has 60 computers loaded with military games, as well as a full complement of Xboxes loaded with shooters. It's a $12-million-dollar arcade that blasts music and encourages hanging out.

This theme park/arcade even has a full-scale Humvee that allows potential recruits to fire upon projections of enemy positions on a huge screen complete with ripping sound effects. There are other simulation actions launched from helicopters. In short, it's a playground that, as with video games, delivers the thrills of battle with no risk of personal harm.

Jesse Hamilton, a veteran of Iraq, has said that the *Experience* and the use of video games are very deceiving and far from realistic. Hamilton, who is member of Iraq Veterans Against the War says, "You can't simulate the loss when you see people getting killed."

So, with a generation that has become increasingly inured to inflicting death through play, and military recruiting and training

145

becoming a form of mass-market entertainment, the U.S. Army is creating a virtual "farm team" of promising, young empathy-free soldiers though game play. Perhaps it makes sense since 3D game graphics technology has its roots in expensive military simulators.

The Military-Gaming Complex

The U.S. Army has even created a commercial game to exploit its "brand." It's called *America's Army* and is among the top 10 first-person shooting games. The Army did its research and knew that males under 34 years of age are more attached to their game consoles than they are to passive TV. According to some reports, 75% of these under-34 male households possess at least one game system. The program is part of what the Army calls its "Digital Generation Initiative," or DGI. The U.S. Army is a serious player at this game and even has a presence at the E3 gaming business trade show. The officer in charge of this game-as-recruiting-tool effort is named, appropriately, Col. Casey **War**dynski.

Any person can just download the basic application from the web and immediately indulge in warrior fantasies while being indoctrinated. Nearly 10 million individuals have downloaded and played the game with a cumulative total of 250 million hours of online play.

Functionally, it is no different from any other first-person shooter game. It, like many others of its genre, is based on the *Unreal* engine. Game developers often use a common skeleton of functionality to create a game. This gives the developer the ability to concentrate on creating the rules and graphical appearance of the game instead of having to invent new mechanics of the gameplay. Many different game titles are created from common engines. Basically, the functions of a 3D first-person shooter are nearly identical. The *Unreal* engine was developed for a game called *Unreal* that focused on killing mutant aliens on their home planet. This setup seems metaphorically appropriate for the missions of today's military. Start with mutant aliens, then substitute the foreigners of your choice based on the political goals and fears of the moment.

Jason Benlevi

The Games of Death

We have been told that military budgets are tight. Half a trillion dollars a year just doesn't buy what it used to at the Pentagon. To raise a few extra bucks, the Army has a deal with a major game developer to create and deliver an "authorized" U.S. Army game. The delicious irony for you fans of "freedom fries" is that the game developer, Ubisoft, is French, headquartered in Paris, and has an exclusive license to publish U.S. Army games around the world. These games are now available on Xbox, PlayStation, and PCs.

The press release, which follows, is titled "U.S. Army and Ubisoft Join Forces in Unprecedented Agreement to Deploy America's Army Brand Worldwide."

SAN FRANCISCO, CA - April 14, 2004 - Ubisoft, one of the world's largest video game publishers, and the U.S. Army, the world's premier land force, announced today that they have entered into a long-term agreement to develop and publish games based on the U.S. Army's industry-leading America's Army game. This historic agreement marks the first time that the U.S. Army has ever exclusively licensed its brand to a game maker and will dramatically expand the reach of America's Army to the vast console game market.

The partnership gives Ubisoft unprecedented behind-the-scenes access to the vast resources of the U.S. Army, to give console gamers the same realistic, action-packed, military experience players have enjoyed with the award-winning PC game. With this agreement, the Army will also exercise ongoing content review with regard to the same features of realism, character progression, and game play motivated by Army values that have made America's Army one of the most popular online games in the world.

"America's Army is an excellent vehicle through which young adults can discover how soldiers are developed and employed in the defense of freedom," said Colonel Casey Wardynski, originator and director of the America's Army game project. "Ubisoft has extensive experience in producing best-selling military games, and we're looking forward to getting their developers in the field with our soldiers."

Too Much Magic

"Ubisoft is in the business of delivering what the consumer wants, and consumers want officially licensed games," said Jay Cohen, Vice President of Publishing for Ubisoft Inc. "When you play a sports game, you want to play the game from the official league, and now, when you play an Army action game, you'll be able to play the undisputed leader."

This French company also has a contract to use the name of Tom Clancy, author of numerous militaristic novels that celebrate war. In the glorious tradition of the Reagan and Bush Jr. administrations's "chicken hawks," Clancy chose not to serve and never actually wore the uniform.

Even those who don't have the funds for computers or game consoles can get in on the fun with the Virtual Army Experience (VAE). Each VAE is housed in a slick trailer containing multiple PCs and giant flat-panel screens that allow visitors to play *America's Army*. These trailers are deployed to public events such as air shows, NASCAR races, and county fairs. The idea is to allow potential recruits to "test drive" soldiering. This "experience marketing" effort and data tracking of potential recruits was sophisticated enough to be featured on the cover of *Adweek* magazine. The Army's marketeers are delighted and probably taking credit for rising recruitment (even though the harsh reality of a collapsing job market is driving many young people into the arms of the military).

Wide-eyed business journals, like *Business First Columbus*, are proclaiming the educational benefits of *America's Army*:

"Imagine kids playing video games in which they drive jeeps and aim cannons — and it's sponsored by the Ohio Department of Education. That will be the case as the state becomes the pilot site for incorporating a free online game from the U.S. Army into science and math curriculum developed by a national non-profit. Clifton, NY-based Project Lead the Way will place modules from the America's Army game in its Principles of Engineering course. Students will use geometry and physics to estimate and carry out virtual ballistics projects and helicopter drops."

Jason Benlevi

Virtual ballistics and helicopter drops? In Ohio, the heart of the "Rust Belt," where the industrial base continues to crumble, could these math and engineering skills be better employed in developing innovative products to outproduce our global competitors instead of calculating how to bomb them accurately?

Machinima Mash-up

Learning to use 3D animation software is a challenging task. So is mastering a musical instrument. Taking a photograph that is well composed and skillfully illuminated requires years of theory and practice. But tech magic has now made it possible to create high-quality media by ripping, sampling, and capturing the work of others with inexpensive digital tools. Enter the "mash-up."

The mash-up (or remix) is the tool of people who have creative impulses, but not necessarily the talent or willingness to learn an actual creative skill. The most prevalent example of mash-up culture is rap — the first form of popular music where actual skill isn't a requirement. Rare is the rap group where someone actually plays an instrument; mostly you just slice and dice other people's music. The video and photographic equivalents of rap are turning up on the web using purloined imagery that has been stolen and cobbled together rather than created. Now the gaming and virtual worlds are exhibiting the latest incarnation of mash-up. It is called "machinima."

The name is itself a mash-up of **machi**ne and cine**ma**. The practitioners create "cinema" by capturing the video output from games or virtual environments, such as *Worlds of Warcraft* or *Second Life*. Since the games/sites have a ready-made 3D environment (no easy task to create on one's own), it is simple to replicate the illusion by just screen recording the actions of one or more characters. Then the video clips are edited together with new voiceovers and storylines. No one will ever mistake these movies for Pixar productions, but they work.

Originally, machinima was used among friends to extract clips for demonstrating favorite gaming tricks. The next step was laying in new dialogue over these short scenes featuring cybersoldier characters. Since the mouths couldn't be seen, there was no need to synchronize sound. A series called *Red vs. Blue* started the ball rolling. The dialogue itself was pure parody with stoner-esque ruminations on the meaning of life spouting from these warrior characters. Someone called it "*Clerks* Meets *Star Wars*." It was much like Woody Allen's *What's Up, Tiger Lily?*, a Japanese spy film redubbed by New York comedians.

Though often sophomoric, when the pieces aim for satire, they can be funny. In fact, arguments have been made that this is an entirely new and creative endeavor. When you look more closely, however, and see the gaming 3D engines powering endless orgies of violence and mayhem, you might well conclude these are the works of angry, frustrated males with too much time on their hands, or fanboys obsessively involved in virtual worlds and sci-fi conventions. Although there might be some raw talent out there, it's clear that the typical machinima maker is in need of an anger-management class — or maybe just a job and a girlfriend.

In the meantime, the marketeers of the original games are still undecided about whether the machinima trend is good or bad for business, since the makers are among their most obsessive fans. There is no doubt, however, that corporate lawyers get chills when they see intellectual property being purloined.

Guitar Hero vs. GarageBand

It is encouraging that there are popular electronic games that do not require shooting, swordplay, or sorcery — just an interest in music. It's natural that music, loved by almost everybody, should find a comfortable niche in the world of electronic play. The question is what experience should "music play" simulate? If the answer is real skills we aspire to achieve, it is curious which games have emerged as the big sellers in the music/rhythm category.

There seem to be two different approaches to music play. One is exemplified by *Guitar Hero* (as well as other games of its genre, such as *Rock Band*.) The other approach is Apple's *GarageBand*.

The guitar in *Guitar Hero* is an array of colored buttons on a toy-sized plastic guitar. You play the game simply by pressing the right color keys in the order displayed on a vividly animated game screen that also shows stage lights and suggests an onstage performance. If you "play" poorly, the audience will boo; do well and the audience will cheer you on.

The object of *Guitar Hero* is like playing "air guitar"; you replicate the theatrics of a rock star or "guitar hero" rather than actually playing music. The term "guitar hero" grew out of veneration for rock's most notable or flamboyant players, starting with Jeff Beck, Jimi Hendrix, Eric Clapton, through Eddie Van Halen, to the various metal and hair-band players who followed. It seems odd that someone who knows how to distort an E-string though a high-gain amp should be considered a "hero," but that has been the term for more than a generation of guitar stars.

Branding the game *Guitar Hero* tips us to what is askew with this popular game. Although it's preferable to the sociopathic interactive training of *GTA*, *Guitar Hero* turns the pleasure of playing music into a competitive event. It's about racking up points. Even that might be okay if the player were actually learning to play real guitar riffs, but that's not what the game involves. The toy guitar only has 5 brightly colored buttons as notes. If the guitar merely simulated a scale of real notes — eight buttons to signify an octave, one for each full note on the scale — the player would at least learn a basic building block of all Western music. But he doesn't.

Although the player follows a vividly animated "tablature" showing which key to push and when, there is no relationship between those buttons and an actual six-string guitar. In short, you could play *Guitar Hero* every day, for years, score an amazing amount of points, become a competitive champion with thousands of hours of the game under your belt, and then, when presented with an actual physical guitar, have no more clue than the average dog has about how to play the thing.

Like most "twitch" games, it is about hand/eye coordination. It is almost like a driving game with the on-screen fretboard substituting as a "road" you "drive" the fake guitar along. Digital magic helps to create a compelling simulation in *Guitar Hero*, but it is a simulation that does not relate to anything in the real world. To further the delusion, a full-size guitar featuring only the five colored buttons, a strum, and a tremolo bar is available for $200. For $100, you can buy a real guitar and actually learn to play.

Countering the *Guitar Hero/Rock Band* model is Apple's *GarageBand*, which avoids the "game" aspect of music play. There are no points to be scored — only the self-gratification of learning to play music.

The *Garage Band* player is presented with real instruments. A keyboard is prominently featured on the screen. A stroke of a controller pad has you playing scales almost instantly. A click of a mouse and the keyboard becomes an organ, or simulates a guitar or a bass, or even horns. Another click and you can record, playback, or edit your efforts. There is a simplified approach to music notation that anyone can comprehend without years of lessons. You can even plug in a real electronic keyboard or have an interface for an electric guitar. The newest versions include music lessons from famous musicians.

The difference between the two approaches is stark. Instead of learning nothing except how to push buttons in sequence like a chimp, time spent playing *GarageBand* yields some ability to actually understand and play music on real instruments.

A drawback to learning music in the digital world is the lack of the sense of touch. Ask any musician about her instrument. She will, of course, mention the quality of the sound it produces, but right after that she'll talk about the instrument's "feel." Musicianship includes exploring the mechanics of the instrument — the touch of the strings, the action of the valves, the spring of the keys. An instrument encourages engagement. Young Jimi Hendrix trying to play a right-handed guitar backwards led him to unlock sounds no one had heard before.

Giving a child a $100 acoustic guitar and a chord chart will teach him more about music than 100 years of playing a much more expensive game console. It may not be as flashy, and in the beginning it will be frustrating. Nevertheless, there is something to be learned from the physical experience of actually playing an instrument that can never be approximated on a computer screen. Music is not about racking up points. Not one real guitar hero will ever emerge from games like *Guitar Hero*.

Flattening the World to Fit a Screen

It is incredibly important for children to play with objects in order to develop their senses, talents, and abilities. Touch is richly informative. The time children spend in contact with a computer keyboard or track pad delivers no illuminating tactile information. The action happens on a flat screen with only a representation of objects from the physical world that cannot be touched, tasted, or smelled. A child's toys are essential to their sensory and emotional growth. Even if they abuse and break them, taking things apart is how they learn to put things together. It's the start of analyzing how things work. What academics these days call "deconstruction" you were doing instinctively when you were only two years old.

Unless you grew up Amish, toys are the products of companies. Whether they were handcrafted or machine stamped by the millions, when you were a child they were personal and emotional touchstones. From the advertising of Cracker Jack prizes to Star Wars toys, the 20th century witnessed a growing relationship between popular media and toys.

When you were a kid, your lunch box probably had artwork derived from your favorite TV shows (mine were *Zorro* and *Looney Tunes*) or toys (Hot Wheels or Barbie). For you, it was a way of making a statement. For pre-digital marketeers, however, it was a tool. But that didn't matter to you — the box was your personal possession and it delighted you. Now toymakers and producers of children's entertainment are almost indistinguishable from one another. There is a symbiosis: video sells toys, toys sell videos.

We don't make mass-market toys anymore in the U.S. In the early 21st century, children's toys, even from U.S. stalwarts like Mattel and Hasbro, are almost entirely manufactured offshore. Imports are the "survival strategy" to lower prices. Driven by the hardball purchasing policies of Walmart, and other mega-retailers, the costs of consumables are continually lowered, contrary to the rules of economics and regardless of the damage to the domestic economy. With toymakers thus squeezed at the retail level, marketeers need to do more to monetize their brands. Digital magic provides the answer.

"Brand-crazed" marketeers are turning every conventional plaything into an on-screen experience. Popular toys like The Littlest Pet Shop, Lego, Ty, Barbie, and the whole Disney-branded universe of characters are being disembodied from physical playthings and flattened into digital apparitions on a computer screen.

There are a lot of powerful business reasons for this, foremost among them the digital magic formula. Real products require manufacturing one item to sell one item. Digital products only require making one and distributing copies infinitely. At nearly zero cost.

Through dedicated websites, toymakers and media companies have built a direct channel to sell kids merchandise, both physical and virtual. Virtual products are "toys" or accessories for toys that only exist as bits, such as an outfit for an on-screen virtual Barbie or a little character figure for a virtual Lego playkit. Real money is exchanged for these virtual objects. An irresistible deal for any toymaker, a website has a dual purpose. Firstly, it provides advertising and promotion for the company's physical products more cheaply than traditional broadcast media.

Secondly, it's a bona fide revenue generator, both through subscription fees and as a direct channel to sell merchandise. As we've indicated, kids need to touch things. Hold things. Possess things. Break things. Touch matters. So, while there are numerous reasons for business to go down the virtual road, there is nothing positive there for your children. Promoted as social or game sites, these are thinly veiled e-commerce outlets. Each site looks virtually identical and offers the same three on screen options: "Product/Play/Shop."

Product/Play/Shop

So what sort of play takes place on these sites? The experiences, regardless of product line, are almost always the same. There's a channel for chat, some simple Flash-based games, and a virtual room where play with digitized versions of the toy character can take place. In these virtual rooms, characters can "socialize" and customize their environs. Some sites require purchase of the physical toy as the price of admission. Usually there is a code number or a USB key that activates the character onscreen.

So what's the point of this play? Many parents mistakenly think that their kids are exhibiting "more advanced" behavior by using computers as playthings. The thought that children are more intelligent because of computer interaction is a vestigial notion that has been carried over from previous decades and generations, when computers required advanced knowledge to be operated. Today's computers, and computer-based play, require no more skill than using a TV remote control — and often the remote is more challenging.

These websites present uncomplimentary aspects of our adult commercial culture. It is a purely a "pay-to-play" environment. It begins with a free trial to hook the child into playing. Then, because kids don't have credit cards, parents need to sign up for a subscription fee that is deducted monthly. There is also the wide adoption of the "velvet rope" business model, where the site provides free access for a limited amount of activities, perhaps a few games, and access to browsing for products to buy. Then, for a premium, kids can have "VIP privileges." Right away, the lesson is that money defines class, with parents put in the uncomfortable position of enforcing that class distinction at an earlier age.

Disney's popular site, The Penguin Club, unapologetically embraces class marketing. Click on the tab for the "VIP section" and the image sums it up. The illustration shows two uber-cool penguins being admitted by a nightclub-inspired doorman, while two other penguins look on longingly in the distance on the wrong side of red velvet rope. In the digital playground, not everyone is a Hilton.

Mattel's site allows kids to dress up their virtual Barbies and chat with other virtual dolls, but some accessories are only available to VIP members and VIP Barbies are distinguished from others by their sparkly tiaras. Non-VIPs? No sparkle. Who wants their child to be the one without the sparkle?

Each of these sites is almost identical in form and function, regardless of the product line. The look features deeply saturated blues and purples with rounded and soft corners and fonts. They all compel children to spend more money and less time within their own imagination. It may be a broadband connection, but it delivers a narrow emotional bandwidth that informs few of the senses.

Let's consider Lego. If you went to a store and bought a Lego playset, your child would look at a diagram or image of a character and build it piece by piece. Play would involve free imagination, swooshing sounds, and made up dialogue.

And Lego's approach to the web? As with most of these toy sites, landing on the home page reveals the typical "Product/Play/Shop" options. "Play" includes a selection of games featuring characters that are fully animated to look as if they're constructed from Lego building pieces. They're already assembled and scripted into games that look very much like what you'd find in a console game. Onscreen pre-built characters do not stimulate the imagination — they become just another form of branded animated entertainment rather than an original construction by the child.

Aside from losing the intellectual and manual-dexterity exercise, scripted games remove the randomness of play and replace it with a pre-scripted experience. There is no sensual experience at all. By contrast, in physical play all the senses are at work and integrated. Crayon and paper are a richer experience than playing in a virtual space. There is the feel of the wax, the texture on paper, the force breaking the crayon, the shuffle through the box to find the right color, and even that unique crayon smell that stays with you your whole life. On the screen there is only a flat world of bits.

The digitization of child play also involves makeovers of "intellectual properties." Classic characters from children's books are receiving makeovers for the digital age. The most hideous example of this is the transformation of the charming, simply drawn characters of Katherine Holabird's book series, *Angelina Ballerina*, into a balloonish, digitally rendered 3D look.

Playtime transferred from the physical world to the screen does nothing to help children develop a full range of senses, talents, imagination or interpersonal skills — but it makes publishers and media property owners rich with little effort.

Wii Step in the Right Direction —

Let's Get Physical

On the road to the Xbox 360 and PlayStation 3 ruling the gaming world, while home entertainment executives were trumpeting "from the comfort of your couch" as the mantra for digital entertainment, there was an unexpected game changer, Nintendo. This one time leader (that was given up for dead in the console game business) made an a-ha discovery of what should have been an obvious fact: People enjoy moving around! Whether it is dancing, playing field sports, ping-pong, skiing, running, or having sex, bodies in motion can be fun.

Thumb-twiddling, even if it is thumb-twiddling on a force-feedback controller while gazing deep into a 3D video environment rendering high frame rates, is a physically passive experience. Nintendo took a different approach than Sony and Microsoft. It wasn't about the graphics, it was about human motion. It was an active game. Instead of a joystick or thumb-action game controller, the Nintendo Wii had a motion-sensing wireless wand that allowed users to simulate real-world physical activities. Wii's wireless controller allowed users to pretend that it was the handle of a tennis racket, a golf club, or a baseball bat.

The gaming magazines and bloggers were unimpressed with Nintendo's simplistic graphics. Analysts projected huge numbers for PlayStation 3, the most sophisticated gaming system ever built. Surprise! By December 2008, while 20 million PS3 systems were sold, the Nintendo Wii sold 50 million units and became the hottest item on holiday shopping must-have lists. The success completely caught Nintendo, and everyone else, by surprise. The Nintendo Wii system got people up off that couch and swinging away at virtual tennis balls and sending bowling balls rolling down screen alleys.

In the late 90s, we had seen another active game title arrive that was a huge hit. In the guise of a game, *Dance Dance Revolution* (or DDR) had sedentary geeky teenagers hitting the virtual dance floor in the guise of a game. The concept was strong enough to be adopted into real dance clubs and even high-school fitness classes. It didn't change the overall metaphor of playing electronic games, but it should have been a clue.

Wii attracted players of every conceivable age. It was intuitive to play and didn't require navigating netherworlds, zombies, avatars, and gunplay though complex storylines. It was play, pure and simple. Nintendo created graphically simple renditions of traditional games that everyone knows how to play. These were games that anyone could pick up and play as easily as swinging a tennis racket, baseball bat, or golf club. This was not for couch potatoes.

The good news is that people are getting hurt. Yes, it can be good news because they are moving muscles that they haven't used in years with free-swinging games like boxing and bowling. For some parents, and even grandparents, the games are a way to engage with children on an equal footing.

One of the most compelling rationalizations to buy a Wii is *Wii Fit* which is an electronic Jack LaLanne for a generation that grew up on Atari. With the Wii Balance Board, lower body movements are fed into simulation of yoga exercises and even downhill skiing.

Of course, none of this simulative activity is as good as the thrill of actually getting out in the world and doing the real thing, but it is way better than zapping among 500 cable channels and shooting the same aliens and zombies over and over again.

Whether *Wii Fit* winds up in garage sales alongside Abdominizers and Nordic Tracks is hard to foresee. But this might be the right combination of physical activity and convenience for many people. It certainly is a better choice than driving the SUV to the closest parking place in front of the gym's door while chugging a whole bottle of sugary sportsdrink.

Not everyone is an athlete, or has the opportunity to get out and play, but at least Wii reintroduced people to their bodies in motion as source of delight. As Katherine Hepburn said in *The African Queen*, "I had no idea a mere physical experience could be so exhilarating." It's easy to forget as we are glued to screens and keyboards all day.

Cycling Back to Simplicity

The other lesson of Wii is keeping the game simple. Frankly, the big game companies have painted themselves into a corner of ever more complex games. Over the years, games have become insanely expensive to develop. More graphics take more worker hours. Even with Nintendo's simple graphics, the company needs to sell a million games to make a profit. Sony and Xbox games require at least double that to be profitable.

As we always see, when too many resources are concentrated on building complex systems with diminishing returns, pretty soon there will be lots of smart innovators looking for simpler ideas.

The most enduring games are often the simplest. You just need a paper and a pencil to play Hangman or Tic-Tac-Toe, and not even that for Charades. On social network sites, Scrabble and Hangman were fairly popular. Simple games are easy to learn and can be casually played. Complex games require a slavish devotion to achieve mastery. Play becomes as time consuming as working or studying, yet yields none of the benefits.

The iPhone and other handhelds have allowed game developers to make inexpensive, casual games that can fill a few nervous moments while waiting in a medical office or pacing for a train. Pleasant distractions, perhaps, but there are other inputs from the real world that are ignored if you are always staring into a tiny screen.

Practice What We Teach

If play is practice for life, think about the world you want your kids to inhabit. What they are playing today shapes how they will be living.

Over the past decades, people in the Western world have managed to put a greater distance between themselves and the realities of the life that sustains us. People used to farm their own food; now food just shows up in a package. Fast food meant people didn't even have to cook those farm products. There were some computer games a few years back that allowed users to create virtual vegetable gardens. (The "social" game *Farmville* has roots!) The simulation or sim games were a lot of work, and in the end, what was the payoff? You can't eat virtual veggies off the screen. Giving children a few seeds and having them get dirty in the garden is a richer and more realistic experience.

What are the skills or experiences that are garnered in video-game scenarios? Learning to shoot and annihilate without risk to one's self? Learning to commit felonious assault? Driving at murderously dangerous speeds? Are these the skill sets for a productive civilization?

Even if these are just fictional escapist scenarios that don't relate to real life, the virtual experience is part of the problem with our economy. We have products on our shelves, but we are losing the skills to make the products as companies outsource to cheap-labor areas of the globe. There is no consciousness about the physical process of creating things of value. Products just appear as if by magic, while games sap our creativity and time, making us less productive and competitive.

As with many aspects of digital magic, we are creating distance between ourselves and reality. All but a few of us are involved in the ongoing war, and it's been made into a spectator sport, with live coverage and color commentary from the front. On our TV screen we have only a distanced, virtual experience, while the victims die for real. We have become isolated from reality as game developers work even harder to simulate reality with greater fidelity.

Unlike any other time in civilization, play has extended well beyond childhood and become a business, as we indulge in simulation for its own sake while we forsake concentrating talent on solving our most serious — even catastrophic — problems. We have literally found a way to play ourselves to death.

2.4

Moving Images:
Seeing Is Deceiving

Movies are the truth. Movies are complete lies. The art is in deftly blurring the line between these states to create an emotional experience that transports the viewer to another time, place or human experience. What makes it work successfully is what I call the "fidelity of illusion" — a convincing rendition of things that may not actually exist or events that may never have occurred as depicted. A film is an exercise in collaborative deception, where the filmmakers' illusion is made possible only when we willingly suspend our disbelief.

From the first days of motion pictures, technology has been part of the quest to create that fidelity of illusion, or "verisimilitude" — to make what we see appear more real or true. Even fantasy depends upon verisimilitude to weave its spell convincingly.

Strangely, in the digital-magic age, the facility to blur truths and lies has the potential to actually diminish the emotional impact of these experiences. This is, admittedly, a contrarian view in light of the development of extraordinary special effects. However, when you factor in our ever-increasing expectations, it clear that we are on a path that dilutes the emotional impact of movies with *too much magic*. That, coupled with marketeers' tactic to have the audience peek "behind the curtain" of digital effects, is making us too aware of the process itself. The simple truth is, once you know how the trick is done, it's no longer magic. Once again, when everything is possible, and then explained, nothing seems special.

Motion pictures are shared dreams, colored luminosity and shadows. They project their illusionary reality because of our brains' peculiar inability to register images fast enough to isolate individual photographic frames when they speed by at 24 times a second.

Hence, we believe there is motion taking place among those rapidly moving stills. There are physics, chemistry, and physiology behind the creation of this illusion, but our brains make this subjective decision about movies: "They are magic."

It is the premise of this book that "magic" is always produced by technical means. It is always a trick — a trick that delights, but still a trick. We are willing to be tricked; that's the deal we make. In return, we expect the filmmakers to do a competent job at delivering the illusion, especially when we pre-pay for the experience. This is why we depend on critics, word of mouth, "brand"-name actors and directors before plunking down our money at the box office or through the Net and investing two hours of our time. However, aside from the truth and falsity, there is another inherent conflict at play regarding movies: Are they mainly an art form or a business?

The Business of Movies is Business

Commercial aspects, as much as or more than creative, have driven the development of movies. The common use of the term "movie INDUSTRY" tells you that. And at every stage, when the fidelity of the movie experience has provided an economic advantage to its business model, technology has been employed by this industry.

It's true that a movie generally begins as a shared dream of the writer and director. Yet, making a film is a collaborative effort — massively complicated, expensive, and risky. More so than ever, creativity, technology, and money are tied tightly together.

Have you noticed that over the past decade or so even local news regularly reports weekend-opening box-office results? "The new Bond movie opened at $70 million, followed by the latest Tom Cruise film." This news, which mainly resided in the back pages of Variety, used to be of interest only to movie insiders. Now every 12-year-old knows the three top-grossing movies for any given weekend. It seems to have become everyone's business how "big" a movie opened. This "blockbuster" mentality has become a self-perpetuating marketing tool. And, unfortunately for all of us, it may be the only real validation for consumers on the tipping point of choosing a movie to see.

Despite the industry's best efforts, research cannot guarantee a winner. Still, there is no shortage of wealthy investors, many entranced by rubbing elbows with screen personalities. Infamous Hollywood accounting makes it impossible to ever state whether a film is profitable. Even without financial transparency, we know that few movies ever earn back what they cost to make, and a smaller percentage yet are ever spectacularly successful.

Buying Tech to Sell Tickets

Well before computer graphics appeared, the movie industry always turned to technology for an edge, whether it was for better photographic film, lights, cameras, sound, color, or special effects. Filmmaking is an industrial process and continuing process improvement is ingrained in its evolution.

Culturally, the 20th Century was "the Movie Century." It was an enormous part of how we were entertained, waged war, communicated information, and evoked passion and fear. It recorded what we were, where we went, and what we did. Political leaders actually made decisions based on what movies they saw — then changed history. Infamously, Richard Nixon watched *Patton* and ordered the invasion of Cambodia the next day.

Time is a filter, and the only things we can judge are those that remain to be seen. Movie truth has always been fluid and flexible. Filmic reality is always an editorial matter: what to shoot, then what to leave on the cutting-room floor. Apart from animation, however, it was never possible to entirely fabricate humans, physical objects, and geography. It was always necessary to actually capture some images from the real world, even if they were manipulated in some manner.

Even in pre-digital days, there were those who doubted that humans landed on the moon while believing that pro wrestling was real. But now you can change the image on the film and, therefore, change the perception of history. With "real" cinematography, we could always go back to the film for evidence of what actually happened. In the digital world, however, we can lose that "first draft" of reality. What is captured on film or video did not necessarily happen.

Let's Shoot the Moon

"We choose to go to the moon, not because it is easy...
...but because it is hard."

I have always loved this quote, despite the fact that is was delivered by John Kennedy to save face after the failure of the Bay of Pigs invasion. The remark announced an acceleration of the U.S. mission to travel to the moon, which was already under way. It stood apart from the usual cold-war rhetoric in its expression of our uniquely American "can-do" spirit. Taking on a difficult task — and a high risk of failure — is more rewarding than successfully leaping a shorter hurdle.

JFK and his team of handlers had a great sense of theater. Kennedy actually had this line written for him by speechwriter Ted Sorenson. A good script combined with a great performance makes compelling viewing. It is as true in D.C as it is in Hollywood.

Up to that point, there hadn't been anything more ambitious than landing a human being on another celestial body. (It is significant that there has been no comparably lofty goal embarked upon since that time. A faster search engine is not rocket science.) The Kennedys had an affinity for Hollywood and mythmaking. JFK easily crossed the line between politician and movie star. This same blurred distinction eventually delivered a washed-up actor as our president.

The first motion pictures were documentaries, filmed slices of real life. Those pioneering cameramen would drag their cameras to locations and just crank away at things as they passed by, recording otherwise ordinary activities that became fascinating on the screen. But soon thereafter, these images became spectacles and took the viewer beyond realities that they could see with their own eyes. Certainly a locomotive engine coming straight at the audience scared them out of their seats at first. But soon even that sort of thing grew stale and they were ready for a more compelling experience. As the early filmmakers knew, compelling experiences sold tickets and more was being demanded by money-paying audiences. Therefore more magic was needed to bring them in.

So we return to Kennedy and the 60s to form a continuum: One of the most significant of the early movies imagined a trip to the moon.

Georges Méliès — Magic in the Shadows

Movie magic has become a hackneyed term, but one of the most influential of all filmmakers, a Frenchman named Georges Méliès, actually *was* a magician. Called "the cinemagician," Méliès blended his knowledge as an illusionist with a keen understanding of what was photographically possible. By any measure, he was the father of special effects. He figured out how to do mattes and double exposures, and he even went so far as to hand color images on the film itself.

Using a prophetic Jules Verne novel as its basis, Méliès's 1902 film, *Le Voyage dans la Lune* or *A Journey to the Moon*, was a playful, magic-mushroom-inspired vision of a lunar trip. (It's worth noting that Verne's book actually predicted that the first moon mission would be built by U.S. defense contractors, launched from Florida, and terminated by a splashdown in the ocean.) By today's standards, the film's magic is transparent, but it's still capable of wowing an audience.

So technology had taken the public from merely watching a streetcar meander up the street to a point where they could see a book as fantastic as Verne's being brought to visual life. While the novelty was terrific for a time, audiences were soon looking for more. At a running time of ten or so minutes, the typical movie was not as satisfying as the standard entertainment experience of an evening at a theater or music hall. There needed to be more of story to grab people's interest and — more importantly — their money. (It is telling that the first places that showed movies named themselves "nickelodeons" after the price they charged to watch a film.)

What the filmmakers had yet to comprehend was that a film could alter human perception of time and space to tell a story as it had never been told before.

Cut to the Chase and a Pie in the Face

One of the first people to grasp this shift in perception was Edwin S. Porter, an electrician and projectionist who became a resident director at the Edison Studios. Edison was one of many claimants to the invention of motion pictures, and, like most studios, produced novelties to be shown in nickelodeons, some of which they owned themselves. The fare, although standard for the time, did include the first filmed pornography. Porter, however, realized that profits could be increased by adding technological magic to this new art form.

At first, Porter borrowed heavily from Méliès's bag of tricks, but soon he invented the template for the modern movie: a composition of multiple shots set in multiple locations spliced together into context. By doing this, Porter altered the perception of time and space for audiences in a way that had never been seen before and which can be expressed in one word: "meanwhile."

Most movies of the era were, in effect, one-act plays — one scene or one set of actions that took place in one single location in a single linear time stream. For example: a door opens; a man walks into the room; the man sits down at a table; a waiter brings him food; he eats; suddenly, a pie hits him in the face. As in a play, all the action takes place in real time in one location or scene. Once the novelty of moving pictures began to wear off, this sort of thing became a bit creaky.

Porter opened up the world of filmmaking. In 1903, he made a film called *The Great Train Robbery.* He decided that his story would be more exciting if the audience could view what was happening in multiple locations at the same time, both indoors and outdoors. Then he would bring these simultaneously occurring actions together into a dramatic climax. Today this is pretty basic filmmaking; back in 1903 it was unheard of.

He started with a western story since the Wild West was still vivid in the memories of the audience. It was also a popular genre for dime novels and traveling events such Buffalo Bill's Wild West Show (at this time, remember, Arizona was still just a territory). What could be more exciting than armed desperados, guns blazing, fast moving locomotives, and things blowing up?

Porter created a film that was 12 minutes long and composed of 20 different setups. The revolution came with the development of parallel story streams taking place in different locations, and "cross-cutting" them. By doing this Porter altered the perception of time and space for audiences in a way that had never been seen before. In regards to movie making, Porter made the most important invention in film – it was just one word, "MEANWHILE."

The Great Train Robbery opens inside a rather stagey-looking railroad station. Desperados enter and overpower the stationmaster. Through a window we glimpse Méliès-style magic: a clip of an arriving train composited into the window by double exposure. This solved the technical problems of shooting in two different levels of light and having to cue the train. Méliès had already conjured this trick. It is what followed that showed how movies would be a unique way of telling a story.

"The Great Train Robbery" on One Page

CUT to:
An outdoor scene. As a train makes a water stop
at the station, the outlaws surreptitiously board
the train. As the train resumes chugging along the
tracks, the outlaws commandeer the train.

CUT to:
A shoot-out with a clerk and blowing up a safe
(with hand-colored smoke.)

CUT to:
The bandits climbing on top of the cars on the
moving train and confronting the stoker (and the
birth of the classic train-top fight). The stoker
is shot (and the first stunt dummy is thrown from

the train by the bad guys).

MEANWHILE:
Back at the railroad station, a girl awakes and unties the stationmaster. It's that glass of water in the face that ultimately rouses him.

MEANWHILE:
In an entirely new scene, cowboys and frontier frauleins are dancing at a hoe down. Enter the alarmed stationmaster and the men-folk dancers form a posse and exit. The chase is on.

MEANWHILE:
Back at the train, the bandits have made their escape into the woods

MEANWHILE:
The posse is tracking them down at full gallop with guns blazing amid more hand-colored smoke.

MEANWHILE:
The outlaws are burying their loot as the posse descends on them. There is much shooting and good triumphs over evil as the last villain falls. And as a parting shot, one of the lawmen fires a shot point blank at the audience.

TITLE:
"That ougta' teach them lawbreakers"

The combination of multiple locations and the use of cross-cutting to show simultaneous action in different places was revolutionary. No earlier film had created such swift movement or variety of scene. More importantly, *The Great Train Robbery* was great "box office."

In the editing there was also something new called a "dissolve," which Porter used to soften the jarring effect of the cuts and, at the same time, show the passage of time. The technique made it possible to blend any two shots together in a gradual transition from one image to the other. In fact, Porter's *Great Train Robbery* introduced many of the techniques that were to become the basic modes of visual communication throughout film history. This film foretold that all future movie structure was to be based on "shots" rather than "scenes" — a convention inherited from stage plays.

Was it hard for people to understand that they were jumping around to view different locations? You couldn't do that in real life. Nonetheless, if one accepts the notion that movies are essentially manufactured dreams, then random movements among filmed scenes were already familiar to everyone since they mimicked the non-linear juxtapositions found in their own sleeping dreams. Movies and dreams share a common logic where realism and fantasy are seamlessly fused.

Film cutting and splicing created excitement, even if there was none inherent in the scene itself. (Over a century later, the cross-cut chase scene is still the spine of any action film.) For comedy, the fast-paced editing allowed multiple explosions of Keystone Cop frenzy and (my personal favorite) pie fights.

When we look back on these films we need to remember that cameras were hand cranked, and that cranking slower would speed up the action and make the slapstick zanier. Filmmakers learned that they could alter the perception of time and space. Cutting and manipulating film enhanced actors' performances. We could now see "close-ups" of faces — an effect impossible to duplicate on the stage of a theater. Different angles could be filmed to express points of view. Changing angles became the standard method that allowed moviemakers to hide their cuts. The actors could redo parts of scenes to improve their performance. Directors could later select the best takes and leave the worst on a place the actors came to dread — the cutting-room floor.

Movie production moved from a single integrated event captured in real time to becoming a sequence assembled shot-by-shot, and scene-by-scene. The "hurry up and wait" method of filmmaking was born. Film time became divorced from "real time." Time and space on screen became entirely fluid and that enabled greatly expanded methods of story telling.

The Movies Get Big

As the movie-watching public became savvier, the novelty of the 12-minute film (also known as a "one-reeler" since 12 minutes were all that could fit on one reel of film) began to dissipate. As mentioned earlier, the movies, despite their cheap admission price, were no match, entertainment-wise, for an evening at a stage play or music-hall revue. Twelve minutes was just not enough time for real satisfaction. It was time for the movies to "get big" and advance beyond being a mere arcade amusement.

Just before World War I, D. W. Griffith had his heart set on being a playwright. He tried unsuccessfully to sell a script to Porter. Instead, he wound up being an extra in Porter films. Some good luck helped him become, first, a lead actor and then a director for the first film company based in Hollywood.

In 1914, after some success directing a few short films, Griffith was inspired by a feature-length film (more than 60 minutes) from Italy called *Cabiria*. Griffith tried to convince the owner of the studio that the audience was ready for "feature films." The studio executives were skeptical and believed that a longer film "would hurt the audience's eyes."

So, as in many Hollywood stories to come, Griffith departed over "creative differences," found some partners with cash, and produced America's first real feature movie. It was called *Birth of Nation*. The movie became a huge hit and broke box-office records. Its star, Lillian Gish, said that it raked in so much revenue that the producers "lost track of how much money it made." It established the technical standards for what a feature film should be, including a running time that is still used for big-budget spectacles, and, apparently, some of the shady accounting practices still employed in Hollywood today.

While it constituted a huge technical advance, it also represented an unfortunate regression in social attitudes. There was no disputing its negative impact on the country's already rampant racial intolerance, particularly south of the Mason-Dixon Line. In a twisted vision, Griffith portrayed white Southerners as innocent victims of the Civil

War and Reconstruction, "victims" whose only salvation was the Ku Klux Klan. While the content was deplorable, Griffith created the Hollywood film as we know it today — including tracking shots, unusual angles, masterful parallel editing, artistic framing, dramatic lighting, real movie stars, and epic storytelling.

Though he was the political opposite of Griffith, Charlie Chaplin called Griffith "The teacher of us all." Whether Griffith was just a good student of other filmmakers or an inventor himself, he absolutely established the rules of film grammar. If Porter opened the door, Griffith let in the crowds and tore down the walls. Movie mogul Louis B. Mayer made the fortune that started his M-G-M studio by distributing *Birth of a Nation* in New England. Later of course, "LB" went on to once again soft-pedal the evils of white Southern culture by distributing *Gone with the Wind.*

The Griffith treatment was the perfect marriage of storytelling and technological magic making movies and money. Movies became an event. The movie had gone big. From this moment forward, the nickelodeon was dead.

The first million-dollar star was Charlie Chaplin, who also was also one of the great pioneer artisans of film technique. When we watch his films we see an amazing grace and fluidity of motion. Was he really that good? Yes, he was. It was not special effects. However, what was not apparent, until recent discoveries of outtakes, was how hard he labored to create his magic by relentless experimentation — filming routines over and over to find new cinematic ways to capture his talents.

Would we call these innovations special effects? Possibly, though they were special only because he was special. It was technical, but only because of his physical technique. The same can be said for the equally brilliant Buster Keaton. It is important to remember when we watch Chaplin or Keaton that what happened on the screen had actually happened in real life. It was edited, but the performers actually performed what the audience saw.

We know that the ability to edit film was essential to the art, but was there a science to it? Was it magic or deception? What could we believe just by seeing it?

Too Much Magic

Red-Faced Truth: The Kuleshov Effect

Meanwhile, in the Soviet Union, a political light year and revolution away from the KKK, filmmakers were dissecting and studying the films of D. W. Griffith, scientifically analyzing the effect that these Hollywood film-editing techniques had on audiences.

Leading this effort was Lev Kuleshov, a young Russian filmmaker and film theorist who started the Moscow Film School, which was probably the world's first. What he discovered has been employed by every filmmaker from Hitchcock to Spielberg. It is generally called the "Soviet Montage Theory."

Kuleshov believed that editing was everything. The juxtaposition of shots was the way in which filmmakers could influence the perception of the viewer. It was the technical and psychological key to altering time, space, and emotions. Simply by sequencing images, even if they were unrelated, people could create their own context for what the combined images communicated.

His most storied lesson, "The Kuleshov Experiment," took existing film clips and edited them into a series of juxtapositions to create synthetic contexts. In this now-famous editing exercise, he used close-ups of the famous Russian actor, Ivan Mozzhukin, then intercut the actor's face with a series of object images such as pretty girl, a bowl of soup, or an open coffin. The edited film sequences were then shown to audiences, who believed that the expression on the great actor's face was different each time he appeared. Depending on whether Ivan was "looking at" the plate of soup, the beautiful girl, or the dead woman in a coffin, he "showed," respectively, an expression of hunger, desire, or grief. The trick was that the footage of the actor was exactly the same shot each time.

Yet the audience saw something entirely different each time. His collaborator on the experiment, Vsevolod Pudovkin, described their reaction with amusement. "They raved about...(Ivan's) heavy pensiveness of...mood over the forgotten soup, were touched and moved by the deep sorrow with which he looked on the dead woman, and admired the light, happy smile with which he surveyed the girl. But we knew that in all three cases the face was exactly the same." Viewers created their own context based on the combination of images. The "Kuleshov Effect" has been exhaustively studied by psychologists and is fundamental knowledge among modern filmmakers and political media makers alike.

It was the artfully blending of cinematic truth and lie. The "truth" was that the actor was actually there, the bowl of soup existed, the young girl was playing, and that the coffin was solid and presumably heavy. The "lie" was the context and the emotions that were perceived in the performance. This was a really handy bit of magic for filmmakers to take advantage of. They did…and still do.

Context, recombined, could yield a synthetic creation — synthetic emotion, synthetic space, and synthetic time — that used photographic images from the real world as its raw materials. They created convincingly "credible untruths." A credible untruth is the core capability of great filmmaking.

As a San Francisco resident, I am always amused to see movie chase scenes in which the sequence of streets shown in the pursuit is unintentionally laughable. A street across town from the one we're on suddenly comes into view around a fast-turning corner. One of the most memorable adventures in synthetic geography is the scene in The *Graduate* in which Dustin Hoffman goes to see his reluctant girlfriend in Berkeley. He is seen driving his two-seater through a tunnel and onto the upper deck of the Bay Bridge, which would actually prove fatal since the direction on the upper deck flows toward San Francisco.

We like movies because anything is possible, if you are willing to believe. We make that deal every time we enter the theater or press play on the remote. Synthetic time and space is fundamental to movie fun. The Soviet filmmakers understood the technique but they ultimately fell short in the fun department when Comrade Stalin became film critic-in-chief.

Silents Were Golden

While Soviet intellectuals were theorizing and dodging the secret police, in California the film industry was creating its own synthetic-time-and-space empire. Using giant enclosed stages and public-relations mastery, Hollywood became a fantasy factory in every sense of the word both inside and outside the studios. They were creating legends in their own time and their own — and everybody else's — minds.

Theory is fine, but practice makes money. The Hollywood movie became the dominant popular art form in the 1920s and the moguls had the receipts to prove it. All of the major studios that we know today had been established by the end of the 1920s (Universal, M-G-M, Paramount, Warner Brothers, 20th Century-Fox, Columbia, and United Artists). Business was good and movie actors were living as large as the movie screens. Money — lots and lots of it, flowing in from all over the world — was blurring the line between a star's screen persona and real life.

There was only one really big problem with movies. The actor's mouths moved and nothing came out. Oddly, the movie moguls didn't consider this a problem at all. From a commercial perspective, silent films were pretty terrific. You only had to make one version of the movie and you could market it anywhere in the world. All it took was changing the title cards to the appropriate language. That was cheap and easy to do. Audiences had acclimated themselves to the silent cinema, which was easy since it was the only type of film that existed.

Hollywood had a good thing going. Then one studio had to ruin it for all the others.

Let's Get Real:

Raising the "Fidelity of Illusion"

How could technology improve the movie experience? Simply by improving the fidelity of illusion — making the experience more lifelike. Sound and color were obvious places to start. In the 1920s, the chemistry for color was still far from perfect or even pleasant. Recorded sound was already of a reasonable quality in records and synchronizing it with a picture was bothersome but not impossible, at least with sufficiently urgent motivation.

Sam Warner was looking for an edge. Warner Brothers was one of the smaller studios and they wanted to get big to survive. Hollywood was dog eat dog, and the Warners, even with Rin-Tin-Tin, were the runts in the Hollywood litter. Their crosstown rivals (M-G-M and Paramount) were among the big dogs. Sam thought going for sound would give them an edge. Elder brother Harry was the money guy. Harry didn't see the point. He famously said, "Who the hell wants to hear actors talk?" In 1926, however, their studio suffered a big loss; now money was talking. So they started releasing experimental one-reelers that featured Vitaphone sound. It was a novelty, certainly, but was it a business? A feature-length sound film would be expensive.

Harry was still unconvinced of the fiscal viability of sound pictures, but Sam made the argument that replacing the live theater orchestra with a recorded version would be a money saver, especially since the company owned some of the movie palaces. Harry could get behind that. The brothers agreed to make a sound picture, but not a "talkie."

Don Juan, staring John Barrymore, premiered at the Warner Theater in New York in 1926. It was a silent picture with a synchronized orchestral score and sound effects. In small towns, it was more impressive than a piano. For big-theater owners, it saved money.

Although *Don Juan* was a success at the box office, it did not earn back its huge production costs. The Warner studio was still in trouble. While the bankers and competitors were closing in, the brothers decided to throw the dice one more time.

You Ain't Heard Nothing Yet

Al Jolson was a huge star. The biggest anyone had ever been. He was a sensation on Broadway, in vaudeville, and on records. He was the voice of his age, like Elvis in the 50s. There is another parallel. Both of them became huge stars by introducing and popularizing black American music to white audiences. Although we think of Jolson's blackface act as horribly racist today, that misconstrues the context of the time. In reality, it was his version of *Black Like Me*. It was an empathetic portrait honoring black musicianship. Throughout his career, Jolson was a champion of African American composers and musicians, even using his clout as a star performer to include black performers in Broadway productions. He was the ambassador of black music in America that opened the door for Louis Armstrong, Eubie Blake, and many others.

Jolson's vehicle for Warners, *The Jazz Singer*, was an unusual story for its day in its ethnic content. The film business was predominantly composed of eastern European Jewish immigrants, and for the most part they were very self-conscious about calling attention to their own ethnicity by presenting Jewish characters to the American audience. Given that Warner Brothers was on the verge of going bankrupt, it is odd that they picked a story about a young Jewish man who was conflicted between his family's cantorial legacy and his desire to be a jazz singer. But it was also a story that could resonate among immigrant families that were raising first-generation American children conflicted about whether they were part of the old world or the new.

Jolson was interested in getting involved with the picture business and *The Jazz Singer* was close to his own personal story. Warner Brothers signed Jolson with a $200,000 guarantee. It was Jolson himself who provided the financial backing. It was a risky venture.

The technology was not totally there to make an all-talking feature picture. Sound recorded directly on film was still in development. The Vitaphone process that Warners employed was actually a dual system of large phonograph records that had synchronized starting points for each reel of film. Vitaphone was optimized for music and serviceable for one-reel "talkies," but with anything beyond one reel, synchronized dialogue was challenging and could look ridiculous if it went out of sync.

For the most part, *The Jazz Singer* is a silent movie, an ethnic melodrama, but it had sound when it mattered, which was every time Jolson sang. The consummate entertainer also improvised his own monologue during the act that added vibrancy to the performance. Those ad-libs included the prophetic:

"Wait a minute, you ain't heard nothing yet."

The Jazz Singer was a smash! Thanks to its success, Warner Brothers was suddenly flush with cash. They followed up with another Jolson film, *The Singing Fool*. This one was all-talking and singing. *The Singing Fool* included the song "Sonny Boy" which became the world's first million-selling record and the first cross-media success. (It worked out better for Warners than that AOL merger thing.)

Sound was now the new standard for fidelity of illusion and silent films were about as appealing to audiences as the old nickelodeon shows to audiences of the time. Hollywood was scrambling, careers were ruined, actors actually had to learn their lines, crews needed to shut up, and cameras needed to move indoors because ambient noises would ruin the scenes. There were questions from many silent film directors and producers about whether it was just a fad, but, of course, there was no going back.

At first, background music in films required a live hidden orchestra on the set. Everything — music and dialogue — had to be recorded at the same time, in the same place. The music helped to set the mood and covered some of the ambient noise. Some critics wondered whether audiences would grasp that the music was just there as atmosphere without any visible source, but since they were used to it playing live for silent pictures, audiences easily made that leap.

Too Much Magic

Some of the greatest movies ever made were filmed in the 1930s. Sound films would actually be made multiple times, with different actors for "foreign" language versions, using the same sets. The fidelity of illusion with spoken dialogue was the new standard. It was obviously more realistic, but that doesn't mean movies were not literally fantastic; in fact, sound allowed the ultimate confection, the movie musical, to be the industry's next big innovation. The uplifting tunes and spectacular art-deco scenery were just in time to take the edge off of the Great Depression — the more nonsensical and fluffy, the better. Hollywood had mastered the next level of synthetic realities and had done it in amazing style. People suffering through hard times also delighted in screwball comedies featuring hare-brained socialites and millionaire buffoons.

Dramatic pictures gained the ability to have intelligent, literate, and witty dialogue by some of the best writers in America, who were churning out scripts in studio bungalows supplemented by the strong drink of their choice. A more naturalistic style of acting was evolving as well, especially as better sound-recording techniques meant that actors no longer needed to shout to be recorded. Given the resolution of cinematography of the day, the sets also had a remarkable verisimilitude and the lighting design was just brilliant enough to convince the audience the actors were outdoors even if they were really in a sound stage.

Editing the World

Hollywood became a time machine reaching back into history, biography, and literary classics for material. Even though the technology was delivering an experience of greater realism, that didn't mean content stayed authentic to the source, or had much resemblance to the truth. These films were not without prejudices or subjectivism. For the many unread or under-schooled viewers, this was indeed a realistic portrayal of history on the big screen. The typical cinematic treatment of Native Americans, immigrants, and blacks horribly misrepresented these groups. In large swathes of the country where audiences had no first-hand experience of the people being portrayed, what was communicated on the large screen tended to create and perpetuate stereotypes.

Events that never happened, or were grossly misrepresented, became ingrained as factual in the popular imagination. Biographies were sanitized, history was revised, and the movies perpetuated these illusions as popular truth. Then, as now, people tended to believe what they saw. As cinema became more technically adept at creating a synthetic reality, it attained a greater emotional power.

Newsreels were a part of the mix at the movie theater. Yet, even those were not necessarily an accurate portrayal of reality. With our historical (sometimes hysterical) perspective, we can look back at newsreels with an upraised eyebrow, knowing that what's portrayed is usually only a partial truth and sometimes an outright lie. Even the documentary film was subject to manipulation. *Nanook of the North* is widely believed to contain scenes that were entirely enacted for the camera. Yet people saw it with their own eyes and believed. Hollywood and partial truth are natural companions; just about every movie ever made has a disclaimer that no one depicted in the film is based on anyone living or dead.

The Acting Governors of California

Most people know that California has had two Republican actors with orange hair serve as governor. What they may not know is that, during the 1934 election in California, the studio moguls took a direct hand in crafting a real-life "happy ending" for themselves by defeating progressive author and gubernatorial candidate Upton Sinclair.

In this campaign, the movie business used the tools of the trade to create a synthetic reality for newsreels. Louis B. Mayer and his studio produced fake newsreels and distributed them to their movie theaters throughout California. These newsreels were often scripted by the dean of yellow journalism himself, W. R. Hearst, Jr.

They did what today we'd call a "hit piece" on Sinclair, portraying him as "paling around" with Soviet agents and otherwise portraying him as a "fellow traveler." They spent $10 million on the campaign, which amounts to 200 million of today's dollars. This is widely regarded as the first modern media-centric campaign.

The problem is that once images are on screen, once they are blazed into our visual minds, we tend to believe them. When it's entertainment, we suspend our disbelief willingly. That's the deal we signed up for. A space in our brain reserves the notion that what we are seeing is a performance. When images purport to be "news" or "documentary" we tend to believe what we see, unfiltered. Unfortunately, it is all too often that the more credible it seems, the bigger the lie.

Fidelity of Delusion

What the Soviets theorized about film technique had become widely known. These editing techniques were not limited to entertainment films. The same editorial approach was applied to documentary films and to films that purported to be non-fiction. Movie magic could take actual events captured on film, synthesize a post-event context, and transform the "true" images into content deliberately misrepresenting reality. Suspension of disbelief was not necessary — in fact it was unwelcome — when these films claimed to be documentaries.

In the early 1930s, the Nazis tried something different. Rather than creating propaganda by twisting filmic reality in post-production, they scripted their own twisted reality and then filmed it. Worse yet, they filmed it faithfully and exquisitely. Using the finest German film and lenses, they would capture the political event of the century.

The Triumph of the Will is a film that documents a 1934 Nazi rally in Nuremburg. The event itself, a Nazi party congress, was somewhat akin to a political convention on a megalomaniacal scale. Rather than sending a crew out to capture an occurring event and edit a version for the newsreels, the entire event was designed with the film production in mind. It was a made-for-media event.

Cost was no barrier for the production. Hitler's personal architect, Albert Speer, built the sets and "designed" the event. Leni Riefenstahl, the director, had a crew of hundreds with at least

30 cameras, including aerial positions. This was not cinema verité capturing events as they were unfolding. Nothing was left to chance.

Nazis such as Josef Goebbels knew the power of the images and coordinated on-the-ground events and cameras with great precision. The effect is overwhelming. This dwarfed anything that Hollywood had ever attempted. Outside of a brief prologue, the film has no narration. The picture tells it all.

For the Nazis investing in this film made sense. While tens of thousands could be at the event, they knew that millions could see the film. The uniformed throngs and thugs were just extras in the movie. What people saw on film actually happened, but without the film the impact would have been dissipated after the event. Instead the effect was multiplied as the film was screened over and over again.

It was propaganda, but not something that was synthesized from elements extracted out of context in an editing room. Everything that happened in the film actually happened. The sequence of actual events was entirely dictated by the making of the film.

From Hitler descending though the clouds in his airplane like a god, to the quasi-military choreography of leagues of workers with shovels performing drills in formation, this is a scripted event faithfully recorded. Leni Riefenstahl, like most "reformed" Nazis, revealed a half-truth in an interview years later: "If you see this film again today you ascertain that it doesn't contain a single reconstructed scene. Everything in it is true. And it contains no tendentious commentary at all. It is history. A pure historical film… it is cinema verité. It reflects the truth that was then in 1934, history. It is therefore a documentary. Not a propaganda film." In her last sentence her "truthiness" goes astray. But if you had the blood of millions clouding your viewfinder you'd have some mental editing to do too.

Ironically, Fraulein Riefenstahl delivered the raw stuff to do cinematic battle with Hitler and his followers, since the most enduring images of Hitler and of his abbreviated "1000 Year Reich" were harvested from this film. While this portrait of ordered militarism comforted the "Master Race" types, the underlying reality of the situation on the ground was a complete lie. What audiences saw were Nazi aspirations — a fiction acted out in the "real world." At the time, Hitler had no real army, and although the Nazis seemed fearsome and omnipotent in the film, in reality the regime's hold on power was still quite tenuous.

The Nazis created a synthetic filmic reality. The rest of the world saw either an authoritarian inspiration or a peculiar madman. While there had been other madmen before him, this one used the cinema as a weapon.

Why We Fight

It took awhile, but on the other side of the world, Hollywood ultimately made good use of *Triumph of the Will* once the war effort was underway. Director Frank Capra, most famous for his idealistic films, *Mr. Smith Goes to Washington, Mr. Deeds Goes to Town,* and later for *It's a Wonderful Life*, made a series of seven newsreels for the United States Government called *Why We Fight*. It was propaganda, masterfully fabricated, but for a good cause: The Good War.

Gathering documentary footage shot in on the battlefields of the Pacific and Europe intercut with footage from *Triumph of the Will*, Capra synthesized a new context for the Hitlerian event of 1934 so that citizens could connect the dots between the evil intent and the cancerous fascism that was spreading across the world. The clear impression communicated by *Why We Fight* is that "if we don't stop this madman we are next."

Capra remarked that *Triumph of the Will* "fired no gun, dropped no bombs, but as a psychological weapon aimed at destroying the will to resist, it was just as lethal." Capra intercut Hitler's 1934 speechified aspirations with the horrors of its fulfillment. It made the case powerfully. It should be noted that one of Capra's more interesting manipulations was actually speeding up the footage of Hitler to make him look even more maniacal than he already was — no mean feat.

Did *Why We Fight* contain cinematic manipulations of time and space? You bet. It was at least five years between Hitler's pronouncements and the formal outbreak of World War II. Capra and his team closed the time loop to show the cause and effect.

The biggest omission of reality in *Why We Fight* was explaining why we weren't fighting in the period between 1934 and 1940, or why world leaders did not challenge Hitler much earlier. Did the impressions of *Triumph of the Will* delude them into thinking he was already too powerful? Or was this just another megalomaniac who managed to capture his rantings on film? Which "reality" did the film convey?

European Intellectuals Debate Reality... Again

After the war, with their biggest troubles behind them, European intellectuals resumed debating the nature of reality, including its relation to the cinema. Was film a mirror of reality or something that was totally artificial? Needless to say, they didn't manage to reach any agreements. At least three intellectuals of note weighed in on the topic, Siegfried Kracauer, Rudolf Arnheim, and Andre Bazin. The debate boiled down to this choice: Was film:

a.) a construction of clips where context was synthetic?

or

b.) an objective reality that could be captured holistically?

In reality, these are not mutually exclusive. What is important is the continued awareness of the conflict between the lie and truth of movies.

While Hollywood came through the war more or less intact, European film industries were broke and decimated. In the ashes of Europe and its economy, a new film industry was beginning to develop a different ethos. These new films, smaller and more realistic, would influence European cinema for the next generation and, eventually, a new wave of American filmmakers.

Italy's neo-realist movement is the clearest example of this new cinema. Rather than shooting on sets, cameras moved out into the streets and the subject matter was drawn from real life. All dancing-all singing was out for the time being. Busy urban settings would work just fine since the Italians tended to post-record (dub) their dialogue later — even into Italian. (In the years to come, the Italians had an advantage when making films that included internationally famous actors, because everyone could speak their own language on the set and be dubbed in later.)

In America, the taste for fantasy lingered longer, but for soldiers who had just returned from the war, the sweeter sensibilities of pre-war Hollywood were set aside for the emerging detective and film-noir genres. Their roots were tied closely to the world they experienced in the war — gritty heroes forced into reluctant gunplay with agents of evil. The cold wet streets, corruption, and darkness echoed what they had already experienced. The Western carried on its tradition to comfort a generation through clearly delineated good guys and bad guys.

What we know, with a hundred years of perspective, is that movies have a natural tendency to oscillate between realism and fantasy. Audiences want different things at different times depending upon social factors.

TV and the Blacklist

Hollywood had a good and profitable ride from 1914 to the late 1940s. Then its comfortable world started to change. The assault on business-as-usual happened in three overlapping waves; technology, a court decision, and a self perpetuated political delusion.

The technology that Hollywood didn't really see coming was TV. While TV is 24/7 by 1,000 channels today, in 1948 it was on the air for just a few hours a day. It was local and it was live. It also wasn't very good in most of the country. If you lived in New York you could see Broadway actors on TV doing plays or big-name nightclub acts, but in most of the country it was birthday clowns and accordion acts. There was no network connection. There was no way to electronically record shows.

Although the movie and television industries are closely interconnected today, back in the early days of TV they were at war over the same audience. Although some of the third-tier studios in L.A were producing TV programming, the major movie studios froze it out. Most of the programs emanated from New York, since the TV companies were offshoots of the big radio broadcasters headquartered there. NBC and ABC were part of RCA, which made radios and TVs. (In an odd twist, NBC in recent times owned by GE, which was started by Edison, which at one time owned RCA.) It was no coincidence that Manhattan was also where the ad agencies were.

No matter how mind-numbing the programming, which included dancing cigarette packs, people were glued to the tube. It had two compelling advantages, it was free and it didn't require leaving the house, both of which were just fine for war veterans cocooning at home with their young families. The move to the suburbs meant that the movie theater wasn't necessarily around the corner anymore.

Since Hollywood studios still owned the movie theatres, every butt parked in front of the glowing tube represented lost revenue in unsold tickets and popcorn. But even worse, they eventually lost a legal challenge that wound up divesting them of theater ownership itself. Now studios had to compete for the attention of a shrinking audience and a cadre of hard-nosed independent theater owners.

Finally, Hollywood shot itself in the foot when it capitulated to the Red Scare by blacklisting actors, writers, and directors. Since the smartest and most talented people in Hollywood tended to veer leftward, the industry became intimidated and consequently dumbed-down in terms of subject matter.

The Big Screen Strikes Back

Down but not out, Hollywood had abundant technology tricks up its sleeve to battle the TV invasion. Taking a cue from its past, the industry's first decision was to make the movie big again. Really big!

Movies, despite being an older technology, had three areas of technical supremacy over TV: color, high-fidelity sound, and wider screens. TV pictures were small, blurry, and blackish-grey and white. The film industry had already developed multiple processes to deliver bigger than life color, while a viable color TV system was still a decade away. Widespread adoption of color broadcasting was a decade beyond that.

Additionally, the dinky confines of the TV box featured sound from a cheap five-inch speaker and buzzing vacuum tubes. Movies were already employing high fidelity, stereo, and magnetically recorded sound processes. The sound in a movie theater was glorious and rich.

The shape of the theater screen changed, too. The screen dimension had been in the same aspect ratio (the proportion of height to width) since the beginning of movies, just slightly wider than a square. Now Hollywood made the screen wider, more like our natural field of vision. This dramatically raised the fidelity of illusion, especially when compared to the little grey TV box. Technically, making a widescreen TV was half a century away.

There were many widescreen movie formats in the 50s and 60s, including VistaVision, Panavision, and CinemaScope. The most innovative and enduring system is the anamorphic Panavision system. The anamorphic widescreen process uses a lens to optically "squeeze" a wide image onto normal-width 35-millimeter film. The movie-theater projector is equipped with special lens that "unsqueezes" the image back into the original wide proportions. Panavision meant that notoriously penny-pinching theater owners didn't have to buy new projectors.

Color, stereo sound, and widescreen — you just couldn't duplicate that with television. Hollywood also monopolized big stars. Appearing on TV meant your movie career was already over; unlike today, "TV stars" were doomed to a career in the little box. Movie studios, in their infinite "wisdom," didn't think that people would pay to see actors in theaters whom they could see for free on TV.

With Hollywood monopolizing "bigness," the films gravitated toward spectacles that you couldn't see properly on a TV screen. Studios had some success in creating movies as events. "Event" movies played in big downtown movie houses with huge screens and advance ticket sales. The films selected for event showings were lavish musicals and ponderous epics.

If anything defines mainstream Hollywood of the 50s and early 60s it is the "epic" — big and colorful, projected on a wall-to-wall screen, and sometimes even shot on location. There were Romans, Vikings, kings, big-sky westerns, Bible epics — all of them "good family pictures." Technically, the fidelity of illusion was excellent, though the art direction was rather hokey. Often the films were so long that they had an intermission. Theatre owners particularly loved that because it revved up candy counter revenue.

It is interesting that the WW II generation had a huge appetite for westerns and Bible epics. Fallacious stories about the Old West and mass-market religion mixed mythology and hero worship with no relation to reality. It is easy to see how this potent mixture could lead to working and middle class people voting for the two phony cowboys, the religion-pandering presidential candidates, Reagan and Bush. The so-called "Reagan Democrats" had their ideological indoctrination in these films and then voted against their own economic interests.

Technically, some big-screen movies were visually impressive. The most impressive of all were Cinerama movies. The Cinerama process used three projectors and a special curved screen to set the three images edge to edge. It was a really deep experience that was wasted by watching Debbie Reynolds sing.

Some films from this era look spectacular but are nearly unwatchable today, while even non-classics of the 30s and 40s more than hold up. The real problem was content. With the Hollywood blacklist, an antiquated, moralistic production code, and second-tier directors from the 30s, the films of the 50s and early 60s were both limp and bloated. The worst of these was *Cleopatra*, a film that went completely out of control and wound up completely unwatchable. Despite the PR build-up, the movie's vast budget overruns and meager box-office returns caused 20th Century-Fox to sell off much of its back lot as a real estate development for what is now called "Century City."

With TV growing in sophistication and networks producing quality shows (relatively), Hollywood got even more desperate.

Actually, it just got downright weird. How weird? Well, how about "Smellovision," or a double bill of *Bwana Devil* and *The Creature from the Black Lagoon* in 3D? Yes, 3D — a technology that is always the future and always will be. Generally, 3D is more trouble and expense than it's worth. We're currently experiencing yet another wave of 3D mania, thanks to digital technologies. It provides some expensive thrills yet remains only a novelty. Creating great movie experiences that endure is never about technology, and certainly not about 3D.

Coming of Age with Sexy Europeans

After WW II, the European movie business took an entirely different course. Smaller budgets and an intellectual culture combined to generate a new style of filmmaking that used simpler production techniques along with more realistic, even artful, dialogue. By the early 60s, this "New Wave" of filmmakers was starting to see some of its films reach the U.S. — at least in a few big cities.

Even though the technical aspects of the filmmaking were usually quite basic (black and white; monaural sound) the stories themselves displayed a realism that Hollywood films had never achieved. People in these films talked like real people, even if we couldn't understand a word of the dialogue, the attitude seemed more natural and believable. The stories were smaller and more personal. Contrast that to the stilted pseudo-classical language of American epic movies and the hammy dramatics of Victor Mature and Charleton Heston.

Urban intellectuals and college students in the U.S. were discovering European films as never before, as independent "art movie" theaters began to take root. Freed from Hollywood conventions and puritanical production codes, European film themes were more mature and even overtly sexual. Compare Doris Day to Bridget Bardot as a sex symbol and you get the idea. Mainstream Hollywood was losing a generation, just as surely as Detroit would decades later.

As the 50s gave way to the 60s, baby boomers were headed out to the movies on their own, and they didn't want to see an aging John

Wayne get the girl, greasy Rat-Packers in sharkskin suits waxing hip, or corny musicals aimed at their parents. They wanted to see their own generation on the screen. What they got instead was *Gidget* and *Beach Blanket Bingo* — exactly what a bunch of over-the-hill movie moguls thought teenagers would want. As for date night at the drive in, the Bible epics were non-starters for "scoring."

Only accidently did mainstream Hollywood make films that had a degree of verisimilitude for teenage baby boomers. *Rebel Without a Cause* and *Blackboard Jungle* both touched a nerve, even though the stories were focused on the illusory parental nightmare of the day, "juvenile delinquency." Still there was more reality on the big screen than what was seen on TV shows like *Father Knows Best* and *My Three Sons* where the all-knowing dad never broke a sweat in his cardigan or worked real hard.

The "Generation Gap" was emerging and the youngsters wanted their own movies. The low-budget tier of Hollywood was all too happy to oblige, making a quick buck from a quick movie. There had always been B-picture makers, and now independent studios were churning out quickies for drive-ins. New, lightweight European cameras and sound gear made it easier to make movies cheaply, "on the go." No need for sets, stars, or big crews. A movie could be made in 10 days or less compared to the months it took to make a regular Hollywood movie. They were called "10-Day Wonders." Youthful producer/director Roger Corman earned the title "King of the Bs" as he churned out hit after teenage hit, often with campy tongue-in-cheek titles.

Quasi-horror and biker films were good drive-in fare. The youth market was being served. The films were so bad they were great. Some went on to immortality, like *The Blob* or *The Little Shop of Horrors* (which came to life again decades later as a big-budget, star-studded musical).

With film students from UCLA and USC as crew and talent, producer Corman initiated a new generation of filmmakers who could make films fast and cheap without the big studios. In New York, a similar independent film scene also emerged from NYU, the downtown underground, and TV ad makers. For these folks the goal was to make movies that were more personal, like the ones from Europe. Among this new generation were Francis Coppola, Steven Spielberg, Bob Rafelson, Martin Scorcese, and a guy named George Lucas.

By the mid 60s the mainstream Hollywood movie was an embarrassment of creakingly old leading men getting the girl, obviously closeted gay leading men, bad music, sanitized war movies and repressed sex comedies. Amazingly, Dean Martin was the biggest box office draw at the time.

Meanwhile, first wave Baby Boomers were tuning out TV, standard Hollywood fare and Top 40 pop music. The Boomers had their own music, an emerging culture of live performance, free-form radio and underground press. A parallel media universe was developing. Mainstream Hollywood didn't get it. The new generation of independent filmmakers was ready to roll.

Easy Ride to Big Money

The availability of hand-held movie equipment was in sync with the "On The Road" cultural revolution of the 1960s. In 1968, during the height of a worldwide generational cultural revolution, Peter Fonda, son of Henry and star of Corman's biker films, conceived and produced an independent film that changed everything. It was called *Easy Rider.*

Fonda's co-stars were Dennis Hopper, who had already plied his trade on TV series like *Gunsmoke*, and a Corman-factory bit actor and scriptwriter named Jack Nicholson. The production was shot on location and on the road with nothing but available light. The cinematographer reportedly said "God is a great gaffer." The production budget was well under a million dollars. The soundtrack music was completely contemporary, featuring the leading bands of the time. The film rocked. It wasn't like an Elvis or Beach Party movie. This was music as it was being heard in college dorms and communal households in San Francisco. The film found an audience and won an Oscar for Nicholson. *Easy Rider* was a huge hit at the box office.

Easy Rider was successful because it had something new: "cultural verisimilitude." It wasn't generationally demeaning like the portrayals of "hippies" that were seen on network TV shows. The fidelity of illusion was excellent, with real locations and contemporary situations. The filmmaking technology did not get in the way. In this case low tech equaled more reality. The film was a journey and the journey was a film. (The pot was probably real too.) Ironically for me, the film was rated "R" (no one under 18 admitted without a parent), so I had to go with my dad.

Because it cost less than a million dollars to make and took in 20 times that (back when tickets were two bucks), Hollywood studios took notice of the new generation. Actually, they took notice of how cheap the film was to produce and how much it raked in. This success launched a wave of independent films that were low cost and culturally connected to the audience. No special effects. No orchestrated soundtrack.

For the next ten years, directors were introduced to the world and they changed the rules of American film, by replicating what they learned from watching European films and older American classics. Realism was key. The fidelity of illusion wasn't a technical achievement. It was provided through character, story, and language you wouldn't hear on TV. The movies were doing what TV couldn't do, and that attracted a new generation of moviegoers and filmmakers.

At the same time, Big Hollywood was hedging its generational bets with big-budget disasters or, rather, "disaster movies." Burning skyscrapers, doomed jumbo jets, sinking ocean liners, hurricanes, comets — anything that could go spectacularly wrong did, spectacularly. These cameo-clogged, special-effects films were technically adept, but completely brain dead. There were lots of excellent special effects and demographically selected, washed-up movie stars. For the WW II generation, I guess it was entertaining to see a much older Shelly Winters in peril of drowning once again.

For younger independent filmmakers, it was a different approach. Following the European model, theirs were personal, often autobiographical, and coming of age films. The era produced Martin

Scorsese's *Mean Streets*, which featured an actor named DeNiro who probably worked for subway fare. Like *Easy Rider*, Scorsese's feature film cost less than a million bucks to make.

Also produced for under a million dollars, George Lucas' coming-of-age picture, *American Graffiti*, was a bit different. Not at all "edgy," it featured a playful nostalgia for the days before widespread hipness. There were no special effects, but plenty of innovative audio, thanks to sound genius Walter Murch. In fact, the term "sound design" was an outgrowth of this film. It's worth noting that Lucas had to craftily dodge union rules so that Murch could work on his movie. Needless to say, *American Graffiti* was a huge hit, returning 70 times its investment. Adding to its revenues was a best-selling LP of oldies featured on the soundtrack.

There was a list of long-in-the-tooth Hollywood executives who turned down making *American Graffiti*. They also turned down a quirky sci-fi film that Lucas also wanted to make. After all, sci-fi movies were beyond dead at that point. (Lucas' earlier *THX1138* was no exception.) But on the strength of *American Graffiti*, Lucas got a shot at the movie he really wanted to make: *Star Wars*. Still, it made studio executives queasy, after all a $10 million production budget was a bit rich for an independent filmmaker.

Personal Films Meet Personal Computers

As we all know now, *Star Wars* is the biggest money-making creation ever put on a screen. From its first day, the lines went around the block, and the ticket sales went beyond anything anyone could imagine. It broke the sci-fi film genre wide open again, a genre that, by its very nature, required special effects to create a credible fidelity of illusion for things that do not exist. *Star Wars* did not disappoint.

Finally we arrive at the point where computing and filmmaking intersect. Before we start down this path, ask yourself a simple question:

Which Star Wars films do you think were better, the first two or the last three?

Moving Images: Seeing is Deceiving

If I'm guessing correctly, your answer will show you the impact of digital magic and computer-generated (CG) imagery on the movies.

The first *Star Wars* films worked because of what always makes a movie work - appealing characters and a story to tell. The films had warmth, adventure, and humor paired with special effects that had not been seen since *2001: A Space Odyssey*. There was detail for the nerds, but also wacky, fun characters that everybody loved. Real "live" characters; even the robots and monstrous otherworldly creatures were played by actors wearing costumes or puppets shot on the set along with live people. There was opportunity for interaction among living beings. From the onset human chemistry was at work. Even if the lines were a bit dorky, the actors were aware of the dorkiness and worked with it. The early *Star Wars* films were just plain fun.

The later films were masterpieces of art direction that utilized acres of CG-rendering farms and hundreds of digital artists. However, the story lines and characters were just not up to the first two films. Although the second wave included some excellent English actors, what was missing was the fun and the live interaction of the first-wave characters. Wave two had hardware, but no humanity or humor.

The cast included computer generated (CG) characters that were not actually there when the film was shot. The actors are speaking to no one, interacting with nothing — and it shows. Inserting the CG characters required a vast staff of graphic artists and computer geeks. They could quantify and codify movements with motion analysis, but the CG characters lacked the spontaneity of live performers.

A real actor can shape a part. Yoda is funnier and more lovable as a Frank Oz puppet interacting with the live Luke than as the CG character he later became. In fact, CG Yoda wasn't even placed in his scenes until after the film was shot. The puppeteer delivered a more compelling performance, simply because he was a performer. Someone at computer screen in the bowels of Lucasfilm just didn't have that skill.

The last Star Wars movies were tedious for the same reason that space-oriented sci-fi movies were always flat because they were about stuff. They have plots that have no emotional connection. There are dazzling effects without personality.

The irony is that Lucas started by making personal films. It surprising that he forgot the lessons. (There was that *Howard the Duck* thing; but it's probably better left forgotten.) Perhaps the machinery of digital filmmaking is so vast an enterprise that the humanity gets squeezed out of it. Certainly, Lucas's Industrial Light and Magic is a huge enterprise that grew out of a strange coincidence of time and place.

Coincidence of Place

How did personal filmmaking somehow morph into a digital box of tricks? It started with a coincidence of time and place. In the early 70s, Francis Coppola and George Lucas decided to base the nascent American Zoetrope film company in the San Francisco Bay Area. The area did have a rich independent film movement, though much of it was supported by making porn. At the same time, a few miles south in the San Jose suburbs, the personal-computer movement was also getting started at the same mid-70s time right before *Star Wars* arrived on the scene.

In the 70s, Intel invented the microprocessor. That meant the electronic components to make computers would become cheap enough for hobbyists to build their own. Just as films went from mega to personal, the same transformation was happening in Silicon Valley. Among these hobbyists were long-haired counter-culture types who peopled the Homebrew Computer Club and the West Coast Computer Faire.

While kids in L.A. aspired to be rock stars and film directors, two kids in San Jose aspired to be computer entrepreneurs in the manner of Bill Hewlett and Dave Packard of HP fame. One, Steve Wozniak, was the classic jokester/nerd armed with a soldering iron. His slightly younger pal, Steve Jobs, had an artist's sensibility and a revolutionary's zeal. Together they started Apple Computer, with the credo of making it possible for artistic and non-technical people to use computers to do creative things.

There were other junctures of creativity and computers taking place in the Bay Area. In 1977, Robert Abel and Associates was hired by the Foote Cone and Belding agency to create a breakthrough computer-generated ad for jeans maker Levi Strauss. Bob Abel transformed the famous orange Levi pocket tag into a cute 3D animated object with dog-like behavior. The tag was seen moving through an environment where both live and computer-generated people strolled along a sidewalk. The 60-second spot used realistic lighting and fully rendered character animation with lifelike fluidity at a time when such things were largely unknown.

After the financial success of *Star Wars* led to the first big-screen version of television's *Star Trek*, Bob Abel's group did much of the computer-generated special effects. Previous computer-generated graphics were flat and no better than what would be found on a game of *Space Invaders* or *PacMan*.

There was also an emerging nexus of video games and movies. In 1982, *TRON* was the first realization of that crossover. It was the first film that completely depended on computer-generated and composited imagery for story exposition. *TRON* required enormously expensive computing resources. To get it made, Disney required a computer company called Information International to invest their own resources in the film. *TRON* cost twice as much as the first *Star Wars* to make, but barely rippled the box office. It showed in theatres sparsely populated by lonely guys without dates. Variety pretty well put their finger on why it wasn't as broadly successful as *Star Wars*.

> *"TRON is loaded with visual delights but falls way short of the mark in story and viewer involvement. Screenwriter-director Steven Lisberger has adequately marshaled a huge force of technicians to deliver the dazzle, but even kids (and specifically computer-game geeks) will have a difficult time getting hooked on the situations."*

Just as we had seen in the 1950s, technology dazzle and spectacle do not add up to compelling movie experiences. Story and character win every time. *TRON* came up short where the first *Star Wars* movies were strong.

Computing made its next crossover into the movie world when Ted Turner, in an attention grab for his networks, announced that he was going to start "colorizing" classic black-and-white movies that came under his control. The film community was enraged, and with good reason: The films looked terrible. It wasn't quite as dumb as his subsequent move to let AOL acquire Time Warner, but at least it met resistance and Ted backed down.

By the mid 1980s, several Bay Area companies were developing computer-based animation technology. Pacific Data Images (later to become DreamWorks Animation) was doing TV commercials, including transitioning the Pillsbury Doughboy from stop motion-animation (à la Gumby) into a computer-generated character. TV networks were doing slick title bumpers and station IDs with motion graphics. Although most of these promotional graphics were essentially flat 2D animations, they required specialized computer systems that only big TV networks could afford.

Movies Get Silicon (Valley) Implants

Then a group of students and professors from Stanford University started a computer company that was entirely dedicated to creating full-motion 3D graphics. It was called Silicon Graphics Incorporated, or SGI. They called their product a "visual computer." The company's first two orders were significant.

The first box was for the U.S. Department of Defense to do visualizations for flight simulators. The second SGI visual computer was headed to George Lucas. Lucas and his Industrial Light and Magic (ILM) group were using their wealth and talent pool to invent and produce CG effects for films other than their own. It was a good business, and Lucas had the vision and cash to develop it. In the period between the two generations of *Star Wars* movies, ILM became the place for Hollywood to buy the most advanced CG effects in the business.

Lucas also had another computer graphics company that he sold to Steve Jobs in 1986, which was renamed "Pixar." Rather than doing special effects, Pixar specialized in doing computer-based character animation and making software for animators. Pixar struggled for many years, supported only by draining Steve Jobs's Apple Computer millions.

In the meantime, SGI became the place to go for 3D "reality simulation." The machines, although expensive, did not require customers to write their own software, which would have been cost prohibitive. There was off-the-shelf software called "Wavefront" that could do full-motion photorealistic graphics. The SGI systems, rapidly upgraded into what were called "Reality Engines," were also being downstreamed to be affordable by less-wealthy creative types.

Doing a full-length CG film was still too expensive and risky. Therefore, many of the new CG projects were short pieces like commercials and music videos. Throughout the 90s, the proliferation of CG into commercials and music videos became pervasive as the price of 3D computing grew less expensive.

Parallel to the activities at ILM and SGI, Pixar produced two excellent short films that were composed entirely with 3D animation, *Luxo* and *Tin Toy*, both of which brought inanimate objects to life. The graphics were lively and nearly photorealistic. More significantly, the short films had a brilliant sense of humor and a richness of character.

The Disney studio realized the value of SGI systems for doing complex animated scenes, mainly to model complex motions, or to render rich, 3D-like backgrounds for their traditional 2D painted-cel animation. The "ballroom scene" in *Beauty and the Beast* is a prime example of mixing traditional character animation with a computer-generated 3D background. Innovative at the time, but now if we look at it in retrospect it seems a bit off and incongruous.

CG character animation reached a critical mass when Pixar released *Toy Story*. Based on their previous short film *Tin Toy*, the feature-length *Toy Story*, which depicts the secret life of toys, was a huge hit. Pixar followed up this success with *A Bug's Life*. Simultaneously, DreamWorks made a movie called *Antz* that "borrowed" Pixar's general concept but without the brilliant technique or humor. Worse, it was burdened by mediocre storytelling. *Bug's Life* scored big, while *Antz* went down the hole.

Meanwhile, 3D graphics from SGI, along with their use in automotive design, medical research, and engineering, were finding their way into advertising, especially ads for cars. Over the years, fewer and fewer actual autos were being filmed for commercials. Instead they were lifelike 3D models that made it easier to put oversized SUVs in more outrageous locations than they will ever reach in the real world. The world of SUV adventure as shown in commercials was almost entirely synthetic. But, since most of these behemoths were destined for mall parking lots, it didn't matter what the truth was about their capabilities.

Commercials That Raise the Dead

A commercial usually requires spending big bucks for a mere 30 seconds of content. It needs to make an outsized impression. In advertising, "brand" matters. No brand is bigger than a legendary pop or movie star, living or dead. With CG as a tool, death no longer was a barrier to getting a celebrity endorsement.

Digital magic took the step of raising dead celebrities for several notable ad campaigns, as long as their relatives, who apparently didn't mind cashing in on their memories one more time, were ready to sign on the dotted line.

The first examples were actually rather fun and had an Andy Warhol sensibility. Hershey's took a fun, artsy treatment that brought Elvis back to life in their *"Huh Huh Huh…Hershey's"* commercial. It was playful and since Elvis had long since been a memory for sale by his heirs it was no big deal.

But soon it started to cross the line in a big way. One unsavory example was the classic *Singin' in the Rain* sequence turned into an ad with Gene Kelly splashing up puddles around his object of infatuation — a Volkswagen.

This tastelessness was soon outdone by a digitally modified version of Martin Luther King's historic 1963 March on Washington. We see the grainy news footage of the civil-rights leader delivering his world-famous "I Have a Dream" speech, but as the camera digitally pans around, it reveals nary a soul standing on the National Mall witnessing the event. Instead we hear a voiceover intone some lame corporate message for Alcatel, a French maker of telephone equipment. Dr. King is reduced to being a pitchman by digital magic. The scary part is how well the ILM team created this spot's fidelity of illusion. With a few workstations and servers, they erased history.

As if that weren't enough, the same avaricious agency/product team repeats their sin by emptying Yankee Stadium for Lou Gehrig's "Luckiest Man Alive" farewell speech. It's pathetic that these people couldn't find anyone actually living to say something good about their products, but instead had to resort to some very expensive tricks to get attention.

The TV campaign was accompanied by similarly altered print ads. We are more used to knowing when still photos have been altered, so the impact was thankfully diminished. I'm not much of a believer in sacred cows, but, again, if you can't find anyone among the living to praise your product, you are in trouble.

The King event is generally credited with propelling the passage of the Civil Rights Act of 1964, which outlawed segregation in public facilities and discrimination in education and employment. Yet even Dr. Michael Eric Dyson of DePaul University seems to have missed the point. "Yes, an icon is being commercialized, but he's also being repackaged for a new generation around the notion of technology.... It does bring that whole civil rights generation into the generation of technology. It says that the Internet is something for African American people, too." Huh?

Brad Burns, a spokesman for Alcatel, said,

> *"We began the campaign with almost no awareness. Now we're water cooler talk.... From a branding perspective, we couldn't be more pleased. It's not like we're selling a product.... We're simply associating our brand with it."*

As if that makes it OK.

In more rational tones, Gary Ruskin, director of Ralph Nader's Commercial Alert was quoted as saying,

Too Much Magic

"If Alcatel thinks it brings credit upon itself by ripping off dead heroes and reducing them to the level of Joe Isuzu and the Taco Bell Chihuahua, it needs to think a little harder."

Forrest Gump introduced the same technique into movies by inserting and compositing Tom Hanks into footage of an awards ceremony with President Kennedy. Overall, the technique and effect in this case is rather dreadful, not at all convincing, and already technically dated. It will stand out like a third thumb when film historians give the ultimate verdict to flush the Gump.

All the News That Fits the Sponsor

TV news organizations have long established their identities through flashy graphics and customized studio sets that surround the news-personality. By the mid 90s, broadcasters started using SGI's "virtual set" technology to plant these anchors in completely synthetic environments. Virtual sets are 3D models that exist only within a computer.

The newscaster is seated or standing in a room that is painted green or blue. Through digital magic, the newscaster appears inside a set that doesn't exist in the real world. This is not just a background, like weathercasters have used for decades. This is a three-dimensional set with a foreground, floor, solid-looking props, objects, and background. Tracking devices on the cameras ensure that the synthetic set is always in alignment with the newscaster no matter what angle the cameras are shooting from.

Each election cycle, the networks raise the bar in terms of making their virtual sets more grand and information rich. The set is starting to become the star in some cases. Companies are peddling their virtual sets according to the digital-economics paradigm of building it once, selling it, and still having it to sell again and again.

Broadcast news use of digital sets raises other issues. It was New Year's Eve, 1999. Dan Rather was positioned in Times Square reporting live. The shot showed a CBS billboard prominently positioned behind Rather. Was this good planning, or a happy accident? Actually neither. If you were actually in Times Square, you wouldn't have seen the CBS billboard, because it wasn't actually there. The billboard was being inserted digitally into the live shot. Using a technique called "live video insertion" (LVI), CBS technicians blocked out the actual billboard and placed their own CBS version in its place.

For entertainment shows we could tolerate playing loose with reality, but this was the news. It would seem that news programming has a special obligation to be faithful to reality. After this event was exposed there was a strong disagreement between CBS marketing executives and the news staff, with Rather, to his credit, condemning the faked shot.

The technique has become pervasive for sporting events where billboards in the stadium are regularly replaced with digital substitutions by TV networks that are being paid by other sponsors. To the home viewer, the swap is nearly undetectable. These inserted billboards and brand logos are becoming more common all the time in broadcast entertainment and, furthermore, we can be assured that digitally inserted product placement is happening in many of our current movies.

History re-Channeled

The History Channel, or as it known by many as "The Hitler Channel" for its abundance of programming from that era, is a satellite-enabled refuge for those who feel a connection to history mainly by watching endless WWII documentaries. Since most WWII footage has already been seen, the History Channel decided to make some of their own, first by taking the Ted Turner approach and colorizing portions, and then by substituting CG effects to recreate action scenes.

These CG animations can actually be illuminating as a graphical device to demonstrate what might be hard to visualize mentally. Slowly, however, we see less and less real documentary film footage in History Channel programs and vastly more CG-animated simulations. I fail to understand why a CG-animated P-51 Mustang attacking a Messerschmidt is as interesting as seeing the real thing. Even if you can't pick the ideal camera angles with footage that was shot 60 years ago (and with CG you can), reality is reality.

It is now reaching the point that History Channel documentaries are becoming more like watching video games involving planes, tanks, and trucks than seeing the real thing. The black-and-white truth of authentic film has much more power than an artist's rendering. Then too, as CG sequences become ever more realistic, there will be a temptation to blend them into the "real" footage. I am hoping, perhaps vainly, that we can keep our rich heritage of documentary film free of digital manipulation and pass it on without modification.

Truth or Virus

One of the issues becoming apparent in the world of virally spread, user-created content is how to determine what is, in fact, a truthful image. Everyone already suspects that an unlikely still image seen on the Net has been PhotoShopped. The same manipulation is becoming more commonplace on video. The tools to alter video are widely available, inexpensive, and require a just bit of patience to achieve near-professional results. Since we are hard-wired to believe what we see, it doesn't take much to fool us — as the following story will demonstrate.

During the ongoing debate about the health hazards of mobile phones, there has been speculation that radiation emitted next to your brain might induce tumors. Would you believe that it was enough to actually pop popcorn? I swear it's true... I've seen it on YouTube.

In the video, four people are sitting around a card table, one to a side. Each has a cell phone pointed at some loose unpopped kernels of corn. Suddenly, the kernels explode and fluffy pieces of popcorn land back on the table. Wow! I guess you just need to keep some kernels in your pocket or purse and your mobile lifestyle will always have a ready treat. It should go great with that action movie on your little 1.5-inch screen.

This video clip "went viral," and was picked up and shown on every TV news network in the world. Obviously, this was the evidence that mobile phones are truly cooking our brains! Soon, however, the makers of the video unmasked themselves and revealed the "science" of it all. In this case, what you didn't see was most revealing.

Off camera, above the phone users, pre-popped kernels were dropped by unseen pranksters onto the card table. What happened, then, to the unpopped kernels? Well, one by one they were digitally erased. It was done carefully enough to ensure that each raw kernel was coordinated to disappear an instant before a popped morsel bounced onto the table. Our brains did the rest to assume they were popped.

The incident blew a hole in the fears about mobile phones heating up our brains — and that's the problem. Yes it was a hoax, just a "harmless" joke, but it may have had the effect of belittling a real health concern. Lies are often better stories than the truth, and usually get more attention than retractions. Incredibly, brand-name global news networks carried the video without trying to duplicate the experiment or check with objective scientists to see if this "demonstration" was even remotely possible.

Reality Goes Up On Trial

As digital manipulation gets better at fuzzing-up the demarcation between truth and lie, we need some sort of rules. Since it is unlikely that we can expect rules to govern those who create visual media, we observers must develop a set of our own. In the past, the photographic negative was difficult to tamper with, rendering it quite reliable as physical evidence; now we have nothing to take its place. In short, we no longer can believe what we see.

As an example, the Zapruder film that famously captured the murder of President Kennedy was physical evidence of a terrible act. Its analyses have garnered controversy and criticism, but nobody doubts the veracity of the film itself. If such an act were to take place today and captured on our digital cameras, there would be no "hard" evidence, given the ease of modifying motion images in the digital realm. The photographic negative was a real positive in terms of telling the truth.

Now the visual "fingerprints" of crime can be erased or fabricated without a trace. So, while DNA can help to vindicate an innocent, digital media could very well convict many innocents. The good guys and the bad guys have the same capacity to modify visual proof. The same tools being used to amuse us at the cinema might become lethal weapons in the hands of corrupt law-enforcement and justice officials anywhere in the world.

We need to doubt what we see in photographs and on screens. This is a radical departure from our instincts and cultural history. Although it will be difficult to construct safeguards to prevent these abuses, we can at least begin to develop some ethics and rules to apply to our news media and video that is captured randomly by observers of events.

Outsourcer's Apprentice

When digital effects first appeared on the scene, or in the scene, there was a sense of awe; these effects were rare and caught our attention. Only a few digital artists were capable of working with enormously expensive software and computers for processes such as morphing, 3D modeling, and digital compositing. Now, there are many CG freelancers creating effects, both for small shops and the giants like ILM and Sony. Special "FX" are turning up in every type of movie. Have you noticed how long the end credits have been getting lately? In large part it's because more productions are turning to CG companies to perform the "magic" of making anything possible.

Digital effects are an industrial process and, as in most industrial processes, time is money. Every shortcut adds to the bottom line. Consequently, there is a great temptation to recycle models, effects, or even "3D objects" that are part of the software packages. Contemporary movies that are effects-heavy have little to differentiate them. How many urban night scenes of buildings, objects being blown up, and physically impossible car chases do you need to see? Action movies, which were already formulaic, have become kits of digital parts with some shots of actors added in an attempt to brand them.

Now even actors themselves have been replaced with digital models. There are some scenes, in what is (hopefully) the last Indiana Jones movie, where we see an obviously digitized Harrison Ford performing physically impossible athletic feats. The overall effect is so implausible that the movie appears more like a video game than a feature film.

The use of digital effects is so pervasive that it is invading traditional movies with no clear reason. In a clear case of Too Much Magic, the filmmakers are attempting to dazzle the audience or obscure basic cinematic weaknesses. Although digital effects, used judiciously, can create amazing illusions to communicate stories, many film productions resemble *Fantasia's* Mickey Mouse character getting hold of the sorcerer's wand and drowning us in uninspired CG images. It dilutes both the reality and magic of the film. CG is a classic case of a digital magic lamp with infinite wishes.

When everything seems possible in a movie, the dynamic tension is diminished. A Superman who is vulnerable to Kryptonite offers more dramatic tension than a Superman who is completely invincible. A good rule for filmmakers is that a solution delivered by an implausible CG effect should not resolve an otherwise irresolvable plot. It is cheating audiences when the only possible resolution of a story arrives as digital *deus ex machina*. Studios should not publicize CG effects as a movie-marketing method, thereby exposing too much of the process…and diluting the experience. Depend on story instead.

Digifilms are Different Animals

As we learn from examples from the 1950s (the age of overblown cinema spectacle and 3D gimmicks) that movies were better in the 1930s and 1940s when story and character ruled over technology.

Yet, technology continues to raise the bar at delivering greater fidelity of illusion and verisimilitude with better cameras and sound. The question is - are the movies themselves any better when CG is part of the mix? It depends. Each subcategory of CG movie seems to have different rules and aesthetics. Here are some of the readily identifiable species in the CG menagerie:

> *CG-Based Animation:* Using 3D modeling software to create 2D animated movies

> *Blendo 1:* Blending animated characters into a cinematographic world

> *Blendo II:* Blending live actors in a CG environment

> *Synthetic Reality:* Entirely CG production simulating live actors and backgrounds

> *Mainstream Fixes:* Conventional movies with CG-enriched scenes

CG-Based Animation

This is the purest and most successful form of digital filmmaking in which everything on the screen has been computer generated. It has also become a killer category at the box office. This is a double bonus for the studios, since CG features are relatively inexpensive to make compared to live action films.

These films are made using 3D modeling software to produce 2D characters and backgrounds. They are similar to traditional animated features, but created without actually painting the "cels" found in pictures like *Bambi* and *Dumbo*. The advantage is that because they are modeled in 3D they look more "realistic." They have a lifelike solidity, which makes them ideal for bringing inanimate objects to life or anthropomorphizing animals. (The savvy studios also know that since these animations are created with 3D tools, they can be re-released as 3D movies down the road.)

This genre offers tremendous creative latitude since everything on the screen enjoys the freedom inherent to animation. As we watch, we know anything can happen, including coyotes falling off mesas yet returning intact to the quixotic quest of catching a roadrunner. The laws of physics are always overruled by imagination. In this realm, there can never be too much magic.

Yet other cinematic rules, such as character and story, absolutely apply. That is why people are still watching *A Bug's Life* and have largely forgotten the contemporaneous *Antz*. Films like *Toy Story* and *A Bug's Life* work extremely well, but as animators cross over to do human characters the results are less satisfying. Even though *Shrek* was a big hit, as was *The Incredibles,* the human characters fall just short. What is acceptable for Buzz Lightyear just doesn't work for the dad in *The Incredibles* or the King in *Shrek.*

The technical possibilities present a quandary: do you make the people look more realistic, or less, to get the right comic effect? Traditional animation has the same conflict, but experience tells us that less realism and more stylized art seems to make funnier cartoons.

The biggest problem facing this genre is the predilection for reusing animated "parts." Because this procedure is very economical, there is a tendency for these movies to start looking alike. Already, the waves of cute animated animals and hero's journeys have become stale and formulaic (though they are, no doubt, good for collateral toy sales and promotions). Overall, studios need to challenge themselves to deliver more innovative stories or they will fall into the Hanna-Barbera world of banality that destroyed children's cartoons in the 60s and 70s.

Blendo I

Even before Jerry the Mouse danced with Gene Kelly, there was an urge to mix live motion and animation, starting with the Fleisher Brothers' Betty Boop and Koko the Clown. The blend was possible with conventional technology, but it is now so much easier and more elegant in the digital realm. In recent history, Robert Zemeckis has done much to revive this particular style of filmmaking. His technique has grown from traditional cell animation to become increasingly dependent on digital effects. The first three of the following films are Zemeckis productions, and they clearly showcase the evolution of digital moviemaking.

1988: Who Framed Roger Rabbit?

Roger Rabbit, a landmark blend of live motion and animation, was a brilliant technical achievement. Though not reliant on computer-generated animation, it nonetheless required a good measure of digital savvy to produce and composite the live and animated "blendo."

The art direction brought the cartoon world and live motion world together in a way that we had never seen before. The use of shadowing on the animated characters made them dimensional. They could walk around in the live-motion world and not look like cut-outs. *Roger Rabbit* worked because it carefully followed its own set of rules, in which the animated "toons" were able to "cross over" into the real world. The storyline was specifically centered around the mishaps caused by this impossible (but charming) conceit and set against an attractive 40s-era Hollywood background.

1992: Death Becomes Her

This black comedy (a genre I usually adore) broke new ground in special effects. Unfortunately, the performers operate in a vacuum instead of interacting each other. Meryl Streep gave an actor's perspective on working on this effects-heavy film: "I think it's tedious. Whatever concentration you can apply to that kind of comedy is just shredded. You stand there like a piece of machinery — they should get machinery to do it…. It's not fun to act to a lamp stand…it was like being at the dentist."

1994: Forrest Gump

I must admit I'm not a fan of "America's everyman," Tom Hanks, and I still find it hard to believe that he qualifies as a movie star. I can understand that many people were taken in by the story and the "life is like a box of chocolates" line, which is now, unfortunately, part of our lexicon of catchphrases. But I'm not at all impressed with what the PR team thought was the selling point, which was inserting Gump into historical and TV-news film clips. First, from a technical viewpoint, it looked terrible. It definitely would have looked better if they had shot the scenes on the set using actors. The much-promoted JFK scene is particularly dreadful. Woody Allen did a better job of mixing footage in *Zelig*. Ironically, the PR campaign heavily promoted the novelty of the effects, which were disappointing and almost immediately dated.

1994: The Mask

In 1994, the next big leap was introducing computer generated (CG) characters into live-action films. An early step was *The Mask*, in which a CG-augmented Jim Carrey became a character that blended real and animated attributes. At the time of its release, the art direction and innately cartoonish performance by Carrey made this bit of magic. Because the techniques employed in this movie are now so commonplace, it's hard to know if it would have the same impact on audiences today.

1994: Jumanji

Generating realistic animals as CG characters was a challenge. *Jumanji* had a story line that required the ability to have rooms of a suburban house suddenly inundated by jungle flora and fauna. The quality of the CG animals varied from excellent to nice try, but the story line was compelling and the performances of Bonnie Hunt and Robin Williams were an added bonus. At the time, the concept was fresh and magical.

1996: Dragonheart

The dragon character "Drago" was probably the first CG character infused with the personality of a live performer, in this case the larger-than-life Sean Connery. The character was crafted by master creaturemaker/ animator Phil Tippett. Given his mastery of the classic art of stop-motion animation and modeling, a great deal of believable motion and character was delivered by the model. The rest of the movie is filmed conventionally with Drago inserted as the story dictated. It was a good balance of plot and character with just enough magic to be enchanting.

1997: Star Wars (Rerelease)

What was George Lucas thinking? The first Star Wars movies were stunning successes, yet Lucas felt compelled to revisit the originals and insert CG characters that were not present in the original, most notably, Jabba the Hutt. The scene is just awful and the scale of the characters is not even correct. There was no rationale to add the character when the story already worked so well. This is another case of "just because they could, they did." The clumsy experiment foreshadowed the disaster of the later *Star Wars* films.

1999: Star Wars I: The Phantom Menace

The ghost of Howard the Duck must have driven Lucas to create this series of films. The temptation to create breathtaking otherworldly locations was the starting point, and these films are graced by gorgeously rendered non-existent architecture, much of it inspired by Frank Lloyd Wright's Marin County Civic Center. Unfortunately, Lucas got distracted with all the technology and skimped on the story and character elements. It missed all the warmth and humor of the original *Star Wars* films.

Lucas also introduced one of the first completely CG-based characters into mainstream cinema, Jar Jar Binks. A real live performer may have been able to dissuade Lucas from the one-dimensional characterization and brain dead dialog. Jar Jar is wincingly awful.

2006: Pirates of the Caribbean: Dead Man's Chest

While this genre's technical attributes are quickly advancing, its story-telling capabilities are declining. The nadir may have been reached with *Pirates of the Caribbean: Dead Man's Chest*. It's true we probably shouldn't expect much from a movie series that started as a Disneyland ride more than forty years ago, but this is

212

a sheer monstrosity of filmmaking. Although they live-motion-captured a real actor on the set, then later successfully blended in CG augmentation, the movie itself is dreadful.

Blendo II

Movie meet game. Game meet movie. It's Sillywood — the ultimate blend of Silicon Valley video gaming and Hollywood.

Given that the electronic gaming world and effects producers are using the same software to create 3D models and animation, it seems inevitable there would be a crossover between the two. For over a decade, hit movies have been made into video games and the better-selling games have become movies. (So far, *Tomb Raider's* buxom but brainy Lara Croft, as embodied by Angelina Jolie, has been the game character who has made the most successful transition to the big screen.)

Often games would start off with a skimpy narrative set created as a full-motion segment before proceeding with the game play, which had even less sophisticated graphics.

As we've noted, the aesthetic of video games is predominantly adolescent and male. Now we are seeing the young gamers growing up into real live moviemakers and bringing their game-world aesthetic with them. Their sensibility is dark, action oriented, violent, and coarse, and their technique features an elementary narrative sense padded with a puerile sexuality.

It's a short distance between the aesthetics of comic books and video games, and the target audiences are nearly identical. However, when these comic books are rebranded as "graphic novels," they attain a certain respectability. Nonetheless, reality and verisimilitude are not requirements in this two-dimensional graphic world.

There are two films that exemplify the Blendo II mode:

2005: Sin City

This new approach to film noir is, in fact, quite noir. The overall feeling of darkness here is amplified by the composited effect. If you are into this pulpy/detective sort of genre, and also like comic books, then this is your movie. A good example of technique.

2006: 300

Damn the history — full-speed action ahead! This movie is based on the legendary and historic battle between 300 Spartan warriors and the masses of the Persian Army. Unfortunately, it comes across like WWF wrestling on a bad acid trip.

Although completely lacking any connection to the historical facts, some of the scenes are beautifully rendered and quite fantastic. Otherwise, this film falls into the ugly realm of cliché derived from using the same tired kit of digital-creation tools employed for other films. If you are a teenage boy, or a gamepad-clutching Peter Pan, you'll probably enjoy this. Everyone else beware!

Synthetic Reality

Technically, these are animated films. However, once you see one, you realize that these are no mere cartoons. And while there are many cues telling you that you are watching real live actors, this technique is not photographic. It uses computer-generated characters within a CG environment. What is different here is that it moves away from the cartoon zaniness of Looney Tunes and *Toy Story* in an attempt to synthesize reality with digital representations sampled/captured from live performers. Once again, we find director Zemeckis's involvement.

Characters are created by capturing their live-motion performance though a series of sensors fed into a computer that tracks every subtlety of their motion. Those motions create the instructions to make the digital model, based on the actor, move realistically. Theoretically, it's a brilliant idea: Fully rendered "performers" with fantastic costumes can be put into physically impossible situations and scenes, or actually changed physically themselves. Unlike a cartoon, the movements of bodies and facial expressions are indeed lifelike, since they're based on live performers triggering the action with their own motions. Unfortunately, characters tend to appear as soulless zombies, empty shells void of content.

2004: Polar Express

While Tom Hanks as Woody in *Toy Story* is appealing, a far more realistically rendered digital avatar of Tom Hanks as the train conductor in *Polar Express* is as creepy as a clown. The attempt to synthesize a live human ruined what was a charmingly-illustrated children's book. This would have been more appealing with traditional animation.

2007: Beowulf

This film was even creepier and more unwatchable than *Polar Express*. Essentially *Beowulf* was a video game without interactivity or fun.

There is no doubt that this particular technology will eventually become more realistic and sophisticated. Right now it's not feasible, but soon it will be possible to photorealistically synthesize actors instead of filming them. The bigger question, though, is "why?" since there is a surplus of talented actors who would be only too happy to appear before the cameras.

2009: Avatar

This simplistic story about colonization could be dismissed as an eco/sci-fi version of Disney's *Pocahontas*. But, instead, it turned out to be the first 3D mega-blockbuster. This was partially filmed live motion, and in other more lengthy and notable segments, synthetic reality.

3D is not really all that difficult in CG since it derives from 3D solid models in the first place. Yes, it was a killer at the box office, but so much of this film was about process rather than the story. People went to see the spectacle after being deluged by hundreds of millions of dollars worth of PR and advertising. Time will ultimately judge whether this was good or goofy.

Too Much Magic

Mainstream "Fixes"

CG and other digital compositing effects have become part of a director's kit. I would venture that there are very few mainstream films that do not include at least a few digital fixes or alterations to scenes. Erasing boom mikes, cables, harnesses, and other nuisances that may have intruded on a shot are good ways to save it. Now radically changing the light, color, and framing of the scene is easily accomplished, making it possible for a bad director to mess up good cinematography. Certainly the coloration needs a rationalization. An otherwise worthy film, Tom Ford's *A Single Man* certainly was overkill and distracting in its constantly shifting color palette.

Here are two mainstream movies that employed digital effects and had very different sensibilities. One worked well, the other no so much.

2000: Gladiator

This is a traditional mainstream movie, which, had it been made sixty years before, would have been populated with thousands of extras in sandals. It was fortunate that the producers hired director Ridley Scott, a man with taste, to create this story. Using digital tricks, Scott was able to scale up the look without adding millions to the budget. More importantly, he told a compelling story based on a sympathetic character. Subtle digital artistry actually helped to lift this movie high above the typical sandal epic of the 50s.

2007: Elizabeth: The Golden Age

No actress before her, regardless of how grand or regal, has ever filled the Elizabeth role as completely as Cate Blanchett. Her first Elizabeth movie made in 1998 was shot in the lush surroundings traditionally seen in a period British movie. Yet when the story of Elizabeth's further exploits was being told, the main star seemed not to be Blanchett, but rather the CG rendering of the castle she inhabits. We see the queen flying around vertiginously in arches and buttresses. Was this supposed to replicate the perspective of Quasimoto through a Steadicam? Why bother? It was a huge distraction that diminished the impact of the performance.

Jason Benlevi

Expect More Substitutes

Since future production, post production, and delivery of movies to theaters will be filmless and digital, it will be tempting for producers to meddle with a film years after it was initially produced and released. As we saw with *Star Wars*, it was clearly a mistake to go back and insert characters.

So imagine these scenarios. A producer could collude with a marketeer to do product placements years after the film was produced. New revenue streams are always attractive, and many films have a long shelf life — why not just change out that beer can or cereal box for whoever comes up with the right price?

If Gene Kelly can make commercials for VW years after his death, it shouldn't be hard to imagine a movie where a dated actor is simply replaced with a more contemporary and popular one. When Hollywood wants to do a remake there will certainly be a lot less to remake.

A step beyond that is using the "performance capture" technology, used in *Avatar* and *Lord of the Rings*, paired with a high-resolution image capture of any given actor. The net effect would be that any no-name performer could wind up "wearing" the physicality of another actor. You can't get Tom Hanks? Just hire another actor to wear him and play the part through motion capture. Or imagine that an actor could simply use the system to wear herself at some previous age when her image had been captured. These things make sense if you are a marketeer and want to leverage every asset. Old Tom Hanks could just keep appearing in films long after his departure to Forest Lawn.

A Film Is a Journey

If you think about the process of producing great movies there is a direct connection between perspiration and inspiration. In the filming of *Lawrence of Arabia*, the crew famously had to wait hours in the brutal extremes of the desert to capture just the right sunrise.

How could the actors not have ramped up their performances when the director was after such verisimilitude?

You can see it in *The African Queen* and many other films. The filmmaker's pain is the audience's gain. The adventure does not take place in front of a 3D workstation. A day in a Burbank studio, a quick stop at Starbucks, and a short trip back home to your 10,000-square-foot house in the Hollywood Hills does nothing to inform a performance

Just Enough Magic

There are some stories in which "magic" itself is the compelling story element. Two series of best-selling books were screaming for someone to capture them on film; digital filmmaking made it possible.

The *Lord of the Rings* had been on the minds of filmmakers for generations, but there was simply no way to create the fantastic world of Middle Earth except for miniature models, costumes, and animation. The animated version of *The Hobbit* was an excellent example of what can go wrong. So this trilogy remained unmade until the digital age.

More recently, a uniquely gifted author infused the *Harry Potter* series of books with humanity, humor, and magic. Both literary series required serious magic to be portrayed in the movies.

Lord of the Rings

Peter Jackson and his company got it right by combining excellent performances from the cast along with art direction that drew upon the best influences. The Maxfield Parrish-like animated scenes in the elf's land were pure flawless digital magic.

Harry Potter

The series started out badly, with cheesy effects in the first movie, but dramatically improved with each subsequent film. Technical improvement was to be expected; what wasn't expected was the advancement of the aesthetic as well. They used digital magic judiciously. Let's hope that the trend continues as they complete the series.

Other films, such as *Chronicles of Narnia*, have tried to follow their lead but, unfortunately, what we are seeing is a cookie-cutter imitation rather than innovation. What is needed is a truly gifted director and art director ready and willing to refresh the model.

Disposable Reality

We began this chapter with the fundamental idea that a film is an artful blend of truth and lies. New digital film and video processes have made it easier to blur the line. This is where the art of entertainment media crosses paths with the serious business of capturing reality and documenting history. All the same tools used to create *Lord of the Rings* are available to manipulate any news or documentary media. The film and video from any moment in our history is subject to revision at any time. The capability and temptation to distort history for political purposes is overwhelming.

The technology has become so sophisticated that perception of reality can be deceived en masse in real time. Dan Rather in Time Square with the non-existent billboard was a preview. A more recent example was when the Chinese government (an entity that has blended the worst of capitalism and worst of communism into one all powerful reality-distortion machine) presented the 2008 Olympics to the world.

The live opening ceremony, televised globally, showed a magnificent fireworks display that was mind-boggling. However, the reality was that this magnificent spectacle, seen by billions around the world, only existed as a figment of computer graphics. Yes, there was a fireworks show there, but the one seen on TV was created by CG and inserted into the live video. They wanted to make a big impression and didn't want to take any chances. Did they think no one would notice? They did. What about 10 years from now, will anyone remember that it was faked? Probably not.

This time it was only something as trivial as fireworks, but next time it may concern events of global importance. Fabricated acts could be used to provoke a war. Perhaps dissidents "making" fabricated statements will damn them at show trials. Digital reality is entirely fluid and, as the fidelity of illusion becomes flawless, there will be no recorded visual evidence that is unalterable. Clearly, proof and truth are being increasingly compromised.

In the age of digital magic, seeing is no longer believing.

2.5

Why Mickey Mouse Has More Rights Than You Do

PART I:

THE BEST LAWS MONEY CAN BUY

On the surface it is a clearly ridiculous question. How could a black-and-white rodent rendered in pen-and-ink 80 years ago can be granted ever-extending legal protections, while your rights as a living, breathing person are being continually and surreptitiously eroded.

Then ask yourself how a fragrant rice, which has been growing for hundreds of years in India, could have just been "invented" by a U.S. biotech company in Texas? How is it that corporations have been issued patents on 20% of the genes in your body which they obviously did not invent? Speaking of "jeans," when did probing inside your pants become an essential factor in assuring "homeland security"?

Welcome to the topsy-turvy world where digital magic crosses paths with intellectual-property and privacy law. Intellectual property (generally known as "IP") means creative works such as stories, songs, movies, and artworks, as well as scientific and technical concepts. But what it really boils down to is the primacy of copyrights and patents over basic human rights.

Intellectual property is the verdant field where fast companies, marketeers, and intermediators of the digital and biotech worlds pair up with lawyers to reap a rich harvest. They have become entitled to reap this boundless bounty by being exceedingly generous to *your* elected representatives. For that generosity the U.S. Congress has rewarded multiple legislative gifts to corporate donors.

Four Letter Fortunes: DMCA and CTEA

Among the most generous of these gifts is the Digital Millennium Copyright Act of 1998 (DMCA). In 1998, by a unanimous vote in the U.S. Senate and with the signature of President Clinton, the DMCA bill extended the reach of copyright to emerging types of digital media.

The DMCA introduced a set of laws that gave media companies something called "digital rights management" (DRM). These laws restrict what you are allowed to do with the recordings and video you've paid *your* money for. It actually makes it a crime to make copies of your media and share them on discs or on the Internet. To make it stick, media companies use various technologies to create DRM codes in the music, software, or video devices that prevent you from making copies of what *you bought*. Not only that, their legislative buddies made it another crime to use any technical means to defeat these codes and unlock the video or music that *you bought*.

The idea was to stem the flow of music-sharing services that were emerging. Needless to say, it had little effect, but it did cause a few unlucky users to be arrested, fined, or sued for sharing songs on their computers. In 2009, one unfortunate woman, Jamie Thomas-Rasset of Minnesota, was fined $1,920,000 for sharing 24 songs.

A second legislative gift was the Copyright Term Extension Act (CTEA), derisively known as the "Mickey Mouse Protection Act." The CTEA, introduced by Congressman Sonny Bono, extended individual-copyright enforcement to an author's lifetime plus 70 years. The previous extension after death was 50 years, which gave immediate heirs at least some control over their family legacy. The 70-year figure principally benefits media companies and heirs whom the original author would have never known.

There is also a separate category for "corporate authorship."

Jason Benlevi

That copyright term was extended to 120 years! Keep in mind that there are few corporations anywhere near that age. Even one of our oldest Fortune 500 companies, General Electric (started by Thomas Edison), had only reached its 120th birthday in 2010.

The copyright extensions had one immediate beneficiary: Mickey Mouse or, rather, the Disney Company. Since old Walt entered his cryogenic chamber some 32 years before the passage of the law, only 18 years remained for the Disney Company to maintain the exclusive use of the famous rodent. Walt Disney and generations of his family have been well compensated for the mouse. This vigilant protection of IP is particularly ironic given the Disney Company has long based its animated features on folktales or stories from the public domain. The heirs of Hans Christian Anderson haven't seen a dime from Disney's use of *The Little Mermaid.*

Life (patent pending)

No matter what spiritual beliefs you may have, even if you have none at all beyond the Big Bang, we can all pretty much agree that life came into being without a single corporate laboratory as the source of creation. Yet Congress and a conservative activist U.S. Supreme Court have been extending the reach of patent laws into areas that are not a product of human intellect.

It started with the patenting of processes to extract and refine chemicals from human beings. The first was adrenaline in 1907, followed by insulin in 1923. In each case, the patent was granted for the process, not the naturally occurring substance itself. Before 1970, well-reasoned courts and the Congress did not allow the granting of patents for any natural raw material or organism derived from nature. Inspired by Luther Burbank, there were some exceptions to encourage botanists to develop hybrid plants to make farmers more productive. Generally, however, *life* could not be patented.

It took a half a century to reach the first inch of the slippery slope. By the 1960s, big petroleum's offshore drilling rigs had gotten into the habit of creating environmentally disastrous oil spills. They didn't cry too many tears about killing fish and birds while on their hydrocarbon quests, but they sure didn't like getting sued for billions of dollars in damages. So how could they get rid of all the oil they spilled and keep their billions?

Fortunately for them, a General Electric genetic scientist, Amanda Mohan Chakrabarty, developed a strain of bacterium that had one purpose in life, consuming and breaking down crude oil into harmless forms. Once upon a time, GE's tagline was "We bring good things to life." Apparently this scientist took it literally. This was a significant development that certainly could have benefitted the world, had it been openly shared. GE, however, saw it as a business opportunity and applied for a patent.

The U.S. Patent Office turned down the request because the law specified that living things were not patentable. In fact, Congress had specifically not allowed living organisms to be patented in legislation passed in 1930 and again in 1970. In his role as the Commissioner of Patents and Trademarks, Sidney Diamond refused to grant the patents.

For all the criticism that conservatives level against "activist courts," they did not hesitate to embrace the U.S. Supreme Court's *Diamond v. Chakrabarty* ruling on June 16, 1980. In a 5-4 decision, the court effectively engineered a new law that contradicted established legislative intent by overruling the Patent Office and creating a new precedent without the benefit of supporting legislation.

Chief Justice Warren Burger, who was joined by his four fellow conservatives, wrote the majority decision, stating:

> *"Whoever invents or discovers any new and useful process, machine, manufacture, or composition of matter, or any new and useful improvement thereof, may obtain a patent therefore, subject to the conditions and requirements of this title."*

The operative words in this decision are "discovers," "any," and "composition of matter." To "discover" is not to invent, and every living thing in nature is a "composition of matter." This basically allows anything "discovered" in nature to be patented. The race was on to privatize nature's own intellectual property just in time for the emerging science of genetic engineering and its spawn of fast companies devoted to the profit machine of "biotech."

One of the first acts of discovery for genetic engineering has been mapping the structure of living beings: DNA. The genetic mappers have been issued patents for what they "discover." Again, they didn't invent or create anything; they simply examined nature and claimed the blueprints of specific life forms as their private property.

Now we have reached the point where the slippery slope becomes a sheer vertical drop. The most egregious example is a company in Texas that decided to patent basmati rice, a fragrant strain of rice hybridized centuries ago in India, where it is a national culinary and biological treasure. The patent was granted in the U.S. If enforced, it would require millions of Indian farmers to pay a company in Texas for the right to grow the crops they had been growing for generations. Again, this Texas company did not create, invent, or in any way earn an entitlement to this intellectual property. They were granted a patent because they "discovered" the rice's DNA. Fortunately the Indian farmers and government have fought back. Still, this law has not been overturned.

Even more outrageous is the patent claim being issued on key genes that are components of human breast and ovarian cancer. The patents on what are called BRCA1 and BRCA2 genes belong to the University of Utah and a Salt Lake City company called Myriad Genetics. Wouldn't it be great if patients could refuse to pay these patent holders, forcing them to take back "their" cancer?

On behalf of thousands of breast-cancer patients, women's health groups, and academic researchers, and based on the First Amendment, the American Civil Liberties Union filed a lawsuit in the U.S. District Court of New York accusing the University of Utah and Myriad Genetics of stifling scientific research with their exclusive hold on the patent. If ultimately successful, this suit would set a precedent that challenges the whole notion of gene patenting in the United States. As of this writing, the district court has found against Myriad, but undoubtedly this case will be appealed and, given the corporatist-friendly nature of the Supreme Court, the prospects of the people prevailing over Myriad is far from certain.

At this point, about 20% of all human genes have been patented. The vast public domain of nature is rapidly being converted into private property. This feverish rush to privatize what has traditionally been public is troubling for democracy and intellectual freedoms. The trend goes back to a 1886 U.S. Supreme Court case called *Santa Clara v. Southern Pacific* Railroad. With its decision, under the 14th Amendment, the high court inadvertently, and disastrously, granted corporations the same rights as persons.

Today, corporations have rights that exceed those of natural persons (for example, those copyrights lasting 120 years). However, when was the last time a corporation voted, drafted, or was executed for murder? And now they are free to make *unlimited* contributions to politicians who write our laws. The Supreme Court's 2010 ruling in *Citizens United v. Federal Election Commission*, which removed any restrictions on corporate campaign contributions, will further erode natural human rights versus corporate rights. A thumb is weighing heavily on the scales against the public interest and toward increased privatization of the common weal.

All of this would have outraged the first director of the patent office, Thomas Jefferson. So we learn once again, that to understand law, you need to follow the money.

What Gift Did Congress Give You?

Since most of us don't have lobbyists and make only modest political donations, if any at all, what gifts did *we* get from our Congress? Remember: these are the people whose salaries we pay, our purported public servants.

While Congress has been busy granting corporations an expanding array of rights, they have been doing their darnedest to scale yours back. Despite our growing digital lifestyle, which allows information to flow anywhere, there have been no serious laws safeguarding personal privacy rights since the *Privacy Act of 1974*. This law was triggered by the revelations of how the Nixon Administration and its domestic-spying agencies were targeting his ever-expanding list of political "enemies." Jump ahead 25 years into the digital age and there has not been one further piece of legislation to safeguard your privacy. Congress did grant you a special treat. Here it is:

Uniting and Strengthening America by Providing Appropriate Tools Required to Intercept and Obstruct Terrorism Act of 2001

Buried in this too contrived acronym is the greatest legal assault on your privacy in the history of the nation, the so-called "U.S.A. PATRIOT Act."

While media and communications companies were buying themselves unprecedented legal protections against you, your Congress's gift to you is a wholesale, broad-brushed invasion of your civil liberties with little evidence to show any effectiveness. In one fell swoop, and with scant debate, a democratically elected government abrogated the rights of its citizens. Okay, maybe at that moment they were cowering citizens, but "the greatest deliberative body in the world" should have spent at least some time deliberating, debating, or maybe even reading the PATRIOT Act before making it the law of the land.

The bill was passed by wide margins in both houses of Congress and was supported vigorously by both the Republican and Democratic congressional leadership. Although it is allegedly in place to interrupt terror plots, the provisions are so broad and sweeping that it can be applied to almost any situation. Domestic animal rights activists and annoyed airline passengers have been subject to the act's reign of rights violations, and are in federal prison for their "offenses."

The PATRIOT Act defies the Fourth Amendment of the U.S. Constitution by allowing law-enforcement officers to search a home or business without the owner's or the occupant's permission or knowledge. The act expanded the use of the Kafkaesque National Security Letters, which allow the FBI to search telephone, email, and financial records without a court order and expanded law enforcement agencies' authority to peruse business records, including library and financial records. Since its passage, several legal challenges have been brought against the act and, fortunately, federal courts have ruled that some of provisions are unconstitutional.

The section of the PATRIOT Act most relevant to our digital-magic world is called "Title II — Enhanced Surveillance Procedures" and includes an expansion of government powers called FISA.

The Foreign Intelligence Surveillance Act (FISA)

Originally enacted to spy on foreign governments and their agents, and requiring the approval of and monitoring by a federal panel of judges, FISA has become a catch-all for unlimited monitoring of electronic communications. The scope of wiretapping and surveillance was expanded under Title II. Wiretaps were extended to include surveillance of "packet switched networks." — in other words, The Internet.

While the courts have generally been friendly to law enforcement when it comes to authorizing wiretaps for bolstering national security and fighting organized crime, they have always required these officials to show "probable cause." It was not a privilege law enforcement requested lightly, for pragmatic (as opposed to ideological) reasons. In the analog world, monitoring communications electronically was an expensive, labor-intensive process. Historically, therefore, it was used judiciously — in both senses of the word.

Monitoring communications got turbocharged in the digital age. In the analog world, monitoring communications required a physical connection to the phone line, tape-recording equipment, and a person or persons to both monitor conversations and listen to hours of tapes. These barriers meant that government agencies needed both a big budget and a damn good reason presented to a judge. Digital technology blew away the judicious practices.

Digital magic makes it possible to electronically vacuum up ALL communications — both foreign and domestic — en masse. High-performance computers then automatically sort through written and spoken key words and phrases. So surveillance moves from being targeted to being a pervasive and continuous sieve.

It was now possible to "listen" to every call and "read" every email.

228

Mickey Mouse Has More Rights Than You

And, as we learned from former AT&T engineer, Mark Klein, that's exactly what Bush's National Security Agency (NSA) did. At a key telecommunications exchange building in San Francisco, at Folsom and Second Street, AT&T simply plugged the cables carrying global communications into a computer network run by the NSA. Every electronic communication – foreign or domestic – to your mother, from your sister – emailed by your shrink as well as your confidential business memos are all being monitored full time, without a warrant. It went way beyond the strictures of FISA.

The Bush regime completely ignored the already generous provisions of the PATRIOT Act and FISA, and just went fishing. The communications of political opposition and whistler-blower employees were all readily available to the Bush White House. We know, in fact, that Republican operatives were monitoring the Democratic Party leadership and hacking into their computers.

When AT&T's Klein, the engineer responsible for the hookup, finally revealed this flagrant violation of the law, what happened? Well, Congress changed the law. But rather than focusing on protecting U.S. citizens, they passed legislation that indemnified the telecom companies from being sued by the millions of us whose privacy was flagrantly invaded. This legislation also neutralized the Terms-of-Service Agreements that carriers had with customers. The telecom giants that broke both federal law and their contracts with customers were congressionally exonerated.

The argument made by *your* Congress was that the poor telecom companies could not afford to pay the damages of every aggrieved citizen — especially after paying lobbying firms and granting generous donations to the candidates of both political parties.

So let's see if this makes sense to you. That woman in Minnesota who copied 24 songs and made them available on the Net was fined $1.9 million. AT&T broke the law and its service agreement with tens of millions of customers and got what? A new law that protects it from prosecution and lawsuits retroactively. To add insult to injury, it got a big fat government contract to continue committing the crime.

The parallel between this legislative duplicity and the meltdown on Wall Street in 2008 typifies what we face as citizens. Overdraw your checking account for $5 and you'll pay a $39 fee. If you are the bank, gamble away billions of dollars, and the taxpayers will be forced to bail you out. End your phone contract early and you will owe your carrier hundreds of dollars. When they violate their service agreement with you, your tax dollars will go to help them trample on your rights.

To put it simply, when it comes to Congress, even though you pay their salaries, you don't get no respect.

Parallel But Not Parity

The problem is that there are two parallel sets of rules evolving for how information flows in the digital age. Separate but not equal. Corporations are being allowed to turn public information into private property, while your privacy is being eroded. Even your digital persona is being bought and sold without your awareness. (Which will be detailed later.)

So here we have the ongoing paradox of technology; the power to do good as well as a dark side being driven by economic interests, two contradictory models for dealing with rights in the age of digital magic. We have one set of rules so that corporations can put more gates around what should be public information set in the commons, and at the same time we have another set of rules permitting invasion of your privacy, which is *your* property.

Once more, for emphasis: *your privacy is your property.* Your information should *not* be free. *You* should be in control of it, just as Mickey is.

Perhaps you believe it's okay for the government to snoop, so long as they're doing it to protect us. Perhaps you believe you have nothing to hide, so why worry? If you didn't cheat on your taxes then an IRS audit is a joyful event, right? Well, here *is* something to worry about: The government is actually the smallest, least intrusive and most benevolent part of the privacy invasion. Digital technologies create new tentacles for private businesses to actively peruse your private life, harvest your personal data, and package you as a "product" to marketeers. What they say about you may be true — or they could be spreading damaging falsehoods that might prevent you from buying a house or finding employment.

So, what have your elected representatives done to safeguard your privacy, your version of intellectual property? Nothing. Absolutely nothing. Less than nothing. A stable set of laws governing privacy and copyrights had been in effect since Jefferson was running the U.S. Patent Office. Why and how did everything change in the past two decades?

PART 2: IT ALL BEGAN WITH FILE SHARING

What sparked massive changes, both good and bad, was electronic "file sharing" among computers.

A file is simply any package of digital information. It could be your credit report or a remix of a Beatles album. A digital file is a digital file, regardless of content. A file can go anywhere that there is a connection for it to flow.

The digitization of all media, especially entertainment, meant that that there was new life in old media and data. It was granted infinite life. It became cheap and easy to make high-quality copies. This process was amplified when the Internet made it virtually free to deliver any information/content to anyone, instantly. That is the power of file sharing.

Media companies eventually understood the value of what has become known as the "long tail." They had movies, books and recordings in their vaults for decades and were just dying to sell them once again in digital form. These were productions that had been created and had their costs of production amortized decades ago. All that was required was a low-cost way to deliver it. It was gold ready to mine itself.

The media companies were slow off the mark in understanding just exactly how information would be shared in the digital world.

Communications and content companies had envisioned a private toll road. Companies including IBM/Sears (Prodigy), General Electric (Genie), and Time Warner (QUBE) invested vast sums in developing private networks or interactive TV systems. All of which failed gloriously. These companies wanted to own every step of the delivery, they were reluctant to share media on the Internet. It was the ideal delivery system but they could not control the media flowing out or the dollars flowing in because the Net was wide open.

By the late 90s, media companies grasped the need for laws to be written that would protect them from the Internet. They sponsored laws like DMCA to fight copying or file sharing of music and video. Although they had the law on their side (and why not, since they wrote it), other more innovative types took the lead and began to develop ad hoc systems to share media. Napster was among the most famous. Suddenly every popular or obscure song was "ripped" (as in "ripped off") from CDs by regular folks and shared on an anonymous network of "peers." You could share the songs I ripped and downloaded to my Mac, and I could share the songs you had stored on your PC, even if we didn't know each other, because the Internet connected my hard drive to yours. No money changed hands among listeners, and nobody paid the media companies for content.

What marketeers and intermediators most feared had happened — the front door of the store was left wide open, without a cashier or security guard in sight. They may have had their shiny new DMCA law, but they had no way to stop the flow of files. As with the proverbial bell that cannot be un-rung, once information has been shared, the content can never be "unshared." It will continue to have a propensity to disseminate infinitely.

Content Wants to Be Free?

There are those among the digerati who believe, in their own words: "Content wants to be free." I find that proclamation to be specious and disingenuous. What most of these people are saying is that they don't want to pay anything for the work of others. If you are an artist, a musician, a filmmaker, or a photographer, you don't want content to be free unless you have a trust fund to pay your rent, or a nice safe tenured position at a university. Creators deserve to be paid for their creations, and they alone should decide the terms of its distribution, just not for generations after their demise.

One particular proponent of this digitally hip notion of "free" is a well-paid magazine editor who is selling books about the "magic of free" for $25, and we can be assured he is well paid on the speaking circuit. Ideally, these proponents of free should publish their books, teach classes and do public speaking for nothing to demonstrate their commitment to the notion that "content wants to be free."

The ability to share music files has meant that record stores have vanished from malls and Main Streets. There is a whole generation that has grown up not paying for recorded music. They have come to view entertainment as an entitlement. Music to the newest generation is not a tangible product, but rather an amorphous download. Not a thing that someone labored to create. Not something that is valued.

Media sharing is a pervasive benign theft, an infraction more common than marijuana smoking a generation ago. Abuses and shoddy business practices left record companies open to "guiltless" downloads by music-loving young people.

In the early 1980s, LP vinyl records were $5 when CDs were introduced to the market at $20. The CD had the same content but sold at four times the cost, even though they eventually cost less to produce. With this proposition in place it didn't take long for music companies to kill the vinyl record and harvest the windfall from reissuing $5 records as $15 CDs. It was easy money as many people repurchased the music they already owned on vinyl LPs. Musicians, except for the most powerful acts, saw little of that gain.

The arrival of digital music, which costs nearly zero to deliver, gave media companies the option to adjust their music to be more affordable. At zero cost they could have provided music at a handy profit while giving the consumer a lower purchase price. The upside would have been selling more albums than ever. Instead, they were undone by timidity, greed and lack of imagination.

Only under the painful pressure of falling CD sales and the ascent of iTunes as a universal delivery system did they get it — maybe.

In the past decade, as revenues fell sharply from recordings, the price of live-performance tickets skyrocketed at a pace far exceeding inflation to compensate for the lost revenue. As music fans have always known, there is no free lunch in the music business. Nonetheless, there *should* be protections on intellectual property for its creators, set for a reasonable time period, that would enable them to derive a livelihood from their efforts.

But what about so-called corporate creators? In the case of movie studios, the majority of the films in their libraries have already recovered their production costs long ago, made a profit, and, in many cases, everyone involved in making the film has been dead for decades. What rationale is there to continue a revenue stream when no one involved in the original creative process can directly benefit?

Films have become a part of our cultural history. If a film outlasts it creators, and still finds interest from an audience in perpetuity, it has become a part of the cultural commons and should be considered public domain. Jefferson wanted copyright to last only as long as the lifetime of the author. A few years later it was extended to provide a legacy for immediate descendents. But recently, just as digital file sharing was emerging and Hollywood realized many of its key properties were in danger of falling into the public domain, the copyright rules changed.

From the widespread attention that illicit music and movie file sharing has been getting in the media, one would think it was a critical issue for humanity. This alarm derives from the fact that these egocentric companies also own the news outlets. They have exaggerated the threat — and its subsequent perception — since they are the ones being threatened.

However, the media companies have spent precious little time talking about habeas corpus, the Fourth Amendment, or Section II of the PATRIOT Act because they have no financial interests involved. No skin in the game. While they have been successful at getting their own interests protected with expanded copyright laws, the erosion of your rights has been ignored by a self-interested media.

So, while you have heard of Napster on the news, the chances are good you know nothing about the companies infringing on your rights every second of every day by sharing files *about you*. Although independent reporting about the PATRIOT Act and FISA called attention to government spying on ordinary Americans without reasonable safeguards, what you may not be aware of is that private firms called "information aggregators," such as Acxiom or ChoicePoint, have been intruding on people's privacy for decades and are virtually unregulated. They are watching you, but no one is watching them.

This Goes on Your Permanent Record

Governing authorities have an astonishing appetite for gathering information about those within their reach. Stalin's and Hitler's reigns of terror were huge information-gathering operations. Stalin already had an entrenched Russian bureaucracy and secret police from the czarist days. It has been estimated that 25% of the Soviet population were paid informants in the darkest Soviet days. At least it was a full-employment program.

The Germans trusted mechanisms over mere men. Using IBM's Hollerith card-sorting technology, they sifted through entire populations for the people they would systematically murder. They blended technology and nominally human informers to assemble dossiers on millions.

In the United States, J. Edgar Hoover crafted the FBI into a personal network of domestic-intelligence resources for gathering dirt on powerful businessmen, political activists, artists, and most importantly for him, congressmen and senators. Why? So no one dared to challenge him by exposing his deeply closeted sexual orientation and mob-connected gambling habits. The root of Hoover's power was the information accumulated in his files.

We have, every one of us, spent our lives being tracked by various authorities. Information persistence as a method to keep you obedient to authority began with the mythic threat of your "permanent record" in public school. Misbehave and — bam! — it's on your permanent record. Later, though, when you opened your first bank account, your *real* permanent record, the one that would truly govern your life, began. It's called your credit report.

Are You Worth It?

The data-collection business started with the three big credit reporting companies. You know their names because they advertise and want you to buy their services. (Yes, they have the audacity — and ability — to make you pay *them* to find out information about *you*.) The big three credit-reporting companies are Experian (née TRW), TransUnion, and Equifax.

You gave your tacit consent for them to start peering into your life the first time you applied for credit. These companies continuously compile a profile of you by gathering files from entities that have a part in your credit life: banks, stores, and finance companies.

Using mainframe computers, that were the supercomputers of their day, they started collecting information decades ago to ascertain just how "creditworthy" you are. By gathering all of your borrowing information together, any of the big three can form an aggregated picture of how much credit you have been allowed and how well you have managed it. Previously, receiving a credit account with a store involved letters of credit from your bank, a background check, or another existing relationship with a merchant. But that was before the widespread dissemination of credit cards. And that development, for good or ill, is directly tied to the advent of the big three credit reporters.

Although at times it may be hard to believe, there is more to life than dealing with money. There are fragments of information about your life scattered in electronic systems around the world. Some you know about, some you don't, but should.

PART 3: YOUR LIFE AS A SHARED FILE

To marketeers, your life is a file (neat anagram, too.) Your life/file is being shared by people and organizations that you don't know, and didn't even know existed! Your most personal information is being collected and sold without your knowledge. Adding insult to injury, it's being sold in bulk for just a few pennies, over and over again, to anyone who will pay the price.

The companies that deal in this domain are alternately called information aggregators or data brokers. They only have one product in their inventory: your private information. The core of an information aggregators' business is a vast database that they actively compile from both private and public sources. Then, by using analytical software, they divine predictable patterns about you. Patterns that are valued by marketeers who (in their lingo) want to "know you better." In other words, target you better to sell you more stuff.

While there are many companies gathering certain types of data for specific purposes, there are two mega companies that "want it all" when it comes to personal information. Called ChoicePoint and Acxiom, these companies are largely invisible to consumers. However, just because you don't know ChoicePoint and Acxiom doesn't mean they don't know you. These companies are buying information about you every second of every day and parsing it, analyzing it, and selling it back to anyone who'll buy — and there's nothing you can do to stop it.

These two giant companies know more about you than your very best friends will ever know. And here's the kicker: All that information about you is not yours; it's theirs. Under current law, your privacy is not your property. In fact, these companies are not legally bound to show you any information they have about you, allow you to correct it, tell you with whom they have shared it, or grant you any power to prevent them from further sharing. While, thankfully, there are certain restrictions on credit-reporting agencies, these data aggregators are under no such strictures.

The Acxiom of Evil?

Acxiom has been called "the biggest company you've never heard of." Founded in 1969, it extends its tentacles from its base in rural

Arkansas to acquire and share information among hundreds of retailers, magazine publishers, and public institutions. Yet, if you read their annual report, you would have a hard time discerning exactly what it is that they do — and that's just how they like it.

Affiliated with TransUnion, one of the big three credit-reporting agencies, Acxiom secures those data that credit bureaus are legally prohibited from collecting. Their business revolves around selling detailed customer "profiles" — comprised mainly of "behavior and lifestyle" information — to marketeers targeting individuals (like you) who populate specific demographic profiles. Acxiom's business is to "data-mine" their enormous database of personal information and then "micro-target" specific individuals with highly customized marketing efforts.

Acxiom's aggregated information is a "product" that they call "InfoBase." You and every member of your family (including children) have their own file at Acxiom, each coded with an individual 16 digit numeric identifier. That file includes information on your religion, education, home value, children's ages, prescription medicines, and unlisted phone numbers. In fact, it is rumored that cell-phone numbers have replaced Social Security numbers as preferred personal identifiers. This makes perfect sense, since such numbers are transferrable among service providers and are possessed by increasingly younger users. Moreover, there are no messy legal issues concerning the use of Social Security numbers.

How did they get these unlisted numbers? You unknowingly gave them out when you dialed a toll-free exchange, which shows your number and name to the recipient of the call. Once captured via caller ID, the unlisted and mobile numbers are sold and transferred among data brokers. From that point on, whenever you dial a toll-free number, the receiver of the call has more information about you on their computer screen than you'd believe possible.

Acxiom's Infobase Telesource is a telemarketer's dream come true. Usually call agents are instructed not to alarm you by using your name before you identify yourself, but in most cases they know all about you, including your age and your net worth.

When you call your bank's toll-free number, the bank routinely uses caller ID to identify whether you are well-heeled or just a poor schnook who is a few bucks away from an overdraft. If you are in the top bracket, you're quickly transferred to a well-trained U.S.-based agent. If you aren't among the select, you get put at the back of a long queue waiting to talk to someone in Bangalore. When you get mailed a new credit card, and they require you to call from your home number to verify that you got it, that's another opportunity to capture your most current phone number – listed or not.

Acxiom is the logical extension of direct-mail merchants. Its roots were in campaign fundraising and in selling Bibles. To add value, Acxiom is continuously expanding its customer base, aggregating ever more information from diverse sources and adding piece upon piece to the composite profiles of individuals. Along the way, it has also acquired major direct-mail marketeers specifically for their mailing lists, and has made deals with a large consortium of retailers called "Abacus Direct Corporation."

Another huge source of information is the warranty card you fill out after purchasing a new product. These cards ask for family information, including income brackets. What you may not — but should — know is that, under federal consumer protection law, these cards *do not* need to completed and returned for your warranty to be honored. Manufacturers have created a side business of selling your information to large data brokers, who in turn sell it to Acxiom. That means at least 30 million surveys per year performed at near zero cost. Each item purchased is matchable to your master 16-digit coded file.

Digital life unleashes a torrent of information captured from our daily lives — a trail of data that is extraordinarily revealing when aggregated. What is dismaying is that no legislative body has set limits, let alone enforceable penalties, for misuse of this information. Is the government even trustworthy for this role? In the days after the World Trade Center attack, the National Security Administration got a full upload of everything Acxiom was asked to serve up — personal information about tens of millions of law-abiding, tax-paying Americans — without the muss and fuss of due process.

Looking at the Acxiom website you can find a place to opt out of receiving promotional mailings for Acxiom's products, but there is no option to review and/or delete the file that they keep on you. In other countries, these agencies are indeed subject to an opt-in provision. In "Old Europe," for example, aggregators need your permission to collect and distribute your information. In the U.S., the land of the free, you are given no such right.

Even when security is breeched by criminals, aggregators such as Acxiom are likely to inform their corporate clients of the violation, but have no obligation to reveal the theft of your identity to you. Your privacy is your property, and yet you have no legal right to recover your property. For now, legislatures seem to express little concern for these issues. Mickey on the other hand received majority votes in the Senate, House, and a presidential autograph.

Flying under the radar is Acxiom's preferred manner of hiding in plain sight to avoid regulation. In fact, they have powerful political connections on either side of the congressional aisle, exceeding J. Edgar Hoover on steroids. Their political aim is simply to avoid any type of scrutiny. One Acxiom executive made the claim before congressional committees that regulating information aggregators would have a chilling effect on the information economy and e-commerce. This well-practiced invocation of digital magic dazzles and befuddles our elected representatives every time. So don't expect much action there to protect your privacy.

ChoicePoint

ChoicePoint, much like Acxiom, was once affiliated with a big three credit-reporting firm, Equifax, and now is part of international data giant LexisNexis/Reed Elsevier. Just as Acxiom collects private information barred from credit bureaus, ChoicePoint has actually created a market in aggregating information about individuals that the U.S. Government is prohibited from collecting for itself. While Acxiom gathers and packages intelligence about "Lifestyle and Behavior" to urge you to buy things, ChoicePoint concentrates on "Rights and Privileges" information that encourages you to heed to authorities.

Based near Atlanta, ChoicePoint originally was in the business of gathering publically available local government records and delivering them to insurances companies to aid in underwriting policies. The data was also useful for investigating fraud within an extralegal framework. Realizing the economic potential of the private investigatory market, ChoicePoint acquired multiple data-compilation companies that specialize in property records, car ownership, driver's licenses, marriage, criminal cases, and court records.

Unlike the stealthy Acxiom, ChoicePoint has made forays into the public eye. In the 1990s, when the web was gaining momentum, they launched what is called a "look-up" service. A look-up service meant that anyone with a few bits of data, or just a name, could easily search data consolidated from millions of public records to find personal information about anyone.

With a crime-centric local news culture, there is a heightened fear of burgeoning criminality. To capitalize on this mood, ChoicePoint created a product that was a "background check in a box," sold by the Walmart spinoff Sam's Club, and priced at a consumer-friendly $39.77. That modest outlay could get you a dossier on any potential employee, teacher, or new neighbor right on your home computer. The World Trade Center attacks were a boon for ChoicePoint. Since fear has been their best sales tool, a panicked nation, already generous at offering up information, became even hungrier to buy it.

ChoicePoint has long and sticky political tentacles. Their acquisition of a company called DBT and a product called Autotrack brought them into public view. Originally a database of car ownership records, the DBT database grew to include driver's licenses, marriage licenses, criminal records, and even handicapped parking stickers.

ChoicePoint's political machinations extended to vetting voter registrations with what appeared to be a political agenda. So where did this review of voter registration take place? Florida, of course! The year? 2000.

Former beauty queen and Florida Secretary of State Katherine Harris commissioned DBT/ChoicePoint to sift through the entire list of all of the state's voters. In the process, Florida eliminated 57,000 voters who were overwhelmingly Democratic, predominantly black or Hispanic, and labeled them as felons. The problem was that the data was erroneous and tens of thousands of law-abiding voters were prevented from casting a ballot, likely shifting the outcome of Florida's already shady 2000 presidential election results. For their "good work" in Florida, ChoicePoint was awarded contracts for the newly enacted the Help America Vote Act of 2002, as well as the Department of Homeland Security, by the Bush Administration.

Now that democracy has begun to flourish in Central America, ChoicePoint has extended its election-registration digital magic south of the border. They bought up the Mexican national election rolls under a $67 million agreement with the Bush Department of Justice and engaged in data surveillance of Costa Rica and other Latin American countries. Was George W. planning to bring back the "good old days" of voter intimidation, rigged elections, and strongman governments?

ChoicePoint continues to grow unchecked, fed by your tax dollars, telling clients who is "safe" for them to employ, and acquiring ever more, and more varied, data. Keep in mind that they can make these recommendations with a full awareness of your political leanings. They have the potential to create a powerful political blacklist against all dissenters of any political stripe. So which legislative or regulatory body is watching these watchers? Here's a clue: They've got mouse ears on.

Getting to Know You

These information aggregators are growing into powerful intermediators because we keep giving them more and more data to chew on. Every day, some familiar activity, such as shopping for food, which we have done for centuries, acquires a digital function or component. The data flowing from those actions is captured, and if information is collected, chances are someone is going to want it and be willing to pay for it. Cash-strapped local governments and struggling businesses see no problem in selling the data in their possession, and there is no governing authority to prevent it. A trickle of data has become a river with the Net making it flow anywhere all the time.

Every bit of information that is created electronically can be captured forever. Everything you do electronically leaves an imprint behind to be tracked. Every time you use your credit card, or make a phone call that information is captured and stored away somewhere in the vast cloud of data that floats around us, becoming permanently ensconced into the dark air-conditioned depths of server farms. Information aggregators have figured out that this information is worth so much more if it is gathered up and analyzed. They are giant J. Edgar Hoovers vacuuming up every bit of digital dirt about you.

Welcome to the Club Card

Look at the contents of any shopping cart and you can tell a lot about the person wheeling it around the store. Admit it: you've played this game yourself waiting in the checkout line. You begin to profile the shopper. Do they have a lot of junk food? Foods that tell you they have young children? A dog? Foot odor? Do they cook from scratch or just heat things up? When you do it, it's just an informal sociology lesson. For marketeers, however, it's a serious business with cash paybacks.

When supermarkets started using Universal Price Code (UPC) bar codes, it was originally to trim the labor-intensive process of sticking price tags on every package, which a checkout clerk would have to read and punch into a cash register. When the codes came into widespread use, during the inflationary 1970s and 80s, prices were changing so fast that some items had multiple, increasing price tags. It was an evidence trail of inflating prices. The UPC was also, somewhat stealthily, something only a machine could read, which made consumers less aware of prices.

The bar code had other advantages. There was information beyond price buried in those bar lines. They could help a store keep track of what was selling, in what volume, and when to reorder. Before bar codes, the clerk had limited options to record what was being sold by pushing a button for categories such as grocery, produce, or dairy. The grocery had no immediate idea what product was selling well or languishing on the shelves. It required having a manual inventory and ordering process to make sure the store was properly stocked.

A supermarket is a rich information environment, and the more information discernable about shoppers and their preferences, the better a store will perform. Makers of soap and soda pop have studied the positions of products situated on the shelves and how customers are more likely to reach for products at specific heights and locations in the aisles. They actually pay supermarkets for the privilege of placing their products in what are deemed to be the prime locations. Prices are set not so much on costs, but on what a consumer will be willing to pay. They'll pay $1.99, but rounded up to a full dollar amount they'll hesitate to commit. It's seems idiotic, but it's true.

With data networks that connect instantly to checkout registers, stores know second-by-second exactly what merchandise is selling. This allows them to adjust prices on slow movers and monitor inventories so that goods selling faster than projected can be quickly reordered and shipped.

Most supermarkets have given up printing coupons in the paper and instead issue "club cards." Why not just give people the sale price? Because the value is in the information gathered about you, the shopper. If you remember, when you signed up for the club or savings card you provided the store with a good amount of your personal data, your address, your phone number, your employer, perhaps a credit card number, and other demographic information.

So why would people give away this information about themselves and violate their own privacy? The reason is simple: to save money on their groceries. Back more than a decade ago, what was "on sale" was the merchandise; today, what's "on sale" is you. Your shopping behavior is data to be gathered, sold, and parlayed into a new stream of revenue for the merchant.

The bar code or magnetic stripe on the club card identifies you when you make a purchase. (They're not able to paste a barcode on your head — yet.) Slide the card and bingo — purchaser and purchase have been identified, cross-matched, and saved to a database. Compile this information among tens of millions of people and billions of purchases and patterns emerge.

Matching specific consumers with specific purchases, and doing it across multiple stores, is like x-ray vision into your life. Think about what you surmised about your fellow shopper in line from looking in their cart. Now imagine every purchase everybody makes being analyzed on a constant basis. Everything you buy saved into a file: every alcoholic beverage, over-the-counter medicine, personal-hygiene product, indulgent dessert, and trashy magazine composes a picture of you. Every bit of that data is parked in a server someplace in Arkansas, with your 16 digit "name" stamped on it.

Why? Because marketeers are interested in what you bought because they believe it is predictive of what you will buy. Some people think, "This is great...I like that they know what I like" Others think that it is "just creepy."

Condé Nasty Tricks

The social science of discerning customer-purchase patterns from databases goes back to the direct-mail business, though at the time, the database was just names and addresses on index cards. Direct mail is the direct ancestor of web-based merchants. The Sears of yesterday is the Amazon of today. Sears's major expense was creating a catalog and mailing it out to millions of potential customers, even though only a few percent of recipients would actually make a purchase. If merchants could narrow that mailing to only the most likely buyers, it would dramatically increase their return relative to the expense of the catalog mailing. Fewer catalogs mailed, more likely customers.

Looking for prospects, magazines and direct-mail merchants have long traded or purchased each other's lists. For example, if you sold cooking supplies, you'd be better off if you could target people who had subscribed to a cooking magazine. Information could be gathered from the contestants' applications to a Pillsbury bake off, or from food-product rebate forms. If you subscribed to a motorcycle magazine and subsequently started receiving catalogs of motorcycle parts you might appreciate the mailings about something that interested you.

There's nothing wrong with asking subscribers of a magazine about their likes and dislikes. It's mutually beneficial for magazine editors and publishers to get feedback and find the right advertisers. A few years back, however, top-drawer publisher Condé Nast stepped over the line, turning their subscribers into unwitting donors of their personal information.

Condé Nast sent out a rather detailed questionnaire, which purported to be entirely anonymous and was presented as a tool to help the magazine develop its editorial content. The problem was that each questionnaire was secretly encoded with a unique identifier that revealed the exact identity of the respondent to Condé Nast and Acxiom. The nature of the questions wandered far from editorial content and into a detailed personal profile of dating, lifestyle, health, financial, and personal-hygiene questions.

When it was revealed that the publisher had sold this extremely detailed information to an information aggregator, there were the requisite apologies. However, even if they claimed the data was destroyed, there was and is no legal or technical mechanism for verifying that claim. The data-collection bell cannot be unrung.

Eat My Cookies, Petitions, and Polls

Milk and cookies are an iconic afterschool treat. Under the cover of this friendly appellation and a good level of technical obfuscation, "cookies" are the magic keys for marketeers to unlock your life secrets on the web. A "cookie" is simply a little marker a website deposits inside your browser that identifies you for the next time you visit the site. Often it will trigger a message to welcome you back. How nice.

What may have surprised many web surfers at first was how much information they were tracking around on their boots as they trod from site to site. These cookies can potentially be read by every other website you visit, Perhaps transmitting information that you would prefer to keep private. As publications and direct-mail merchants made the transition to the web, they began using cookies, as well as other tools, that vastly increased their ability to gather profiles on customers. Even companies that you have never heard of or visited can deposit and read your cookies. Go ahead. Take a look at cookies saved on your browser if you know how to do it. Chances are it is even more revealing than what is in your shopping cart at the supermarket.

It is no secret that there are no secrets when it comes to the Internet. The biggest problem for security on the Net is the gullibility of the people who use it and their unwitting surrender of personal data. Everyone is already familiar with spamming and phishing and letters from the wife of the Nigerian ambassador. For the most part, the media has accurately portrayed these as criminal enterprises. These same media companies have done far less to explain how the very businesses that they own are also using questionable practices to exchange and collect data.

Ever wonder about those sites for online petitions? Why would someone go through the trouble of setting up a business to gather "signatures" for petitions on the web, even allowing others to set up their own petitions on the site? Does anyone using these sites believe that anybody is ever going to receive these petitions? Do you think that a TV executive is going to bring back some obscure TV show because a few thousand people added their names to a list? In reality these are generally phony websites that are in the business of gathering lists that match personal identifying information with specific interests.

These are lists that can be sold to direct marketers or added to the information aggregator's dossiers about you. The whole idea is to gather names and email addresses where people self-identify their interests. Sign a petition about shelter dogs and pretty soon you can expect to see solicitations from ASPCA, pet-food companies, and other entities that know you have an interest in animals. Sign a petition about gays in the military and you might wind up receiving hate mail from some unsavory group. Fake polls are particularly popular on social network sites and are nothing more than tools for data brokers. They already know your identity, your personal associations, and now your opinion on a specific issue. You have just painted a target on yourself.

The reason big media companies are interested in social networking ventures is because people have voluntarily revealed so much about themselves and their activities as members of these sites. Facebook accidentally tipped their hand with a technology called "Beacon." Without explicitly informing participants or getting approval, Facebook and a number of online merchants decided to share information about users.

I became aware of it when I purchased a pair of Ecco shoes from Zappos, a large online shoe retailer. Imagine my surprise the next day, when Facebook announced to all the visitors to my "wall" an announcement that I purchased Ecco Track II high tops from Zappos.

Obviously, I was not the only one ticked off about this activity and Facebook ceased their most blatant application of Beacon technology. But keep in mind that this sort of thing is probably taking place anyway, even if it is in a stealth mode. When you are using a social network site, remember it's their playground and there is no legal authority that can truly safeguard your privacy.

The web is about sharing information, so don't expect privacy because there is no way to enforce it. Assume files will be shared and that the data about you will persist forever. Assume every Google search you do and every click-through will be recorded and archived and searched by others.

PART 4: EVERY MOVE YOU MAKE

I spent two decades helping companies envision scenarios of what would be possible when things became increasingly connected. There was no shortage of brilliant engineers who wanted to change the world for the better. Being a believer in technology myself, I shared their optimism. Yet there was a lingering negative in the darkroom of Silicon Valley where visions were developed.

Connection comes at a price. That price is intrusion. Every

time you look out through your connected devices, you let an intermediator look back *into* your private life. The web is a two-way medium whether you granted access to your privacy explicitly or inadvertently. Every time you search, you leave a record of what you were searching for. You may not have any big secrets, but the cumulative violations of small privacies, and their aggregation, adds up to an overwhelming invasion over the course of your life.

A theory holds that the value of the Net grows exponentially with the number of things that are connected to it. Not long after the first web browser was created, an engineer in the U.K. aimed a camera at a coffee pot so he could see if there was freshly made coffee before trekking over for a cup. Soon cameras and weather sensors were regular features of the web. Now network-connected sensors and transmitters are becoming embedded in all manner of devices at work, at home, in your pocket, and in your car to make them "smart" (a term of dubious exactitude, which allows many opportunities for abuse). The reality is that the invasiveness of the web is proportionate to its pervasiveness.

With the proliferation of these sensors, we are moving from voluntary web participation into a realm where autonomous "machine-to-machine" messages are exchanging information without human involvement, awareness, or permission. Even the highway is becoming aware its own congestion and can communicate that status. There is not much disagreement that increasing connection is the future. The question is who will be in control of the information as it flows?

GPS — Worldwide Watch

As an example, the global positioning system (GPS) is a terrific invention for those who are geographically challenged. As a participatory and voluntary technology, GPS is brilliant and a boon to public safety. For decades it has been an asset for trekkers, the U.S. military, and public-service agencies. It was introduced as a one-way system, like radio. The signals were received from a sky full of satellites, you knew where you were, and that was it. GPS's two-way capability arrived when it became linked to cellular communications networks. Your GPS data isn't just providing your position to you; it's also beaming your location to a network of computer servers.

In 1996, General Motors merged GPS and cellular communications into a service called "OnStar." The result was sort of a roving concierge service that knew where you were and helped you find what you were looking for. At the same time, it captured information about the condition of your car and transmitted it to the OnStar service center, all without the driver's participation.

All this was great if you were in a car accident, totally lost, or looking for a Starbucks to help you keep your eyes open. OnStar could even unlock your car remotely. If you value your privacy, however, it wasn't so great since you were being tracked everywhere you drove. Who owned that information? Was it for sale? Was it accessible to law-enforcement authorities, and for what reasons? Lastly, what would happen to all of this information should the company go bankrupt (which indeed General Motors did)? Who would own your data?

Help! I'm Being Followed by My Phone!

Emergency calls were problematic for mobile phones. Most 911 call centers were built by land-line phone companies. The 911 systems identified your phone number by caller ID and automatically matched it to your address so the agent would know where to send help. Brilliant for saving lives in many medical emergencies and fires. But because mobile phones were not fixed in one location, coordinating phone numbers and addresses was not automatic. This caused delays in providing emergency aid, since people were often calling a 911 center that was not local. To solve the problem the FCC required all new mobile phones to contain a GPS-like technology by 2005.

Not to waste the opportunity, the mobile-phone service providers sought ways of turning this public safety requirement into revenue-generating products. "Turn-by-turn" directions were worth a few extra subscription dollars a month. Another "premium" product allowed the service subscriber to track the location of all members of the family plan. In the case of young children, that would be a comfort; for teenagers, not so much. There was no requirement that limited which family member was tracked. One spouse could easily keep tabs on the other, without his or her knowledge, depending upon whose name was on the account.

With most recent devices, every minute your phone is on it is capable of determining your location and transmitting it to the network You might be able to find the menu to turn off your Bluetooth, but try to find the menu to turn off your GPS. There is currently a controversy about why some makers of smart phones are actively monitoring the GPS data from every new phone they sell. There seem to be no good answers. Given the nature of hacking, you can also assume that your location information is available to anyone with devious or destructive intentions.

Another troubling question is what the service providers — the telecom companies — are doing with this stream of GPS data. They have their hands on great amounts of information valued by data aggregators. Judging from the disregard these providers exhibited for privacy agreements in violation of FISA, one could expect government agencies to tap into location information without consent. Illegal? Probably, but you won't know it if and when they do.

On the marketeer front, telecom companies, media companies, and ad agencies have now become an unholy trinity rolling out "location-based services." Because your phone, and perhaps your car, is a beacon letting the entire network know where you are, location-based marketeers are targeting advertising at you based on your proximity to their store or restaurant, or even predicting what location you will arriving at soon. You will be increasingly bombarded by highly localized mobile spam aware of your shopping proclivities. Thanks to database connectivity, they will know you, and know where you are.

There seems to be a generational divide about the issue of location awareness and privacy. Social network services are offering applications that allow you to continuously transmit your location information to a network of your friends. That's appealing to members of the younger "look-at-me" generation who hunger for social encounters and hookups. It's easy to see, though, how this could become a nightmare as relationships shift and someone gets in the "wrong" position with the "wrong" person. Too much magic can accidentally deliver too much information.

EDR: Driving Big Brother

Aside from your phone, other objects you own are busy tattling on you. You are probably not aware that your car carries a "black box," a data recorder similar to the ones on airliners that report data after a crash. Your car's device is called an Event Data Recorder, or EDR. Most modern cars carry EDRs. The "events" that EDRs record are car accidents, performance metrics, and, increasingly, driving behavior. Carmakers started installing them around the same time that they started installing air bags. The initial idea was to record and measure the effectiveness of the safety equipment. By 2005, nearly 65% of passenger cars were equipped with EDR. Beginning in 2011, EDR will be mandatory in every new car.

As you move along the highway, the EDR records your speed, the position of your brakes, and dozens of other metrics about your car's performance and safety equipment. The data, encoded so that only the car manufacturer can read it, has been of some assistance in improving car safety, and is useful for research and development purposes.

However, as we often see, even well-intentioned technology has a way of being used for less noble purposes. It didn't take long for insurance companies and attorneys to demand the data as evidence in court. For the time being, courts have ruled that the data is admissible. Less clear is who owns the data. In some states, a subpoena is necessary, while others say the information is not private since it records your behavior on public roads, making it no different than being observed by law enforcement while you are driving.

EDR might well be a great idea for affixing blame in contested traffic accidents. At the same time, it is not infallible, especially at the moment of impact, when car systems are headed toward major failure. (Think about how well a computer will work when it's slamming into a brick wall.) Aside from limited reliability, EDR is also subject to data manipulation by parties interested in influencing court decisions. Often after a car is totaled the EDR becomes the property of an insurance company, and their agenda could — and probably does — differ from yours as the insured party. And what if an accident occurs because of a malfunction in the car itself? If the car company owns the codes, how will you prove it? The codes need to be open and independently verifiable.

Currently, EDR records only the moments before impact. But we can expect the capability and capacity of the device to allow monitoring of driving over a longer period of time; combined with wireless connections, your actions could be transmitted in real time. The question is to whom? Law enforcement? Insurance companies? Who is entitled to know?

It's disturbing that this invasive technology has been deployed so widely without public awareness. When people buy a car, they should be made aware in no uncertain terms that an EDR is installed. There are three reasons for this. One: It would safeguard their rights of privacy. Two: It is possible that real benefits could come from people knowing that their driving is being monitored. Three: Drivers should be offered an opt-out of EDR activation if they feel that it violates their privacy.

RFID: Radio Freq-out

Tracking people and things has long been a dream of technologists and now the technology has caught up with the imaginings. After the collapse of the dotcom bubble, the moribund computer industry stood up and cheered at the prospects of marketing radio frequency identification equipment, or RFID. The idea was to implant tiny radio-frequency transmitters ("tags") into all sorts of merchandise to report information back to scanners that would read the data and pass it on to an Internet protocol network.

These tags would have their own addresses on the Internet. The mantra of the day was:

"Millions of computers, billions of users, trillions of devices."

Most people are familiar with RFID from dog and cat chip implants. In a creepy development, there have even been some people chipped for access to high-security locations.

A huge driver of the RFID initiative was Walmart, which had issued the requirement that all goods arriving at their stores have preinstalled RFID tags. It was harder to do than they imagined. Radio waves are tricky and subject to interference. Nonetheless, Walmart did succeed in getting RFID tags attached to each of their shipping pallets so that inventory could be tracked in what they called their "global supply chain." The vision had been to extend those tags down to each and every individual item of merchandise and eventually replace the UPC bar code which required human interaction to aim a scanner. Items implanted with tiny chips would allow people to check out of a store by just walking through a checkout area.

For payment, Visa and MasterCard have already rolled out "touchless" RFID debit/credit cards. Such a card, implanted with RFID tags, remains in your wallet and is automatically debited wirelessly. Obviously, since these credit cards are constantly capable of transmitting information, there is a huge potential for identity thieves to easily steal your card number while it remains in your wallet. Imagine a massive RFID hijacking in a crowded subway car.

RFID has been successful in speeding up transportation systems with automatic bridge and highway toll collection systems like EZPass, FastTrak, Clipper, and public-transit passes. Nonetheless, privacy activists are wary of the government and private contractors acquiring and recording this data, since these tags identify individuals coming and going in public spaces.

These activists are also dubious of RFID tags imbedded in items that find their way into your home. Interested parties could simply drive through a neighborhood and have the tagged items in your house respond as if they were being polled and inventoried. It would let both marketeers and potential thieves know exactly which houses have big-screen TVs and other high-ticket items.

Think about this: you're shopping at the mall, and, after making some purchases, you walk into the next store and the RFID tags in your bags are telling the store's computer exactly what you have already bought. It might also check your "touchless" credit cards to find out how much credit you have available. If the store has already done business with you, they might bring up your profile and dispatch a salesperson. If they don't like your profile, they could purposely ignore you. Just like the caller ID at the bank, you will be analyzed, classed, and dealt with before you say a word.

The RFID tag is finding its way into its way into other parts of daily life. Nike and Apple had this great idea to embed sneakers with tiny self-powered GPS/RFID tags. As you walk, it transmits information wirelessly in real time to your iPod. It's great for monitoring your training regime. Except the radio waves don't stop at your iPod; they continue to broadcast locally, and anyone so inclined and equipped can track another person without detection. It's a perfect setup for you to be stalked while listening to the music of your choice.

TV That Watches You

Nielsen has been using technology to record the viewing patterns of TV watchers for generations. From seeing the resultant shows, I'd say they have a curious criterion for success. The process has been implemented by logbooks, "People Meters," and wacky infrared sensors that gaze into viewer's eyeballs to see if they are paying attention to the ads. The subjects called "Nielsen Families" have always been willing participants in this monitoring.

When digital video recorders (DVRs) such as TiVo were introduced, advertisers panicked about people fast-forwarding through the commercials. Marketeers had a ready workaround. Most DVR, satellite, and digital cable services are two-way systems. Digital cable systems are inherently two-way, and newer satellite TV systems are usually connected to a phone line that sends your personal-viewing information upstream.

Although they don't disclose it, these services have the capability to track every flip of your remote. From that data they "get to know you better" and can target ads based on your behavioral patterns. TiVo now has the capability to place advertising in the pause when you are skipping forward — ads targeted just to you. By TiVo's own admission, they are in the business of "giving advertisers insights into audience behaviors and help them better attract and retain consumers' attention." And you thought you were paying them so you could *skip* the commercials.

Now, Microsoft and other game console makers have introduced motion sensor controls that use video cameras to detect your body movements, and that can also recognize your face. Since these game consoles are connected to the Net your face can easily be matched to other databases about you. Marketeers are drooling over this opportunity to *play* with you.

Oh Brother, Are You Watching?

The other way TV is watching you is akin to that envisioned in *1984*. Digital technology has made video cameras amazingly cheap and small. TV cameras are everywhere. There are cameras on the street, and in both public and private buildings. Questions remain as to who is entitled to view and retain those images and whether they actually stop crime or just document it. Certainly we have seen many crimes committed in full view of cameras. After all, criminals are not always shy. To actually stop crimes, the cameras would require direct feeds to police; at that point, which crimes would qualify for police intervention?

During the past three hundred years, we have often seen massive police responses to "quell" protest marches. Civil demonstrations are not a crime; they are the heart of democracy. Nonetheless, we have seen people demonstrating for labor rights and civil rights, and against illegal wars, clubbed and tear-gassed in the streets. But I don't remember ever seeing police clubbing anti-choice activists, Tea Partiers, or jingoistic pro-war marchers.

Now technologists are using generous Dept. of Homeland Security funds to develop "facial recognition" technology that would allow authorities to target people in crowds. Judging from our experience with Nixon and others, the "targets" would be political enemies. The police are always going to be an extension of authority, and authority is always going to protect itself. It will always want the most sophisticated tools it can get. Will it take capturing images of Mickey Mouse at a demonstration to raise alarm bells in Congress?

Looking Through You

Fear sells almost as well as sex. The cascade of privacy abuses rationalized after the World Trade Center attacks now has citizens baring their privates just to board a crowded, overbooked airplane and eat oversalted peanuts. The Transportation Security Administration (TSA) has rolled out 19 "whole-body scanners" to airports around the country and more are on the way in the wake of the "Underpants Bomber of 2009."

Using a special low-powered X-ray scanner, these new systems peel away the clothing of passengers to reveal them in all their anatomical glory, thereby putting the T&A in TSA.

While the TSA claims complete neutrality in its procedures, such claims counter-indicate the very notion of profiling people. Profiling is obviously not neutral or it would be pointless. They also claim that they don't save images, but the there is no technical prohibition since the files can easily be saved and viewed on any standard computer. They would have to be able to capture and save images as evidence if someone had contraband.

You can bet that, sooner or later, surreptitious celebrity sightings will find their way to the TMZ website and less unsavory places. Your spouse and kids can easily wind up in someone's private collection. If it can be done, it will be done. You might want to do your own casual survey while waiting at the airport to see what body types are most frequently scanned.

After the Underpants Bomber episode over Detroit various Bush Jr. administration ex-officials popped up on TV news pushing for wide adoption of the machines. Most journalists did not bother to note that these talking-head, termed-out bureaucrats were actually being paid by the makers of the scanners.

Owning Your Private Parts

Nude pictures of you are only the beginning. Now that they've seen you naked, they want to use biometric identification to "get into your genes." Biologically, only you are you. The first biometric ID was the fingerprint. Over the past two decades, DNA has become the most convincing identifier. On the positive side, DNA evidence from crime scenes has vindicated falsely-convicted felons. These capital convictions, overturned decades after the crime, display all too clearly the massive imperfection of our pay-as-you-go justice system.

But the troubling question remains: Who owns your genetic material? Once you have given a sample, who gets possession of it, and beyond that, who is entitled to decode your genetic secrets? If your employer wants a sample to make sure you are you, are they also entitled to run a scan to see if you are predisposed to illness? If you have a blood test at a hospital and the test is paid for by your insurance company, does that entitle the insurance company to test your DNA for congenital diseases that have not yet appeared? Could they decide not to cover you without disclosing your condition to you?

Your Genes Head to Court

The genetic issue takes us back to the beginning of this chapter and intellectual property versus privacy rights. According to the U.S. Patent Office, 20% of your genetic material is the property of someone else. Private companies have been granted patents because they have "discovered" your genes. The idea would be laughable, except that biotech companies hold exclusive rights to diseases — and their genetic codes — extracted from patients. These patents are crippling the ability of scientists to freely study diseases, and are restricting patients from getting the information they need to make important medical decisions about their health.

Chris Hansen, of the American Civil Liberties Union, simply states the objections: "The reason why everyone thinks this isn't right is that it isn't right. This is common sense. Patents were designed to protect human inventions, and you can't invent the gene." On the other hand, Myriad Genetics, a notoriously aggressive defender of their breast-cancer marker patents, said in a recent statement that they will "vigorously defend our intellectual property rights" against breast-cancer patients.

There is research about breast cancer, heart disease, Alzheimer's disease, and countless other diseases that we, the public, could use. Instead, the patent office has decided it's more important for private companies to make money by holding this information hostage. So if this is the age when information is supposed to be shared because of the Net, someone needs to let Congress know it…or better yet, write them a check.

PART 5: WHAT'S YOURS IS MINED

A world of information could have been available to us with a few keystrokes. Yet our elected government, either by omission or design, has consigned this treasure to private companies. We are being laid bare in every conceivable way as private companies encircle us with their enhanced and extended rights. Even where we have been given the right of privacy, there is no enforcement or punishment for the violators.

The concentration of data accumulates. The big information aggregators continue to collect more data on us while making sweetheart deals with military and domestic security agencies. Hiring, rental, and scholarship decisions are being made behind our backs as data miners report on us with neither our consent, nor our right to examine and challenge the records that they keep on us.

Take the example of a company called "Clear." With the promise of speeding a customer though airport security, people paid Clear a fee and gave them unfettered access to personal and biometric information. Then they went belly-up and sold off their private information in a bankruptcy sale. To whom? Well, uh, that's none of your business.

No matter what political philosophy you subscribe to — libertarian, progressive, or that vast space down the middle— it is outrageous that in America information is being locked away from you, while *you* have become an open book, subject to the whim of unchecked corporate and government power to sift through your life. Your life and privacy are your property and deserve at least as much protection as has been given to a cartoon mouse.

2.6

Electiontronics: Who's Counting?

"It's not who they vote for that counts...
...it's who counts the votes."

— *Josef Stalin*

Daunting Digital Democracy

In this, the later part of first decade of the 21st century, we have turned to digital magic to attempt to resolve long-standing political problems.

The digerati, mainstream media, and many young citizens firmly hold the belief that we have entered an age of "digital democracy." It's hard to dispute that digital technology shaped the 2008 U.S. presidential election, though at the moment the resultant political changes look modest, at best. More radical changes took place in the days of newsprint and vacuum tubes.

Many people have also pointed to the social network-powered emergence of a vociferous opposition following the sham Iranian presidential election of 2009. Yet, despite all the fuss, the level of oppression in Iran may be even more pervasive than before the election. Twitter has been no match for the truncheons and torture dungeons of the theocrats.

Digital democracy exists under the illusion that advancing technology inherently and inevitably advances the cause of social justice while fostering progress and democratization. As is a constant in the digitization of any human process, the results are subject to intermediaries and authorities who control the machinery, the process and, therefore, the outcomes.

The Two Halves of Digital Democracy

There are really two halves to what is being declared "digital democracy." The first half is information dissemination — the ability for ordinary citizens to share information widely and rapidly at virtually no cost. Specifically, I refer to the blogs and social media that can raise awareness and money for virtually any cause or initiative. With a combination of video, image, and text, this half is a "new media" story, but as Hitler and his gang of thugs made us painfully aware, new forms of media can be flipped by authority figures to convey faithfully rendered lies. New media is not inherently progressive.

The second half of digital democracy is the mechanics of the election process itself. Specifically, it's how citizens' votes are registered and counted — and who's doing the counting. As the quote above from Stalin indicates, the counting is what matters most in the outcome of the election. Despite all the campaign money raised by millions on blogs, hundred of thousands of votes may be erased by a single programmer with ill intent, and such a massive theft leaves no fingerprints. In both information dissemination and vote tabulation — as in all things digital — the process requires intermediators who often have their own agenda.

Are the promises of digital democracy falling short? If an irresistible force for positive change truly has emerged, it will work only by understanding technology's flaws and strengths.

Democracy Is Simple

Democracy is actually a very simple process that has a very low technical requirement. The Greeks are credited with the official start some 2,500 years ago, though most likely its origin goes back even further. Think about a tribe or small village electing leadership or making group decisions. If the group was small, chances are everyone had access to the same information. A show of hands, a stone in a

Jason Benlevi

box or a mark on a piece of papyrus was all that was required for the group to reach a majority agreement. Information was shared. Votes were counted by a group of voters. Simple.

For a small town, like those in the American colonies, the process was equally simple. Information was shared by townsfolk, or perhaps by a broadsheet, pamphlet or newspaper. Chances are that everyone knew the candidates or at least knew the printer/publisher of the newspaper. There was a social contract of trust within the community. A newspaper that was consistently skewing the facts would either be shunned or used as a yardstick by which to judge objective reality. People would know from experience whether to trust what the paper reported.

When it came time to vote, a town hall and a show of hands might suffice. A simple handwritten name on a folded piece of paper dropped in a ballot box was an irrefutable private expression of public opinion. The votes were counted by fellow citizens. Any citizen could challenge, audit and verify the vote. In Dixville Notch, New Hampshire (the first precinct to vote in every U.S. presidential election), they still perform the vote as they did in the 18th century, and its veracity has never been challenged because this small community of fifty voters all know each other. Generally, a small democracy using ink and paper works well. The problem comes when democracy starts scaling up.

Scaling Up Democracy

When a community grows beyond the size where all the citizens know each other and have first-hand knowledge of current affairs, the potential for a breakdown of simple democracy appears. Citizens become more reliant upon newspapers and the opinions of leaders to inform them. If the town is large enough, you may not personally know the publisher. If there are multiple papers, chances are the facts will be colored differently by different papers, which is only natural.

In these larger civic entities, instead of gathering together in one room to vote, the governing authority will be in charge of conducting the election process. A group of citizen volunteers will likely count the ballots. There is undoubtedly room for corruption, but, at least, awareness of the players involved insures some accountability.

Once we scale up to a metropolis, rather than voting for people whom we know first person, we depend entirely on media to tell us about the candidates, and this proxy for our own personal experience is vulnerable to manipulation. Instead of having ballots personally counted by people we know, we turn this process over to paid officials and whatever system they have put in place.

Ultimately, we don't really know that much about the person we are voting for, beyond superficial impressions, and we don't know for certain that our vote has been counted. Digital democracy presently solves neither of these problems and may, in fact, exacerbate them, since we have transferred much of the election process to digital intermediators who introduce potential biases into the process.

Into this mix, we must also add one more cultural factor: the preference for "fast" over "good." Tens of thousands of fast-food emporia and "billions and billions served" are evidence of this detrimental impatience. The need for speed coupled with digital magic is an accelerant to the deterioration of the democratic process.

Let us now examine, in order, the two parts at play in democracy and how they are being affected by the Cult of Tech.

Part one is getting the word out. Part two is counting the votes.

DIGITAL DEMOCRACY, PART I:

Getting the Word Out

No matter where you are on the political spectrum, winning converts to your point of view means reaching the most people with the most persuasive information. The history of the U.S. and its emergence into independence shows a strong linkage between information technology, the movable-type printing press, and democracy. From the beginning, America has been media-savvy. Pamphleteers, such as Tom Paine, and printers, such as Benjamin

Franklin, were the architects of our democratic revolution. News reporting has co-evolved with our democracy, and each has worked synergistically to shape the other.

Early newspapers were small operations where the writer, publisher, and printer were often the same person. This medium was small, personal, and passionate, but still factual enough to warrant credibility among readers, especially if they personally knew the particular subjects and events described in the articles. As towns grew and there was more news to cover, the paper grew as well, with more pages and more staff. In order to pay the expenses of an expanding newspaper venture, advertising became increasingly important factor. Instead of selling papers to people for a few more pennies, the business model became selling the readership to advertisers.

With advertising as a driving force, it was irresistible to turn the editorial slant of the paper toward the merchants and business community. Publishers served up just enough truth, along with the requisite amount of sensation, to do the community a reasonable service, while delivering more readers into the arms of paid advertisers. Throughout the 19th century, newspapers grew along with the population, becoming substantial businesses in their own right.

Old ink-stained publishers were becoming increasingly wealthy and conservative as they served the interests of the social class to which they belonged. Yet, the overall instinct of journalism stayed intact: to expose the long-lived and corrupt nexus between business and political interests. The founding democratic instincts of the press remained alive in city rooms, even if the publishers became more interested in sipping brandy in exclusive clubs with fellow business moguls. To this day, surveys show reporters to be overwhelming progressive, while newspaper publishers tend toward conservatism. The political influence of publisher endorsements became overwhelming. Newspapers, the biggest megaphone in town, ruled.

By owning a widely read newspaper you could shape the public agenda. Men of immense wealth began purchasing or collecting independently owned newspapers, even when they weren't particularly sound businesses. For example, financier Eugene Meyer of San Francisco used his wealth to purchase the *Washington Post* to provide himself with a political soapbox in D.C. More notoriously, mining heir William Randolph Hearst acquired enough papers across the country to become the world's first mega media mogul, while seeking to fulfill his political aspirations, both as candidate and kingmaker. Indeed, Hearst was the first publisher to lead us into a war of his own choosing. The Spanish-American War and the jingoistic distortions of "Yellow Journalism" will forever be associated with "W.R."

Newspapers continued to wield enormous power throughout the first half of the 20th century. It was still feasible to start a new newspaper. There were no laws stopping you, but the economics were brutal. Joint operating agreements (JOAs) kept newspapers from cannibalization in some markets, such as San Francisco, where the two morning papers became one evening and one morning paper with separate editorial staffs but joint advertising, printing, and distribution operations.

Alternative or underground weeklies emerged in the late 60s to serve the counterculture and later found a market as community-service and cultural voices. However, these weeklies had no real capacity to drive public opinion with narrow circulations of a few thousand copies a week versus the hundreds of thousands, or millions, served by the daily papers in their markets.

Most American cities today have just one daily paper and, for the most part, the printed daily paper, is limping toward extinction. But we are getting ahead of ourselves. For most of U.S. history, newspapers were essential, closing the chasm between the ordinary citizen and the newsmakers of the world.

Radio Plays Politics

The first electronic medium in our democracy was radio. Because radio sets were entertainment devices that served music, drama, and comedy for free they were rapidly adopted by users. News and politics were not driving factors. If there was news, it most likely was wire copy being read by an announcer. With the beginning of radio-network hookups connected by phone lines, a politician's voice could be heard from coast-to-coast. For some old-line politicians, being heard was not an advantage — their grandiose speech was appropriate for a Masonic hall or the courthouse steps, but clearly unsuited for living rooms. Radio, however, could work exceedingly well for politicians able to use the medium's intimacy and drama. People could hear their actual intonations and make judgments about their temperament and demeanor.

Franklin Roosevelt's personal warmth came across in his intimate "Fireside Chats." His manner, though aristocratic, was also easy — pitch perfect for a frightened public in search of reassurance. Churchill's timing and language served him well for making stirring radio addresses during WW II. Hitler and Goebbels took full advantage of aural spectacle with the sound of their adoring, maniacal crowds.

Both truth and deception worked well on the radio: you had no idea what was actually going on in reality since you couldn't see it. Orson Welles's *War of the Worlds* broadcast proved beyond a doubt the power of radio coupled with the human imagination. Voices engaged the audience more than print ever did. Radio was hot, live, and immediate.

In America, radio was democratic. Radio stations were licensed by the government, but there were few requirements. Stations were local, plentiful and not extremely expensive to start. While the big networks, like NBC, CBS and Mutual, had the biggest audiences, local and regional voices were also heard. Radio transmitted a broad spectrum of opinion. A turn of the dial could bring you the spirit of Woody Guthrie, the lefty troubadour, or the twisted hate speech of Father Charles Coughlin from the Shrine of the Little Flower Church in Detroit. At night, signals traveled far and wide, allowing listeners to catch programming from distant cities.

Opinion was magnetic on the radio. Religious zealots and political extremists who were skilled at soaring rhetoric discovered that verbal pyrotechnics were incendiary to their flocks and profitable to themselves. These radio voices were like dog whistles specifically tuned to their sympathetic human receivers. Outside listeners might find the rhetoric horrifying, but could just turn the dial. Today, radio is still a huge driver of popular opinion. One major party in the U.S. can't make a decision without an on air blessing from a certain Mr. Limbaugh.

The Narrowing Tube

For reasons both technical and financial, TV started the process of narrowing the spectrum of opinion. Where radio had plenty of open frequencies and relatively low operating costs, TV required so much broadcast signal spectrum that it was possible to have only six stations in any market — and only the biggest cities had that many. These signals also didn't transmit as far as AM radio, which was the dominant broadcast technology of the day.

That technical limitation became a huge advantage for marketeers of products and politics. With only a few TV broadcast slots available for any given media market, getting a TV broadcasting license was often the result of political clout. Lyndon and Lady Bird Johnson's fortune was greatly enhanced by grabbing the only TV frequency slot available in Austin, Texas. This monopoly made them the only choice for advertisers.

The big radio networks (NBC and CBS) got first dibs on TV channels. The lower-frequency channels were at a premium, since those bandwidths transmitted farther for the same amount of wattage and reached a bigger potential market. In most metropolitan areas the big networks seized the lower frequencies.

The FCC of the day was keenly aware of the political influence and financial power of the big networks and wisely limited them to owning a maximum of five stations. The networks then could offer their national programming through affiliates, which had local ownership. The idea was to avoid media concentration and prevent the type of informational hegemony that the Hearst newspapers had once exercised. With New Deal DNA still in their blood, the FCC's goal was to ensure a diversity of opinions or, at least, fairness. In 1949, they specifically instituted the Fairness Doctrine to foster the airing of a wide range of opinions on TV's relatively few (compared to radio's many) stations.

The FCC also restricted newspaper companies from owning TV stations in their home market. The idea was to prevent one company from dominating the delivery of public information, or from monopolizing advertising. Fortunately, the big networks considered delivering news and current affairs as part of their public obligation. The networks invested mightily in building global news organizations. CBS had already become famous for its radio news coverage and, within a decade, TV news went from reading dry news copy off the teletype to reporters and camera crews jetting in film and shortwaving in the voiceover from around the world.

A new species developed at the center of the TV newsroom: the anchorman. The first superstars were Chet Huntley and David Brinkley (in the *Huntley-Brinkley Report* on NBC) soon to be eclipsed by Walter Cronkite, who became "The Most Trusted Man in America." So important was "Uncle Walter" that when he turned against the Vietnam War, President Lyndon Johnson said, "If I've lost Cronkite, than I've lost America."

The 1960s saw a huge expansion of the power and influence of network news operations — along with the rise of powerful enemies of the media. The most famous enemy was, of course, Richard Nixon, whose distain for the news media stretched back to his California congressional days. With Roger Ailes (later the president of Fox TV News) as his media czar and disgraced former vice president Spiro Agnew as his hatchet man, they launched a campaign of intimidation on the "eastern elite" news media. Authority and truth were mortal enemies and it was clear which side Nixon and his mob were on. In 1974, truth got the better of an increasingly authoritarian regime. Nixon resigned and various members of his gang were dismissed, disgraced, or jailed.

Was it a triumph of a free press, or did Woodward and Bernstein just catch a few breaks? The truth is that the mainstream TV news organizations really missed this story until it was already in motion. Quite possibly, they were just too intimated to pursue the story, fearing they might lose their broadcast licenses which the

Nixon-appointed FCC controlled. On the other hand, unfiltered live TV coverage of the Watergate hearings was a revelation and probably led to the creation of C-SPAN, which has been good for democracy.

The News was Making Money on News

The 70s and 80s were a time of massive changes in TV news. Technically, videotape replaced film while global satellite uplinks vastly sped up the process of news gathering. The new model was called "electronic news gathering" (ENG). CNN was founded at this time because it was technically and financially feasible to use these resources to re-engineer the news-gathering process. At the same time, the TV networks had changes of ownership that made them look at the news differently. News departments started to be pushed from public service to serving up profits to the network. A languishing *60 Minutes* moved from its Tuesday-night graveyard to a sweet prime-time spot on Sunday nights.

The perennial TV-news ratings loser was ABC. Roone Arledge, the guy who produced the network's flashy sport shows, was put in charge of adding some production dazzle to the newscast. He enticed Barbara Walters to jump from NBC to ABC with a million-dollar salary, an outrageous sum at the time. News was now expected to be a moneymaker and the talking heads in the anchor chairs wanted their share too.

The original founders of the networks (Paley at CBS and Sarnoff at NBC) were slowly retiring from daily operations. It was becoming time to sell their interests. Like any moneymaking business, it's not hard to find buyers who think they can manage it more effectively and rake in greater profits. Add in a measure of glamour, and broadcasting companies become very attractive to mogul types. They arrived with accountants in tow to squeeze out profits and wanted news to be more "business friendly."

Local stations were the first place where news stopped being news. Media consultants created cookie-cutter formulae that made the local news look and sound the same no matter what city you were in. City council and school board meetings were replaced by mantras of "If it bleeds, it leads" and "Tits, tots, and pets." Local Edward R. Murrows were transformed into well-coifed Kens and Barbies with mix-and-match ethnicities. Every rating point on local news was money in the bank the local station didn't have to share with the network.

The war on news continued as the Reagan administration and his horde of right wing ideologues declared war on PBS and the so-called "liberal media." For PBS, the severity of the cuts meant that public broadcasting, which had been non-commercial, now airs "funding messages" that are essentially commercials for the same oil giants, military contractors, pharmaceutical and chemical companies found on the for-profit networks.

No matter how middle-brow, hagiographic, or timid the network news had become, it still was not conservative enough for the new crowd in Washington. The Reaganites ended the Fairness Doctrine that had ensured balance since its 1949 inception. They also began the decade-long deregulation process that unraveled FCC ownership limitations to allow their friends to acquire more stations, concentrate their power and gain greater influence. Any TV network could now own more than five stations, and newspapers could buy TV stations in their hometowns, both of which had previously been prohibited.

Big newspapers were also buying their competitors or expanding beyond their home cities. Radio-station ownership rules now allowed broadcasters to own multiple stations in a single media market. Overall, media concentration has delivered an ever-more conservative tilt. The flight of music programming to better-sounding FM frequencies meant that there were a lot of AM stations available on the cheap. Right-wing and politico-religious interests were buying up these stations and starting networks to spread their ultra-conservative "gospel."

Even the emergence of the innocuous *USA Today* as a national newspaper was evidence of media becoming homogenized and narrowed. And as all of this narrowing and rightward skewing of the mainstream media was taking place, the greatest expansion of human communications was developing on the Internet.

Dialing for Democracy

Although people usually credit the campaign of Howard Dean in 2004 for the rise of new media in digital democracy, it really started right before the dawn of web browsers. The Democratic presidential primary campaign of California's visionary Governor Jerry Brown in 1992 was the opening volley of this revolution. Brown's long-shot, widely ridiculed campaign ran on a shoestring, but he still needed funds to run the machinery of a campaign. Governor Brown, who had spent some of the previous decade doing a call-in show on non-profit radio, had learned the value of "pledge week."

Given any airtime on the news or in a debate, Brown would give out his toll-free 800 phone number so that potential donors could use their credit cards to make small contributions to his "people's" campaign. All the big-money establishment candidates, except Bill Clinton, ran out of money, while Jerry Brown carried on his campaign due to his ability to raise grass-roots funding from people not in the habit of attending rubber-chicken dinners and writing fat checks to politicians. The Brown campaign signaled something new; bypassing the usual channels of fundraising with an electronic medium — the toll free 800 number — to gather money and network supporters. Like many of Governor Brown's ideas, it was ahead of its time.

In 1992, Bill Clinton was elected without a majority. Media consolidation, propelled by a new, more virulent conservative tide in the Congress, continued. Corporate-friendly "business" cable channels emerged. Amid a wave of corporate takeovers, and abandonment of civic responsibility, TV news departments went from being loss-leading public services to huge profit centers. Lead by celebrity-studded "news-lite" shows such as *60 Minutes* and *20/20*, news was making money, and news personalities were bringing in millionaire salaries. Reporters and the powerful people they were supposed to be covering belonged to the same social class, attended the same parties in Georgetown, and "summered" together on Martha's Vineyard.

Mainstream media got softened by reporters who didn't want to rock the boat. This generation of reporters, ostensibly inspired by the Watergate exposés of Woodward and Bernstein, were surprisingly quick to sell out. The star-power achieved by the *Washington Post* duo was a greater influence than their drive to get the truth out. Tough questions could put reporters on the social "outs" with the powerful newsmakers.

Radio, always a rumbling voice of dissent and controversy in the background, took on a new role. Without the Fairness Doctrine to keep any balance of political viewpoints between right and left, radio station owners switched to all-right-wing-all-the-time talk formats to cater to angry middle-aged white men. Not surprisingly, this programming was a comfort to those very same owners, since they shared the same political outlook. The abdication of meaningful ownership regulations, along with no local-content requirements, meant that an owner could string together many stations playing one national talk show. It was cheaper and easier than producing and promoting local programming.

While all the established broadcast media outlets were becoming more bowed and cowed to authority, less substantive, and more celebrity-infused, the newly emerging Internet was exploding with hundreds of get-rich schemes and truly boneheaded business ideas. While it was possible that anyone with certain technical knowledge could create a webpage to espouse their ideas, it was not particularly stylish in laissez-faire Silicon Valley to be political. The folks with the requisite technical chops were more interested in the IPO possibilities of pets.com than in civic affairs.

Reinventing Defeat

The 2000 presidential campaign should have been a turning point in electoral politics. For the first time, there was a viable candidate in the race who was truly knowledgeable about technology — the Internet in particular. Although the mainstream press liked recycling the misstatement that Al Gore "invented the Internet," in reality the senator was an early advocate and champion of the "Information

Superhighway," much as his father, Senator Albert Gore Sr., was a champion of the Interstate Highway System in the 1950s. Gore Jr. may well have been the only senator in 1988 who even knew there *was* an Internet.

By any measure, the 2000 presidential election was a lot of things it shouldn't have been. Instead of Al Gore being himself and taking advantage of this new media, he put the same old Beltway insiders who had been helping Democratic candidates lose for years in charge of his campaign. These people make their living from commissions and fees for TV and radio ads buys. They had no particular interest in or knowledge of the web since it didn't cost anything.

What should have been the first Internet Age election was, instead, a dull repetition of Beltway processes that didn't connect Gore with the younger and more socially and environmentally conscious voters. Combine this failure with those of the election mechanics themselves and a serial failure, George W. Bush, wound up holding the reins of the nation.

Despite spending billions of dollars on the most sophisticated computing and signal-gathering resources imaginable at the NSA, Bush's first summer in office found him asleep at the switch when the nation's capital and biggest city came under attack from 19 Arabs armed only with box cutters.

The attacks on the World Trade Center drove the bewildered mainstream broadcast media deeper into the arms of the powerful and paternal. News organizations became willing cheerleaders for military adventures, and reporters who had a history of challenging authority became in*bed*ded with the military. TV news organizations hired ex-generals who were still on the payrolls of military contractors as "news analysts." The news media became either a willing or unwitting instrument of authority, which was about to run afoul of our democracy.

Web 2.0

Although the dotcom boom had crashed in 2000, innovation was continuing with guys working in their parents' basements.

This time it wasn't about making 22-year-olds Internet zillionaires. In what would be called "Web 2.0," innovation started shifting services toward the community. Craig Newmark introduced "Craigslist" as a free ad-listing service, and Jimmy Wales introduced "Wikipedia," which became a community-compiled encyclopedia. This was clearly not 1999.

It should be noted that MoveOn.Org, started as an email list in 1998 to oppose the impeachment of Bill Clinton and increasingly became a sounding board for those with progressive views willing to donate money for their causes. Even with millions of albeit loosely-associated members, it was still not much more than a voice for the leaders of the organization, who were web technologists.

One of the most important ideas adopted by the Net was actually relatively old. It was called a "web log." A web log was a simple web page of text, coupled with a few images that had none of the slick animation or polished design of commercial websites. It looked like the very first pages that were ever viewed on the web in the early 90s. The difference was that you didn't need to know a thing about writing the underlying HTML code required to create a web page. The term "web log" became contracted to "blog" and soon anyone with anything to say could offer attractive and readable pages on the web with simple applications that only required a bit of typing.

War of the Webs

In the background of Web 2.0, a war in Iraq was alienating at least one post WW II generation. Politically aware baby-boomers and their tech-savvy children came together quickly to protest in the streets, in the established fashion of the 60s, but more than that, they began to author anti-war blogs. Voices of opposition were becoming an alternative to what was called the mainstream media.

The time couldn't have been better for Governor Howard Dean of Vermont and his progressive political consultant Joe Trippi. They had their finger on the technical and political pulse that was emerging to oppose the Bush-Cheney agenda. Picking up where Jerry Brown had left off 12 years before, they turned to the grass roots to raise money and spread their campaign message. To the surprise of the political pros, their web contributions were outpacing the big checks from the big-donor dinners of the established Democratic candidates.

The Washington establishment was taken by surprise, especially the Beltway Democratic Party consultants. The amateurs were doing better than the highly paid pros. The media at first embraced Governor Dean since it was a fresh take on what was going to be a dull field of candidates. A trained doctor, Dean was a brainy iconoclast like Governor Brown and sixties icon Senator Eugene McCarthy. But still, no matter how smart and how insightful, these candidates were ultimately belittled by mainstream media organizations. Dr. Dean turned out to be their latest candidate for ridicule.

On Jan. 19, 2004, the night Dean didn't win the Iowa Caucuses, and spoiling Beltway media's predictions, he was rallying a crowd of volunteers when he let out a rather raspy scream into his handheld microphone. The "Dean Scream" became the ideal opportunity for mainstream media to dismiss the doctor as a non-serious candidate. With endless showings of the "Dean Scream" video, the governor's campaign soon tanked. Nonetheless, Dean and his team proved that the Net had become an important tool for raising funds and awareness.

The mainstream media and the Beltway crowd quickly anointed Massachusetts Senator John Kerry as the front runner, but Sen. Kerry's campaign hacks were unable and unwilling to pick up this torch of digital democracy ignited by Dean and Trippi. Kerry's consultants *did*, however, manage to pocket a good amount of money in commissions for placing traditional — and ultimately ineffectual — TV spots. If there was a significant web victory in the 2004 election, it went to the GOP. They managed to get their slanderous anti-Kerry "Swiftboat" spots plenty of free airtime on the web and right-wing cable TV talk shows.

Give Us This Day, Our Daily Blog

As the mainstream media continued a "sleep of complicity" through Bush's economic and foreign policy disasters without serious challenges, a whole new medium was being born. The ad hoc collection of bloggers began to revolve around a few key locations on the Net. The entire universe of politically oriented blogs became called "the blogosphere." Although the name was originally coined in jest years earlier, it was widely adopted in earnest by bloggers and worn as a badge of honor.

By 2005 the popular blogs were in full swing on both the right and left sides of the spectrum. For the right wing, which already had Fox News and talk radio, the blogs were just another part of the echo chamber but for the progressive side, it was a fresh channel of citizen journalism that magnetized people hungry for news and thirsty for change from the Bush and Reagan years — needs unsatisfied by the atrophied and tamed mainstream media.

Instead of a few dozen insular national reporters dominating the big print and electronic media, suddenly there were tens of thousands, hundreds of thousands of citizen-journalists with a place to post their local, state, and national political stories, insights, and opinions. Better yet, these blogs were drawing millions of readers.

Daily Kos is the most visited of these blogsites and has become a huge megaphone, not just for its publisher, Markos Moulisatas, but for anyone on the left side of the spectrum. With myriad personal diary postings and links to other sites, including YouTube, it has become clear that Daily Kos is the big gorilla in progressive blogsites. Savvy political reporters were getting scooped by DKos and its band of volunteer "Kossacks." The *New York Times* and *Washington Post* started checking it frequently for leads on stories. Clearly, the blogosphere was out in front of the mainstream media — and by days on many stories.

In 2006 MoveOn.org, DKos and ActBlue, were powerful information outlets for senatorial and congressional campaigns, as well as conduits for raising funds for causes and candidates. News aggregators like Huffington Post and Salon.com combined original professional journalism with the energy of the blogosphere and also became an alternative to the MSM. Sensing that it was falling behind, reporters from the mainstream media started their own half measure toward the blogosphere with Politico.com, which unfortunately relies heavily on inside the Beltway sources and reportage.

In the closing years of the Bush Jr. nightmare, tools, talent, and cause came together to generate a key part of digital democracy: an aggressive, free flow of information. Citizen-journalists were on the job, and politicians began to listen to voices beyond K Street K Street lobbying firms.

A phrase from the 60s says it well, "When the people lead...the leaders will follow." That is exactly what democracy is all about.

The Stage Was Set

Barack Obama's presidential campaign focused on the Net from its inception. Although he was a national celebrity, gifted writer, and speaker, the freshman senator from Illinois, nonetheless, seemed an unlikely candidate. But the generation that grew up with their own computers, the Internet, and a non-stop war in the Muslim world was ready to cast their first vote for president, and before that first vote, they pulled out their credit cards and started making donations — not large in individual value, but massive in the aggregate.

Obama was pitted against mainstream media's front runner, the savvy and well-funded Hillary Clinton, who had spent years collecting donations for a presidential run. However the professionals were stunned when they learned that candidate Obama vastly outpaced Hillary in campaign contributions. He had gone from zero to 60 million dollars in three months. It was a jaw-dropping revelation for every candidate, consultant, and reporter who had ever worked in politics. It wasn't a flash in the pan, either. Quarter after quarter, the Obama campaign outraised every candidate in both parties. Young people were voting with their credit cards, and spreading the word in meet-ups and online social settings. Giving dollars for democracy was as easy as buying music from iTunes.

The Obama campaign, well aware of the power of the Net, hired people who knew how to do business and social networking on the web. The same process was taking place in Senate and congressional races around the country. The progressive grass roots, or "net roots," had finally started generating the green stuff to make progressives competitive. For the very first time, insurgent candidates had a better set of tools than Beltway insiders of either party, and a receptive, generous base of donors.

However, the web wasn't just an information-delivery system or campaign-fund ATM for the Obama campaign. The campaign used the Internet blogs and social networks as listening posts to gather input, opinion, and even talking points from smart folks all over cyberspace. There was intelligence funneling into the campaign that no pollster could have ever equaled by traditional methods.

On the night of November 4, 2008, shown on high-resolution screens in downtown Chicago, the country's first digital democrat took the stage in victory. But it didn't stop there. In the Obama administration's battle for universal healthcare, the blogosphere didn't let the newly elected government become the exclusive property of the usual K Street lobbyists who have dominated both parties since the Reagan Administration. Though still coming short of the public option goal, the Internet helped to level the playing field and to steer the conversation, much to the chagrin of Washington insiders.

Though I suspect many of them voted for Ron Paul, most digerati would stop the story here and point to the victory of digital democracy. However, there is also an inherent problem with the speed, malleability, and vulnerability of digital media. As explained in an earlier chapter, "Seeing is Deceiving," digital-media tools make it easy to fabricate and propagate convincing falsehoods and fake grassroots groups, such as the Tea Party, which is, in fact, funded by corporate sponsors. Because of speed of the Net, erroneous information can circulate unchecked on the web explosively.

Old-line media are now chasing stories that surface first on blogs, and in their haste, they often rush to publish stories that are not adequately fact-checked. In some ways, the daily newspaper and nightly news did a better job of filtering than the 24-hour net-enabled news cycle. Still it's hard to argue against more voices being heard.

We are reinventing or disintermediating the traditional news organizations because the Net is a common media to move information from any source to any reader or viewer. Yet when we look at the Net itself, we see a looming threat that can squelch this unfettered freedom of information.

The Choke Points

Although the Internet is built on common standards that everyone shares, there are just a handful of companies that actually own and control its physical network. As we are learning from watching other nations, this flow of information is the lifeblood of digital democracy, and it is vulnerable. Network providers are the choke points of digital democracy. In the U.S. they are the telecom companies, ISPs, and wireless services providers. You know their names from the bills they send you. Despite talk about free markets, most areas have only one or two providers. Without their services there is no Internet for you.

China may be the most obvious example of the clash between the openness of the Internet and the institutions that control the flow of information. China is famous for building walls. Hundreds of years ago, the Chinese built a 3,945-mile wall of stones to protect themselves from foreigners. Shortly after the end of Mao's days, elements of the Chinese government famously plastered a long brick wall in Beijing with message posters to create what they proclaimed a "democracy wall" used to vent disagreements between contending political factions.

Now China continues to work on another wall — the world's most pervasive Internet firewall. A firewall is usually used to protect businesses or private citizens from having their computers invaded by cybercriminals, or by parents to filter out offensive materials on the Internet. The Chinese are using their firewall to filter out the free flow of ideas.

For all its pretenses of progress, the most fundamental of modern ideals — the free flow of information — runs into a wall of authoritarian resistance in China. They have introduced so-called free enterprise, while still clamping down on political freedoms. In China, you are free to buy anything you want, but not free to think or learn anything you want. Citizens have developed clever workarounds, but it is very easy for the Chinese government to pull the plug if the political situation turns against them. They are in control of the discussion. China is not alone in having this power, but they are by far the largest nation to use it unhesitantly.

Most shameful is the complicit role of America's top technology providers in China's clampdown. These are companies that ironically talk up libertarian ideals in the U.S., yet sell the products that are giving anti-democratic authorities the capacity to filter out information and track down those "outlaws" who dare to exercise what should be their basic freedoms.

The Twitter Flickers in Iran

In the spring of 2009, the world watched as presidential elections unfolded in Iran. It was surprising to see information being freely communicated in a country generally under the strict control of religious authorities. There were debates among the candidates and opinions being expressed in print, on TV, and on the web. In the Islamic republic's peculiar form of "democracy," any candidate for president had to be officially approved by a board of governing religious authorities. So, obviously, no matter which candidate won, dramatic changes would not be allowed to occur. Nonetheless, the sitting president, Mahmoud Ahmadinejad, was clearly reviled by the urban population of Tehran.

Despite the narrow field of candidates, change was in the air. As in the 2008 U.S. presidential election, there was a generational split. Many young voters were not even born when the Shah was in power, and they were tired of religious police treating them like misbehaving children. As with young people all over the world, this generation of Iranians was restless, rebellious, and connected, toting mobile phones with cameras, texting and connecting with friends and family abroad via email, Facebook, and Twitter. Twitter was particularly useful because it made it possible to exchange messages between personal computers and text-capable SMS mobile phones, which virtually everyone in Tehran had.

Surprisingly, an opposition candidate, Mir-Hossein Mousavi,

emerged from the field. He seemed an unlikely opponent of the power structure since he himself had once been prime minister and the editor of the official Islamic Republic newspaper. People proudly flew the green flag of their reformist candidate. On Election Day, their ink-stained fingers proclaimed proudly "I voted." From all appearances, democracy was being revived in one of the oldest civilizations on earth.

When the election authorities announced that President Ahmadinejad was reelected in a landslide, the streets of Tehran erupted in outrage. The world media was watching the eruption of massive protests against the authoritarian government. Soon, the powers that be had enough, and the government restricted or expelled all global reporters, including those from al-Arabia and al-Jazerra. As the media organizations were shut down in Iran, the citizens on the streets of Iran became the ad hoc reporters, sending Twitter text messages ("tweets") and uploading mobile phone video to YouTube for the world to view.

Twitter, which had only been rolled out in 2006, was a modest application and had no viable business plan that anyone could discern. It was free and simple. So simple that it could only transmit 140 characters of text. If broadband Internet was a Series 7 BMW, Twitter was a VW Beetle. Its simplicity allowed it to work with virtually any mobile phone and send messages quickly to anywhere in the world. Overnight, Twitter became the conduit of news from inside the Tehran resistance.

As the story unfolded on the streets of Tehran, Twitter was deemed so important that the U.S. State Department asked them to delay their scheduled maintenance shutdown. Soon the Western media was all abuzz about Twitter, dubbing the Iranian situation the "Twitter Revolution." Despite the initial euphoria, people forgot something important: The tweets and Internet traffic that allowed the news to reach the world were exactly the same communications that allowed the Iranian authorities to track down and arrest the resisters. Although partially privatized, the regime retained ultimate control of all phone and Internet traffic in Iran. Every message could be read, every transmitted location revealed, every user of

Twitter identified. Although it looked like a new light was shining, the Iranian mullahs pulled the plug on digital democracy. The intermediators, whether state or privatively controlled, ultimately dictated the digital discussion.

2011: The Winter of Arab Discontent

Although the northern hemisphere was suffering through one of coldest winters on record, in the warmer climes of the Arabic-speaking nations, the political situation was simmering to a boil in the Winter of 2011. The governments' of Tunisia and Egypt were festering with the sort of excessive authoritarian corruption so often found in the region. The wealth was headed to those at the top and the game was stacked against those who were not connected to the ruling oligarchies. Those who were young, ambitious, and well-educated felt deprived of the opportunities and freedoms that they knew existed in Europe, Asia and the Americas. Unlike their parents, they had a global cultural awareness garnered through media that came to them via the Net and over satellite TV.

The "Arab-street" led collapse of the Tunisian government became a signal to many in Egypt that change was possible from the ground up. The seeds sown by Tunisian people-power spread instantly in Arabic social media circles. A young, globalized and urban population did not hesitate to seize on the social network application Facebook, as well as Twitter, to voice their discontent for being underemployed and culturally thwarted. Soon their unrest and frustration spilled into the streets, and then on to the screens of the global media beast.

One face, one Facebook page, set the spark. Wael Ghonim put up a Facebook group to protest against the government of Hosni Mubarak. For his efforts he was spirited away by the not-so-secret police and disappeared for more than a week. His worried family and Facebook friends sounded the alarm to the global media.

Experience tells us, that there is a tendency for news media to create a "narrative" or "package" a story to make it more appealing. When it involves a nexus of technology and politics, the media will often double-down on creating linkages. No matter how tenuous the connection, the media will stamp the movement with the "brand" of the "next big thing" in technology. The failed uprising in Iran was called "The Twitter Revolution." The Winter 2011 uprisings in Egypt and Tunisia were quickly branded "The Facebook Revolution" by the media. In this case, the branding may have gotten out ahead of the reality.

During that first week of February 2011, Tahir Square became the focal point for the overwhelming discontent of a generation. Facebook became the brand name instantly associated with this movement. It was an easy connection for the media to make since graffiti and protest signs clearly heralded "Facebook." They had the pictures…and it played well on TV. Facebook had already become a global media darling with a big movie about its youthful billionaire founders and bubble-valuation. However, it is still not exactly clear what the impact of social media might have been in the larger scheme of what transpired February 2011.

The naïve optimists of the digerati profess that the Net is an unstoppable force for freedom, yet the case is not nearly so clear-cut because control of the Net was still within the grasp of the autocrats. As previously stated, we know with certainty that Twitter and texting eventually worked against those who rose up in Iran.

So here are some factors worth considering as to whether the Winter of Arab Discontent was indeed a social media-based uprising:

> - Although the Net has an open architecture and multiple pathways for information to transit, the Egyptian authorities had a choke point that connected the national parts of the Net to the rest of the world. (They also made the Net inaccessible by using a scheme to interrupt the DNS system, which actually directs Internet traffic.) This may be the first time that the term "Internet Kill Switch" was discussed in public media. A term that is self-explanatory.

> - The mobile phone network was deployed and managed by European and U.S. companies. Although the Egyptian

government ordered a shutdown of the mobile network, and succeeded for a while to shut down it down, Western governments were interested in the success of the uprising and encouraged wireless phone companies, based in Europe, to not comply with the government order. The U.S. State Department worked with Twitter directly during the Iranian uprising.

- Only a small percentage of people in Egypt were Net-savvy. Less than 20% of the people used computers. More pervasive in spreading the word, was satellite TV, the medium that 99% of the Arab world had within view.

Although the spark may have been set on the Net, it was TV – uncensored and uncontrolled by government – that fueled the flames. There is no discounting the notion that Wael Ghonim using Facebook to dissent, and his unjust arrest, was a compelling story. However, it was his face on TV, in an impassioned appearance after being freed from custody that re-stirred the action in Tahir Square. He was the face of the revolution. While only a few saw his Facebook posting, the whole Arab world saw him on TV.

Here's where the story starts to take a twist. After his release, and grateful that he didn't get fired by Google for his absence, Wael wanted to meet with Mark Zuckerberg, the CEO of Facebook to thank him. However, the leadership of Facebook took great pains to distance itself from this democratic yearning. Why? Perhaps Facebook didn't want to jeopardize business relationships with other countries that were under authoritarian regimes. On the other hand, "Do No Evil" Google expressed pride in their employee Ghonim for fighting the good fight. The question becomes, what is more important to the world's leading social networking company, fundamental human rights or business relationships? We'll get to that answer later in this book.

Mubarak was forced out of office by protestors in the streets and other forces that were not readily apparent. The Egyptian Army was largely supplied and funded by the U.S. Government.

The Obama administration was increasingly uncomfortable in the position of backing the faltering and corrupt regime. We can pretty much bet that high-level U.S. diplomatic and military officers were in communication with the Egyptian military and short-circuited any attempts to attack peaceful protestors in the square – a case easily made since the Egyptian Army regularly received over a billion dollars a year in U.S. aid.

The fall of the government may have been sparked by social networking, but it took Egyptians willing to put their bodies on the line in concert with diplomatic actions occurring out of public view to bring down Mubarak.

The social network-rooster crowing made a lot of noise, but did not actually make the democracy-sun rise. Many digerati will attempt to sell that impression. Had Mubarak been given the green light by the U.S. to clamp down on the demonstrators, shut down the Net, use the phone network to track down dissidents the results would have looked more like the long suffering Iranians. No amount of "friending" or "liking" on Facebook could have prevented it.

We can expect that authoritarian governments will prepare counter-measures to stymie future expressions of discontent from their citizens over the Net. They will spread disinformation on social media and they will deploy "Internet Kill Switch" capabilities – most likely developed and deployed by U.S. and European companies, as has been the case in China. The euphoric claim that the Net, a social network, was the power that brought down a dictator may be so much digerati magical thinking. Many of these same freedom-espousing digerati will wax poetic about new products, or accept sponsorship from the very same companies that will also supply that autocrat-empowering Internet Kill Switch.

It Can Happen Here

We Americans may smugly feel this sort of usurpation of our freedoms can't happen here because our laws protect the free flow of information on the Internet. Yet there *are* no laws to ensure that the Internet remains open and free. Believe it or not, there is no legal framework to keep the service providers from deciding what you should and should not be able to see.

"Net Neutrality" is now an issue before the FCC, the courts, and Congress that touches on full and fair access to the Internet. It would prohibit Internet service providers from preferring or blocking content from one site or another, ensuring a free flow of information without prejudice. While Net Neutrality looks good on paper, can we trust the companies that have already violated their own agreements with customers and have received immunity from legal action?

Suppose the telecoms make a deal with an oil or insurance company to filter negative blogs or debate. How would we even know? Suppose a government in the future decides that it wants to direct control. How would anyone be able to stop them? The FISA laws didn't stop them the last time the government made an illegal request.

Although digerati celebrate cyber-modernity and laud the demise of printed newspapers, the sole dependence on digital media via intermediators is a huge vulnerability. Without an archive of print we are going to be subject to an ever more elastic version of the truth. As an example, there were the silly claims from the "birthers" denying that Obama was legally elected because they claimed that he was born in Kenya. No amount of computer-generated print-outs of his birth certificate from the state government was as powerful as libraries around the world possessing physical copies of the Hawaiian newspaper that originally contained his birth announcement. As one right-wing congressman finally admitted, "Unless the Obama campaign was capable of time travel, he was born in America."

It's true that digital media levels the playing field for candidates, but it also puts a compromised version of the truth on a level playing field with objective reality. It's often been said in politics, "You are entitled to your own opinion, but you are not entitled to your own facts." The first requirement of democracy, digital or otherwise, is a truthfully informed electorate.

DEMOCRACY, PART 2:

COUNTING THE VOTE

Having a reasonably informed and motivated population of voters will not deliver digital democracy if their votes are never counted. The second stage of digital democracy is ensuring accurate results. The question we need to ask ourselves is whether speed matters more than accuracy.

Over the years media have raised our expectations about how fast we are supposed to know the fates of victors and vanquished in elections. It is not actually the media's fault, because we are like little kids who want to sneak a peek at our birthday presents.

We've become increasingly addicted to polls. The arrival of computers in the 1950s allowed statisticians and pollsters to create models of the electorate and predict the outcome of the elections with some level of accuracy.

Despite all the science, sometimes it's just too close to call. In 1960, for example, the contest between Nixon and Kennedy was razor thin. Although the 1964 election was a slam dunk for Johnson, there were some stirrings in the country that it was time for our voting systems to move past "X" marks on pieces of paper. The claim by the computer companies of the day was that digital machines could do the counting quicker and with greater accuracy than people. After all, if we were heading to the Moon, democracy itself should be launching into the Space Age.

Introducing the Votomatic

"Votomatic," the perfect 60s name for a product, became the first voting machine of the coming computer age. Based on the already familiar IBM punch card that was fixture of life in the 60s and 70s, the Votomatic was actually an incredibly low-tech device. Using a small sharp stylus, voters would punch through the pre-perforated holes in the card, which corresponded to the names of the candidates and issues they were voting for. The punches would be read by IBM machines and tabulated with lighting speed compared to hand-counting ballots. They also were very portable and cheap unlike earlier mechanical voting machines.

Because the names and issues printed on the card would be too small to read, it slid into a holder that formed the spine for a loose-leaf collection of plastic-coated pages that were printed with the choices a voter could make. As you flipped the pages, you would automatically be switching columns on the punch card. This was commonly known as a "butterfly ballot." Completed punch cards would be dropped in a locked ballot box and taken to a central location to be machine-read and tabulated. The punch-card ballots were kept in case there was the need for a recount.

Los Angeles County, June 1968

On June 4, 1968, in a presidential primary race that would be historic for other, more tragic, reasons, Los Angeles became the first large city to completely embrace the Votomatic system. The machines were very easy for voters to use. There was even some visceral pleasure in poking the ballot with a sharp instrument. The main drama of the election was the contest between Senators Robert Kennedy and Eugene McCarthy. During that warm spring, campaign activity had the town completely abuzz.

When the polls closed that night, the locked boxes of punch-card ballots were placed in the trunks of big American cars and headed to freeway entrances across L.A. County. That's where the Votomatic model encountered it first problem. All those cars headed downtown to City Hall, where the tabulation machines were located, created a massive traffic jam. All those cars descending into one location and the physical act of unloading boxes from hundreds of vehicles created a chaotic mess. The results that were supposed to be tabulated instantaneously were, instead, delayed for hours by traffic jam on the L.A. freeways.

Everyone knew it was going to be a close race in this winner-take-all primary. The expected victory statements at 9 or 10 p.m. Pacific Time were going to be delayed for hours by the process.

It was past midnight when Robert Kennedy took the stage in a victory that was short lived, as he was brought down moments later by gunfire. Lost in the larger story of the day, and despite the automotive snafu, the Votomatic had indeed delivered results faster than hand counting.

Optical Scan

Another popular voting system that emerged shortly thereafter was the "optical scan" system. Using a black marker, voters indicated their preference on a paper ballot with a simple line. That marked paper ballot was then scanned by a light-sensitive automatic reading machine and tabulated. If you ever took an SAT or standardized test in school you are familiar with the technique, except that a #2 pencil was not required and no one would be telling you to "time is up, put your pencil down."

Both optical-scan and Votomatic-type systems were paper-based, meaning any citizen had the ability to read the results on the original ballot, which was important in the case of a recount. The Votomatic system and its clones were so widely adopted, that by 2000, over a third of all votes were cast with such machines.

Then something strange happened, and by no surprise, it happened in Florida.

Florida, Left Hanging by a Chad

Maybe it was just Florida. Maybe it was because the guy running for president was the governor's brother and the guy was in charge of the election. Maybe it was because the election officials in West Palm Beach needed to put on their reading glasses when they were laying out the ballots. Somehow, the usually reliable and indisputable punch-card ballot system was yielding weird results as votes were being tabulated in this state, the state that would decide the presidency.

Normally, a presidential election — actually 50 state-by-state elections — is relatively decisive and by midnight Pacific Time, we know who is headed to 1600 Pennsylvania Avenue. But, as Al Gore said, "You win some, you lose some...and then, there are those other ones."

Given the razor-thin margins, and other voting irregularities in Florida overall, the Gore campaign asked for a recount. In fact, by state law, the narrow margin of the race mandated a recount. That's when a hand count of ballots was set in action, specifically in Broward and Dade counties, which both employed a Votomatic-type punch-card system. Hand-counting meant literally looking at punch-card ballots that encountered problems being read by machines. There were "overcounts" (in which voters accidentally may have voted for two presidential candidates) and "undercounts" (where no vote for president was tallied).

Looking at cards revealed that many were poorly punched. The debris of the punching process left little rectangular bits of paper called "chads" hanging on the ballots — the infamous "hanging chads." There were also "dimpled" and "pregnant" chads that both revealed failed attempts by the voter to punch the chad out of the ballot card. A visual inspection with magnifier revealed the voter's intent, even if the machine could not read the ballot. Individual readings of ballots did not make for a fast process.

A complication was the design of the ballot itself. Places to poke the stylus through the cards were not necessarily clearly aligned with the choices on the ballot, and quite a few of the voters were older with vision difficulties. It is believed that the ballot design had otherwise Democratic-leaning voters erroneously voting for Pat Buchanan (though it could be argued that any vote for Buchanan was erroneous).

The Florida Republican Party, which had already unleashed a barrage of dirty tricks to suppress Democratic votes, wasn't going to stand by as the individual counts revealed more votes for Gore with each new day. They reached out for their most zealous ally on the U.S. Supreme Court, Antonin Scalia, to stop the recount before their candidate, Bush Jr., was "harmed" by finding out he didn't actually win.

On a black day in American history, the U.S. Supreme Court interrupted the process of democracy by not letting officials count duly cast votes. They suspended the counting of the ballots that were already in process. The conservatives knew that one more day of counting would leave Al Gore with a victory in Florida, and therefore the presidency. In a final ruling they forbade the counting of any more ballots.

It was a stunning development that shocked and bewildered the world. However, it should not have been surprising, since Bush Sr. and his predecessor, Ronald Reagan, had picked several of the sitting members of the U.S. Supreme Court, and these conservative activist justices returned the favor by crowning Bush Jr. president. In retrospect, this was the first volley in an authoritarian attempt to short-circuit our constitutional principles. It portended an administration that would suspend habeas corpus, posse comitatus, abuse FISA, and commit a whole shopping list of constitutional violations.

Ironically, this hijacking of the democratic process and legal enjoinment from counting the votes became the rationale to discard paper-based voting and switch voting to an all-digital process. Just so election outcomes could never be "in doubt" again. Ha!

Politicians Don't HAVA Clue

A confused and cowed bipartisan Congress passed, and Bush Jr. signed, an Orwellian-named legislation called "The Help America Vote Act," or "HAVA." The core proposal of HAVA was to switch away from paper-based systems, such as the punch card, into digital systems, called "direct recording electronic" voting machines, or "DREs." Technically unsophisticated members of Congress, as well those who *did* know the power of DREs and wanted that leverage in an election, granted billions of dollars to states to implement these systems.

The immediate beneficiaries were an exclusive troika of companies that manufacture and sell the all-digital DREs: Premier Election Solutions (formerly Diebold), Election Systems & Software

(ES&S), and Sequoia Voting Systems. The net result was to cast election outcomes in more doubt than ever, both by accident and by design. The nation was sold a system that was non-transparent and inherently prone to both malfeasance and malfunction — and would leave no evidence of either circumstance.

Dreaded DREs

A DRE system is a computer that has been specifically designed to perform a single function. Most are based on clunky Microsoft operating systems. With a touch screen as its only user interface, a voter is presented with a page of choices. Voters make their selections by touch and continue through subsequent "pages" of candidates and issues. Their votes are directly recorded into a memory card like the one you would find in a digital camera. Data from those cards are transferred to a central reporting location, which would involve physically moving the cards, or having the DRE machines "phone home" to a central computer via modem over regular telephone lines. (Yes — a modem!)

DREs present two problems that are interrelated. Technologically, they are flawed. They are computers and all computers are subject to the same problems: software errors, hardware failures, and hacking. The cases of failures and manipulation of data are numerous and well documented both academically and in practice. Other cases have happened so surreptitiously that we have only circumstantial evidence, or the testimony of guilty individuals who performed the hacking.

Unlike a paper-based system, such as punch cards, there is no physical record of the vote, nor is there any way a human can count the votes without the aid of a machine. That means that what used to be done by people has been transformed into an intermediated process. Direct citizen involvement has been passed off to a third party. Therefore the outcome of a public function has been handed over to private, for-profit companies. Like so many other things in our age, the process of running an election has been outsourced. Private companies supplant the army in warfare. Private companies run prisons and public schools.

Then, when private companies circle the drain on Wall Street and in Detroit, the public comes to their rescue with hundreds of billions of dollars.

It could be argued that the Votomatic and optical-scan systems were outsourced to third-party vendors, but there is a critical difference. With a paper-based system, any registrar of voters, or any citizen could look at the ballots and tally results with no third party involvement, just by examining the ballots. This is what was attempted in Florida — and then blocked by the U.S. Supreme Court. DRE machines have removed that capability and assurance entirely. The DRE vendor becomes the owner of the democratic process. That is a huge shift of power.

The DRE companies that sell these systems have two purposes. The first, of course, is to make money. The second is to, whenever possible, influence the outcome of the election. The most obvious example of the latter was when the CEO Walden O'Dell of Diebold Election Systems (now Premier Election Solutions) sent out a letter stating that he would do whatever was possible to deliver the state of Ohio to Bush Jr. in the 2004 election. "I am committed to helping Ohio deliver its electoral votes to the president next year."

For those on the right wing of the political spectrum, there is cause for concern, as well. At one time, the ownership of what is now called Sequoia Voting Systems was connected to Venezuela and Hugo Chavez. That ought to give them chills.

The concern is that a digital process sold as a method to ensure that every vote is counted has instead delivered exactly the opposite result. It has enabled the wholesale disappearance of votes without a trace — and for those who cynically trade in these systems seek profit and power though their exploitability.

Chuck "I Bought the Company" Hagel

In 1996, talk-show host Chuck Hagel of Nebraska ran for his first political office, the U.S. Senate. A well-known conservative and Vietnam veteran, he also owned a partial interest in a company called American Information Systems that distributed computer-based voting machines. Although Nebraska had a long tradition of sending moderate Democrats to the Senate, including fellow-veteran Bob Kerry, Hagel was, nonetheless, a very attractive candidate. He was running against the popular Democratic governor Ben Nelson (who ultimately was elected to the Senate in 2000). Much to everyone's surprise, Hagel pulled off a stunning upset, garnering 56% of the vote. Not only did he win, he won among demographic groups that generally reject conservative Republicans.

Six years later, Hagel ran for reelection. The results were even more stunning, with Senator Hagel winning 83% of the vote, which was the biggest election victory ever in the state of Nebraska. What was not common knowledge is that 80% of the voting machines in Nebraska were built by, programmed by, and managed by the company in which Hagel had a financial interest.

Is there a way to prove that the election was rigged? Or even that Hagel himself participated? That's the problem. Digital voting, sometimes called "black-box voting," can't prove guilt or innocence because the machine creates no physical record of the vote. The vendor of the DRE, which is a "closed" or "proprietary" system, is the only party allowed to view the internal workings of the computer program that records and tabulate the votes. Even local voting officials are in the dark as to the inner workings of their DREs, and they have no independent means to audit the machines. For DRE vendors, a candidate is declared to win "because I said so." With no human-readable, paper-based ballots, no one can dispute or verify the vote.

Though Hagel may be guiltless, certainly any programmer could have been given instructions to flip a few votes along the way from one candidate to the other or to record non-votes for senator as a default to the Republican candidate. It can be done with enough subtlety to avoid suspicion. It's essentially a skimming operation that embezzles votes.

It is interesting that Hagel had been mentioned as a VP candidate by both parties and even by third parties in the 2008 presidential campaign. One wonders what makes him so appealing.

Oh, Ohio!

Outside of Florida, no state has a spottier record of electronic-voting irregularities than Ohio. Long considered a bellwether state, it has been at the center of elections for better than a century. More presidents have come from Ohio than any other state. Even if local officials can maintain good physical security of their voting machines and are operating on the level, secretaries of state can have a powerful influence over the entire system, as was evidenced by Bush Jr's heroine, Katherine Harris of Florida, in 2000.

The equivalent in Ohio was a Republican Secretary of State Ken Blackwell. Blackwell, like Harris, was both the chair of the Bush campaign and his state's chief election officer. The obvious parallels of their roles yielded parallel results, an unlikely victory for the candidate they supported. Blackwell resorted to the usual bag of tricks, including using a partisan data-mining company to purge the voter rolls of valid voters who were likely to vote Democratic. He also rejected voter-registration applications that he deemed to be printed out on paper of improper thickness.

In Ohio, the counties are strongly partisan by geography and each selected its own voting system. How could an election be stolen if both parties were in positions of authority? The vulnerability would have to be introduced at the point where the votes would flow together into one set of results. Most voting systems transmit results electronically to a computer that is under the control of the state government. In Ohio, the path from the precinct to the state house was a rather crooked one.

Secretaries of state normally host statewide election tallies on their state's own servers. Ohio's Blackwell did something a bit different. He contracted to send the data on a roundtrip to Chattanooga, Tennessee, before it arrived in the state capitol.

The vote-fraud scheme was simple. Before being tallied as the official Ohio vote returns, the raw voting totals from the counties were reported electronically to a privately-owned servers in Chattanooga, where it would be possible to digitally flip votes from Kerry to Bush. From there, the altered results could be sent to Ohio's official election servers.

It had all the hallmarks of a "man-in-the-middle" computer-fraud operation, where raw data was collected, altered, and then sent to an official website without suspicion.

As was later revealed in legal proceedings, Blackwell had paid hundreds of thousands of taxpayer dollars to a contractor named Mike Connell to create Ohio's official, real-time state election website, election.sos.state.oh.us.

Connell was the "go-to" information technology guru for Republican candidates. He supplied web services and Internet strategies for the Bush campaigns of 2000 and 2004. His companies, New Media Communications and GovTech Solutions, were employed by a who's who of right-wing candidates, including John Thune, Heather Wilson, Tom DeLay, and Rick Santorum. He was the star GOP IT geek.

It is known that Connnell was Karl Rove's chief IT consultant. Connell had another company called SmarTech that hosted websites for the Republican National Committee, as well as hundreds of web domains registered to Republican organizations, including the domains involved in Bush's "missing" emails regarding the Valerie Plame case.

In this vote manipulation scam SmarTech servers in Tennessee received raw voting totals from the all of Ohio's counties electronically, from there, results could be altered and sent to Ohio's official election servers, with no outside observers becoming aware of the actions.

In 2008, after a change of administration in Ohio, Connell was facing a subpoena in connection with fraud in the 2004 election. The allegation was that Connell enabled this "man-in-the middle" scheme on behalf of high Bush Jr. campaign officials.

A whistleblower and GOP IT security expert, Stephen Spoonamore, said he was prepared to testify for the plausibility of electronic vote-rigging having been carried out in 2004. Spoonamore, a conservative Republican reportedly had evidence that Karl Rove, with the help of Mike Connell, electronically stole the Ohio 2004 election for Bush. According to Spoonamore, "This centralized collection of all incoming statewide tabulations would make it easy for a single operator, or a preprogrammed 'force balancing computer' to change the results in any way…." He also stated that the only reason to have a man-in-the-middle arrangement was to commit a crime.

Connell appeared for a two-hour, closed-door deposition on November 3, 2008, just 18 hours before the presidential election. Connell was reticent to testify after reportedly receiving threats from high party operatives involving members of his family. Despite Connell's insider status as a Republican IT consultant for years, his requests for witness protection from the Bush administration were denied. Just a month after his testimony, his single engine plane crashed in Akron, Ohio, on his way home from D.C., just three miles short of the runway. He was an experienced pilot and his plane had been recently serviced. The cause of the crash remains unknown. The timing of the crash is noteworthy and raises suspicions, since without his testimony there was no legal case, because whatever transpired inside the computers left no trace of a crime.

Congressman Rush Holt, Democrat of New Jersey, has tried to introduce legislation to require that computerized voting systems produce a voter-verified paper ballot and that the software code be publicly available. The bill, in the House Administration Committee, has 60 co-sponsors, none of whom are Republicans. Holt recalled a conversation that was indicative of the problem: "Someone said to me the other day, 'We've had these electronic voting machines for several years now and we've never had a problem.' And I said, 'How do you know?' "

Dr. David L. Dill, a computer-science professor at Stanford, said: "If I was a programmer at one of these companies and I wanted to steal an election, it would be very easy. I could put something in the software that would be impossible for people to detect, and it would change the votes from one party to another. And you could do it so it's not going to show up statistically as an anomaly."

Retail Politics vs. Wholesale Fraud

The Net has allowed ordinary people to be politically involved, express their opinions and have influence as they never have before.

The dominance of big mainstream media has been fractured by hundreds of thousands of voices being heard through blogs. There is a feeling that one person can make a difference in what politicians call "retail politics."

Technology is a powerful magnifier, but it cuts both ways. It is ironic because the efforts of thousands of bloggers and tens of millions of voters can be short-circuited by a single individual who has the technical knowledge to manipulate the data that comes from digital voting systems, and yet that is what has happened. In 1996, only 7% of citizens voted on a touch screen. In 2004, it was 29%. In 2006, it was 37%. The pressure on local voting officials to rationalize systems on which they spent millions is strong, but the vulnerability to fraud on a wholesale level is largely unchecked (though suspicion of the machines' flaws appears to have caused a drop in their use in 2008.)

While we have overcome the problem of scaling up democracy with a democratization of media though blogs, paradoxically the voting process has become more centralized and intermediated by three or four companies. A single individual with access to digital DRE systems can undo all the individual efforts of millions of participants. Compare the influence of a solitary blogger to the power of a single hacker to steal an election and the problem of digital democracy is obvious.

TWO SOLUTIONS:

I propose two solutions to the voting problem.

Plan A: Open, Free, and Trusted

If you think about it, a DRE is a lot like an ATM. DRE and ATM machines have been made by the same company. So why are ATMs not a problem?

The answer is that a bank has a vested interest in making sure that an ATM machine is relatively secure and trustworthy for both the bank and for customers. If customers' money is suddenly missing, you can bet the banks will be hearing about it from depositing customers. With an ATM, customers have a paper record of the transaction, as well as online and in-person access with which they can monitor transactions for accuracy. Obviously, the bank is watching out for its side of the deal, so there's no need to worry about them. ATM transactions give bankers and customers access to the same information so they can verify each other's actions. With DREs, if your vote should be wiped out by accident or design, you would have no way of checking whether your vote was counted. There is a simple solution for touch-screen voting systems:

- **Voter uses touch screen to make choices.**
- **System prints out a paper ballot that users can read and verify.**
- **The paper ballot is dropped into a locked box in the traditional manner.**
- **Votes are being sent live in real time to a central location.**
- **For same-evening election results, the electronic system would be provisional.**
- **The certification comes after counting the physical ballots.**
- **The physical ballots are the authoritative total.**

The second part of making DREs more trustworthy is to change the business model from proprietary to open. There should be a single, open design that is generic. It worked for telephones; it can work for voting appliances. This would remove private vendors as owners of codes that can't be audited by the public. The DRE would have one national standard. If companies want to make voting machines, they can conform to the standard and bid for the business. The machines would be less expensive and no politically ambitious DRE maker would have exclusive access to alter results.

Plan B: A Slow Democracy Movement

This is by far a more radical approach — and yet is vastly simpler and more participatory. We have seen a global movement toward Slow Food. Maybe it is time for Slow Democracy. Although we are all anxious to see results of elections, maybe we should just stop worrying about speed and spend our time getting it right. It used to take months and weeks to know the results of hand-counted ballots. Maybe we should go back to that. Get citizen volunteers to help count ballots, encourage all those bloggers and voters to get out and help count. We could make it a month-long celebration of democracy that is personal and hands-on.

After watching the glacial pace of the U.S. Senate in action, can we really say that adding few weeks to know results will make much difference in the overall scheme of things?

2.7

Naked on the Net:
Let's Get Social!

Caught in the Act

There's a reason that this chapter has been written last. From the time this book project was first conceived until the date of this writing, what we call "social networking," "social media" or simply "social" has been surging along at a frenetic pace. At best effort, commentary about social networking applications and business models catches only a snapshot of the moment. What is of more enduring importance is comprehending the trajectory of social media, where it started, why it has caught on, and where it is headed.

The first step is, of course, is defining "social network."

For us users it is:
A way to stay in touch with friends...a conversation.

For the Cult of Tech it is:
"A platform for engaging brand relationships."

For us users, that conversation or chat may be happening in text, in real time, or as an asynchronous string of messages between two people (or more), and it may contain links to shared images or video. In every case, however, the principal "interaction" is conversational and since the technical requirements for digital conversation are rudimentary, any mobile phone is now a ticket to the social network. But no matter what glittering new facade or branding is cooked up (such as the delightfully low-tech Twitter), in social networking "chat" is always the primary function. Sharing pictures and videos would not be "social" unless there was a capacity for the comments to be attached to the images, either by the poster, or by the viewer.

Business and popular news media have breathlessly conflated "Web 2.0" with "social media." Web 2.0 is a generalized marketing term for web-based ideas that crawled out from under the wreckage of the dotcom crash of 2000, such as the collaborative WikiPedia, the community-oriented Craigslist, and the mediasharing Flckr and YouTube. Social media actually predates all of these applications by decades.

Rather than critiquing specific — and transitional — social network applications, it will be more useful to postulate a unified field theory, or what I call a *unified friend theory*, to explain why social networking is both surging and failing at the same time. It is surging in popularity and (despite what you hear in the press) failing as a business because fundamentally opposing forces — commercial and personal needs — are in direct conflict.

Once again, what we want from technology is at odds with what the purveyors of technology want from us. With social networking, the contradiction is staring us right in the Facebook.

What We Want

What we want is easy to figure out. It's not rocket science to postulate that social media sprang from the basic human need to connect. The rapid adoption and reach of the mobile phone into the most primitive villages, even where there is no electricity, testifies to our hunger for interpersonal contact. The visual connection is strong, as well; sharing a photograph of a friendly face is a powerful tug across most cultures. That's because, along with voices, facial expressions are our most natural communication. Our malleable, emotion-filled faces allowed us to be social beings before language was ever spoken.

In modern life, all of us have friends who have become scattered across time and space, located in the places where we used to live, used to go to school, and used to work. Many of these personal relationships have lapsed out of benign neglect. Although the bonds seemed strong at the time, over time and distance the magnetism and gravity of these attachments became weaker. There just isn't enough time to call everyone, write everyone a letter, or pay a visit. Most of us can't afford the time or emotional commitment, though we still crave the connection. It is part of our life story. We have the overwhelming desire to get back in touch with those whom we miss.

For those still young enough to be in school, it's not about threading together already-established connections — it's a way to establish connections in the first place. For teens, texting from the safety of your bedroom is a low-risk, almost passive, way to engage in social activity. You can "call" a potential girlfriend for the first time with a simple text message versus the sweaty phone call experienced by previous generations.

The social network frees all users to explore common interests without threat or commitment. However, for those who are young and unworldly, revealing their still-evolving persona through digital magic introduces future issues unimaginable to them today. Teenagers are fully exposed, without any comprehension of privacy, even as they write secret diaries, hide behind bedroom doors, and answer parental questions in monosyllables.

While boomer/hippie long hair can be cut and Gen-X tattoos concealed, every "youthful indiscretion" of this unwitting generation will live on forever in digital memory. We are forever changing. How much of the past should persist to haunt the next generation as they mature? The network doesn't forget and will not be forgiving. Remember: the political activists of the 1930s paid a unforeseeably heavy price in the McCarthy era for their past public opinions — and this was long before digital media.

Joining a social network, such as MySpace or Facebook requires only disclosing a few lines of personal identifying information. (Judging from the profiles of my ex-girlfriends, data about age doesn't even need to be accurate.) Combining the innate human desire to connect with the low barrier to participation has made social networking grow in popularity at a faster rate than TVs, PCs, or even the Internet itself. Baby boomers are now the largest group of participants on Facebook. As of this writing, Facebook has reportedly surged beyond 500 million users.

The key to growing a social network "platform" is making it easy and free for users. There are no setup fees or subscriptions siphoning off your credit card. However, as we all know, nothing in life is really free. To build out a system to support millions of online users requires acres of computer hardware, staffing, electricity, and lots of cash. As a system grows more popular it grows more expensive to maintain. So who's paying for all of that?

This is where the contradiction between the two drivers of the social network head for an irresolvable conflict. We have established that users want to connect with other users, so what do fast-company investors want?

What *They* Want

If users are spending nothing to participate in social networks, why are wealthy investors and media companies plunking down billions of dollars to own companies such as MySpace, Facebook, and Twitter that give away these services? Why pony up cash to own businesses that appear to be ephemeral and "free"? If you attend any conference or read any publication on social networking, the magic words you will hear over and over are "engagement" and "monetize." Just exactly how does this occur with a free service?

For the Cult of Tech, "monetizing" means turning hundreds of millions of users (or, in their parlance, "eyeballs") into cash. Much like broadcast radio and TV, the idea is use social media as yet another advertising conduit. Unlike TV, where marketeers have to guess about what might interest you, social media networks already know about your interests, your relationships, and your life — after all, it's *you* who've told them. The business concept of a social network is to mine your friendships and interests into opportunities to target advertising.

Despite everything you've seen or read — all the magazine covers, the billions being invested, and the news stories about Facebook, MySpace, and Twitter — they are all terrible business models that have yet to stem continuous losses, much less produce significant income. Your response may well be, "Huh? What's going on here? I thought these guys were the smart money?"

This is where our *"unified friend theory"* of social networking comes into play. Simply stated, **the more commercial a social network application becomes, the less appealing it will be for users.** Add more annoying ads and you chase users away. If you monitor and track their personal relationships and interests to target them, you'll creep people out, again chasing them away. The concept of social media as platforms for advertising is about as appealing as having an Amway salesman in the cubicle next to you at work. For younger users, the more mainstream and commercial a social network becomes, the more they will want to move onto something newer, an alternative, something of their own.

With billions of dollars spent on startups, is there any innovation taking place within the social networking area? Astonishingly little. There is an extreme paucity of thought. The basic technology of social media has changed surprisingly little. What changes are the business models, which are extremely ephemeral and quixotic. We do know that each new wave of social networking adds vastly more users, giving rise to more pervasive societal changes.

Each new model of social networking first grabs the attention of an initial select group, then generalizes to a wider population, crosses into popular culture, and finally becomes a media obsession. Then, relatively quickly, the parade starts to fade, people move on, and a vestige of new social behavior is left behind. Let's look at the history of this phenomenon.

Hookups on the BBS

Digital social interactions have been going on since computers and modems first came into our homes. In the early 80s, people would use their computers to dial into bulletin board systems (BBSs). These were the electronic equivalents of cork bulletin boards where users could dial in one at time, post text messages on a thread, and share downloadable software and images. Not surprisingly, given the nerdiness of the participants, there were reviews of restaurants, erotic service guides, and downloadable porn images. (You can always judge the future success of a technology by how quickly it becomes a conveyance for porn. It was the desire for privacy-of-your-home porn that drove the growth of the VCR business, not the tepid participation of Hollywood studios.)

BBSs were also the beginning of serious discussion groups among a highly literate base of users. The best-known such group of the era was called The Well (Whole Earth 'Lectronic Library), which is the spiritual antecedent of the blogosphere. The Well lives on today as part of Salon.com. There were also live text discussions through what was called Internet relay chat (IRC), even though the Net was largely undiscovered by even the most knowledgeable computer users and the World Wide Web had yet to be invented.

Given that you needed to know how to set "parity bits" on your modem, the BBS user base was miniscule, though global. Was it social? Well, tying up your phone line for hours on end wasn't the most "social" act imaginable.

You've Got Mail

Then, later in the 80s, along came AOL (America On Line) with a handy self-install disc, a friendly graphical interface, and automated software for logging into what were essentially massive BBS systems. Suddenly it was possible to have hundreds, thousands, and eventually millions of users all online at the same time, connecting through the same service. GE, IBM, Sears, and others tried and failed to create a similarly simple and affordable online service. Does anyone even remember Prodigy or CompuServe? (Even my spellchecker doesn't have that one in its vast memory.)

AOL put email on the map for the general population, and it also opened the doors to "chat rooms." These were live real-time text conversations that were ostensibly about topics of mutual interest. As expected, the greatest mutual interest was sex. It became a famous playground for flirtation set within the safety of anonymity. It was being social, but only in virtuality. It was a microcosm of social behaviors with curious searchers, liars, lonely folks, lurkers, and "cyberstalkers." Some of those cyberstalkers unfortunately convinced the vulnerable, particularly sexually-curious teenagers, to meet up with them in the physical world — to ill effect.

With fictitious "screen names" as pseudonyms, AOL users never knew for sure who they were chatting with. There were chat sessions and electronic bulletin boards reviewing consumer products, particularly electronic and computer products. Much of it purported to be by fellow consumers, sharing grassroots opinions. As was revealed later, corporations would often dispatch their own agents in the cloak of anonymity to tout products or squelch valid criticisms in what we now call "astroturf" campaigns. Microsoft was the most famous and obvious of the astroturfers. Their complex and poor-quality products supported by arrogant customer service gave them plenty of reasons to be defensive.

For a while, AOL was a killer business, taking in cash from all directions. People were paying monthly service charges for the privilege of being AOL members. AOL itself realized that they had a lot of eyeballs looking at their screens and decided to fill every bit of the screen territory with advertising. It was a goldmine, a "virtual" dream come true: getting people to pay you a monthly fee so you could make them watch annoying ads. During this fat time, in the silly season of the Internet Boom, AOL merged with Time Warner to achieve "synergy" — in other words, more ways to sell you more things. AOL became a massive barrage of ads and quietly sanctioned spam associated with its media-giant sibling.

As users became more comfortable with the web, however, they kicked off the training wheels of AOL and went with independent service providers or big telecoms to connect to the Internet. They got real email addresses and started creating personal web pages. Although creating personal websites was not extremely technical, it was still beyond the skill set of most people to make an attractive page, and finding pages could be a challenge since search engines were not completely effective. Finding someone's email address by search was all but impossible.

As users became more sophisticated, AOL slowly collapsed under its marketeers' overblown synergistic ambitions, though the greeting of "You've Got Mail" lived on in popular culture and an email address became as fundamental as a social security number and a phone number.

MySpace or Yours?

From under the dust cloud of the dotcom implosion, one unemployed ex-programmer came up with an application called "Friendster." Drawing millions of users upon its inception in 2003, it was the first site specifically designed as a social network application. Although it introduced the idea of "friend requests" and other fundamentals, it had technical problems that made it fall out of favor quickly in the U.S.

Coming on its heels was "MySpace," which fared better. It may have initially succeeded by combining two groups that already had a natural symbiotic relationship: rock bands and members of Generation E who had never seen the inside of a music store, let alone bought a CD. MySpace became a playground for Generation E "screen-agers." First, these kids had screens in front of their faces as infants, absorbing dubious "educational" software. Then, as toddlers, their peanut-buttery fingers were banging on keyboards — all to soothe the anxiety of parents who felt disoriented by the computers entering their own workplaces and were afraid their kids would be left behind.

As kids grew beyond *KidPix*, *Reader Rabbit*, and *Millie's Math House*, they wanted to express their own creativity and identity on the web. Most didn't have the technical skills to build a web site or have the resources to host personal pages from their bedrooms. MySpace became the relatively easy way to create and host personalized web pages at no apparent cost.

It was an immediate hit with teenagers, becoming much like the wall of a teenager's room or the inside of their locker door at school. They could cut and paste a pastiche of images — pictures of their favorite bands, movie stars, and friends — and use the decorated page as a place to post information about themselves. A message board was included and the socially necessary chat function was included.

MySpace was designed to allow for the addition of "widgets" which are small bits of software that allowed new functions, such as playing music or videos, and sharing pictures. The video-sharing site YouTube (now part of Google) originated as a MySpace widget.

For bands, the attraction to MySpace was similar to that of the teens. With no monetary investment, musicians could put up a web page with samples of their music, pictures, a calendar of concert dates, a bulletin board to communicate with fans, and, most importantly, links to buy songs online. For bands, MySpace made MTV exposure and record contracts irrelevant. They completely avoided the record companies and radio stations that were ignoring them anyway. MySpace was a way to establish an identity for the band and publicize concert dates. It allowed both bands and teens to create and present a persona/identity to the world. And for bands it was a way to sell music, but what were the teens selling? Whom were they trying to reach with these pages? The friends they already had? Or was it a way to attract new friends?

Perhaps they were seeking to "brand" and market themselves. Certainly they had grown up in a world where shameless self-marketing was a pathway to popularity. The 00s were an age that seemed rich with demi-celebrities such as Paris Hilton and Tia Tequila who also used MySpace as their digital home address. High-school students and suburban teens could feel that they were on equal playing ground with the dubious celebs of MySpace. Suddenly teenagers were exposing themselves in ways their "unshockable" boomer parents could not imagine. The so-called "me generation" had spawned the "look-at-me generation." The question is whether that exposure was the result of innocence or narcissism. In any case, this age group, which regularly dwells behind closed bedroom doors and discloses only minimal information to their parents, was disseminating limitless data about themselves on the web.

For many middle- and high-school students, assembling a MySpace digital persona became a consuming activity itself, as if by fashioning the right image of themselves on the web they somehow could create a new reality. They've absorbed the notion — widely circulated in our culture and politics, though patently untrue — that if you lead with imagery, reality will follow. There were myriad stories about obsessive teenagers spending hours a week updating their pages when they could have been socializing with their peers in the physical world. A cottage industry grew up around teenagers designing and selling design templates and other decorative objects for MySpace pages. Given the no-cost-per-copy nature of digital economics, many teen entrepreneurs reportedly made tens of thousands of dollars.

On the darker side of the magic, MySpace became a stage for something new. Acts of love and cruelty were regularly being played out in public. With egotistical strutting and plaintive cries for help, MySpace became a soap opera. The social network became the host of starkly unsocial behavior, particularly what has come to be called "cyberhazing" or "cyberbullying." Such behavior could involve users defacing each other's pages or posting hateful, intimidating messages. For those already working out self-esteem questions, having it play out on this public stage was devastating.

As with other digital media, MySpace's anonymity left openings for those with ill intent. The most extreme example concerned a middle-aged Missouri woman, Lori Drew, who fabricated a teenage-boy persona on the site. This "boy" began a deceptive online friendship with a girl, Megan Meier, that led to tragic circumstances.

Drew, who lived four houses away, was under the erroneous impression that Megan was spreading rumors about her own daughter. In a plot to vengefully humiliate the neighbor girl, Drew fabricated a false MySpace identity of a 16-year-old boy she named "Josh Evans." A borrowed photo of another boy showed him to be attractive. Drew fabricated details about the boy and started a chat with Megan. At first the fake persona of the young man was flattering toward Megan and showed a mutual interest.

Then came a turn in their dialogue, with "Josh" saying,

> *"I don't know if I want to be friends with you anymore because I've heard that you are not very nice to your friends."*

That statement touched off a firestorm of increasingly hurtful messages assaulting Megan and shared by those in Drew's circle of tittering co-conspirators. They even posted the exchange of confidential messages on public bulletin boards that anyone could read. Lori Drew fired off one more volley in her fraudulent guise:

> *"Everybody in O'Fallon knows how you are. You are a bad person and everybody hates you. Have a shitty rest of your life. The world would be a better place without you."*

Megan gave this heartfelt response to the vile and fraudulent message:

> *"You're the kind of boy a girl would kill herself over."*

As with many her age, Megan was struggling with emotional problems; in her case these were exacerbated by lifelong struggles with clinical depression and attention deficit disorder. She was found twenty minutes later, hanging by the neck in her bedroom closet.

Lori Drew's role in the death was revealed and found its way into the press almost a year later. Officials were not able to adequately prosecute the case since it was an occurrence that was beyond the imagination of lawmakers. However, a less formal justice was served up via the Internet as the Drew family's phone number, address, pictures of their home and other personal information were widely circulated on the web. Just because a network is social, doesn't mean it is friendly.

Teens to Rupert: "Drop Dead"

So why would media mogul Rupert Murdoch spend mightily to get control of MySpace? The weed-like growth of the site was largely due to the fact that it was a free service, which made it easy for teens, who generally don't have credit cards, to set up accounts without parental involvement. They may not have had credit cards, but they were still discretionary spenders in a big way for music, clothes, makeup, and junk food.

Media companies thrive on one thing: advertising revenue. What Murdock's News Corp. and others saw were millions of users who were generating their own content and who were also a prime demographic group for advertisers. All that News Corp had to do was increase memory on their computer servers for MySpace so users could add more content and advertisers could place more ads.

The key difference between so-called old media (print, radio, and TV) and social media is "behavioral marketing." Users have given their MySpace hosts a vast amount of data about themselves. That knowledge about their activities and relationships gives marketeers a hook to reach them. On the surface, MySpace was an attractive proposition: no cost for content and a revenue stream from ads directly targeted to the audience.

But oh how fickle is the teenage heart! It wasn't long before a whole new crop of kids started to shun MySpace for the next big thing. A visit to MySpace today reveals a mess that looks an awful lot like the waning days of AOL. Its user base is declining fast and its relevance as a social network site is marginal; however, it remains the leading marketplace for musicians as they disintermediate the record companies.

The lesson of MySpace is that ***the real magic of any social network is its directory***, that searchable central "address book" where a person can connect with someone else without having prior knowledge of the other's email address. The directory is the key social-media development that will carry forward into succeeding iterations.

SMS 4 SAS Text Us

Text, chat or SMS (Short Message Service) messaging exploded in popularity partly for technological and partly for sociological reasons. At the point when even the most ordinary mobile phone was capable of sending text messages, students started carrying their mobile phones to school. The long tradition of passing messages among each other as social discourse continued in a new form. It was nearly free and always available. The only impediment, the initial lack of a keyboard, actually begat an entire language of acronyms that even political figures and mainstream journalists have adopted. WTF!

Of course, having these concealable pocket messengers-cum-cameras made cheating on tests vastly easier. And then came "sexting," where every 15-year-old can become an overnight sensation on the Net by exposing themselves. Beyond that, there is a sociology of texting in the dating life that avoids, rightfully or wrongfully, the awkwardness of proposing or declining romantic encounters. At the same time, this minimal communication is useful to mask activity, until someone else has possession of your phone. I don't think Tiger Woods is going to be doing any ads for a mobile phone carrier any time soon.

Text, plain old written words retain their power.

Second Life: Chat Takes on a Life of Its Own

Despite all its media attention and digerati pretensions, Second Life, a virtual online experience created by Linden Labs in San Francisco, is essentially a revisit of the AOL chat room in a graphical environment. Here we find people enveloped by pseudo-identities meeting in non-existent spaces. "Rooms," instead of being simple frames of text, are computer-rendered environments straight out of an early-90s video game. A user is participating in an alternative life

— a "second life" — different from the one in which they actually live and breathe. The concept of creating an alternate reality space and "inhabiting" it with other live human beings is intriguing; it's like being an actor on stage. Second Life "in-world" experience makes each visitor in this computer-generated landscape an actor of sorts, or more exactly, a puppeteer in control of an avatar. Avatars are digital 3D cartoon marionettes in which the "player" pulls the strings. (If nothing else, the movie *Avatar* has at least relieved me of the necessity of providing a detailed definition of avatars.)

In Second Life's synthetic reality you can portray yourself as anything you desire to be. Pick a costume. Pick a gender. Pick a species. It's up to you. In your new virtual getup, you engage in activities with other people assuming *their* alternate identities. Despite the elaborate costuming and graphics, the social interaction is mainly text-based chat. You will either be typing dialogue on a keyboard or using a headset to engage your "in-world" voice. If you are voicing a strip-teasing babe named "Amber," however, it could present a problem when you sound like Bruce from Brooklyn.

Although Second Life can be compared to acting, there are huge differences. Acting is all about presence, being in the moment with all the human senses in play. An actor is looking into the eyes of other actors, smelling them, feeling the same space and ambience, being in the moment. The Second Life player is gazing blankly into a screen and tapping away on a keyboard, moving an empty shell of an alter-ego through imaginary real estate. There is no sensory awareness of anything other than a cartoon world. Every move requires obtrusive and clumsy keystrokes. For those who are heavy sci-fi fans, remedial in social skills, or both, Second Life is ideal. It is a world long predicted by sci-fi authors. Second Life is partly inspired by Neal Stephenson's seminal novel, *Snowcrash*, which was required reading in Silicon Valley during the 1990s.

Second Life players exhibit a paradoxical display of both immense creativity and wasted effort. It is a convergence of highly intelligent participants who create costumes, characters, objects, buildings, and businesses that live only within the "in-world" of Second Life. In fact, there is a whole economy of virtual goods built on nothingness and denominated in a currency called "Lindens," which should have no intrinsic value except inside the game, but are traded outside the game for real currency or other tangibles. Keep in mind that because all of the objects bought and sold in a digital world are infinitely duplicable, making one costs the same as making a billion copies of the same object. There is no scarcity and therefore no actual value. As with all digital media, everything is just a low or zero-cost copy. Not long ago, someone made a name for herself by becoming the first in-world millionaire, a dubious achievement signifying only that she could probably find something more productive to do with her entrepreneurial skills.

You might ask yourself, then, why tech heavyweights such as Cisco and IBM have gone so far as to organize industry conferences within Second Life. Well, they are in the business of pushing virtuality in the First World because it requires selling very tangible and profitable hardware. But you can be sure neither IBM's nor Cisco's CEO has given up his executive jet or stopped taking face-to-face meetings in luxurious executive suites.

For major chain store merchants there is the ultimate opportunity to sell virtual branded goods "in-world" that cost nothing to produce. Those actual Nike sneakers cost $5 to make in Vietnam and ship to the U.S. or Europe. The manufacturing cost of those Nike sneakers for avatars is zero dollars, American Apparel t-shirts, zero dollars. Dell Computers in the first world, a few hundred dollars while in Second Life, cost of goods is zilch.

While there are many Second Life participants, the number is a fraction of that of a conventional social network site. The complexity of the engagement method interferes with the experience. Although it is a social network, it really doesn't encourage social interaction in the real world. It remains a hothouse garden for those with too much time, money, or social disorders. After all, there are still Star Trek conventions.

The sadness of Second Life is that smart and talented people are throwing skills and time down a rabbit hole of illusion, a game of digital dress-up for people who have not found a productive outlet. It is akin to the trend of people playing video games well past their teenage years. Even if they can't be vixens and warlords, most of these folks would be better served by just getting out of their rooms and interacting with live human beings in real life.

Facebook: Behind the Friendly Face

Directory as Magic

As previously stated, the real magic of a social networking site is the directory. Finding people by using their actual name, city, and associations is way easier than having to know their email address. It allows for establishing or reestablishing a personal network of friends from all stages of life. Type the name, and soon you are presented with the all the people whose names and possible associations come close to matching what you typed.

The old phone company put your name and number in the phone book by default to build their directory. A social site has to be irresistibly attractive in order to get users to sign up and grow the size of the directory to near universality. What was required was a concept that was easy, free, and attractive enough to create that critical mass. Forcing users to author a "page" was deal breaker for many people.

Facebook, the monster of all social networking applications, learned these lessons from MySpace and then went on to eliminate barriers to participation. Unlike MySpace, users didn't need to create a page to represent themselves or to divulge excessive demographic information to get started. It was simple enough for your grandmother to use. Facebook transformed the word "friend" from a noun to a verb as people *en masse* began inviting others to sign up by "friending" them.

Facebook didn't start out as a universal way to socialize online; it had much more pragmatic origins. Its genesis was an attempt to replicate the photographic directory of incoming college class members, informally called a "facebook." Each page had a photo along with a name and a brief personal profile of interests and contacts. A book of faces builds conviviality among strangers on a large university campus.

Allegely, one evening, student Mark Zuckerberg, in a fit of amorous rejection, slapped together a prank mash-up application called "facemash" assembling student ID pictures from the printed facebook with the intention of creating a "Hot or Not" website. The original "Hot or Not" was a website in the early 2000s where dating-age people would submit pictures of themselves to be viewed and scored from 1 to 10 by members of the opposite sex. Showing some skin helped to up one's score.

Zuckerberg's computer-enabled tantrum introduced an idea of surprising utility: your photo, personal description, and interests consolidated into a single-page view made available in a firewalled, web-based central directory. It was very useful for finding out who's who — who's already attached, who's gay, who's in the glee club, who's a math whiz, who's into tennis — all from your WiFi laptop. It was great way to hook up, in both senses of the term.

This app was cooked up in a dorm room, not in a Silicon Valley incubator, so it didn't have the burden of conventional expertise. Soon this simple and popular application was spreading to other schools, including Stanford University. The fast-company birds of prey were within striking distance. In 2004, Zuckerberg and his pals came out to Palo Alto and were quickly fortified with a wad of Silicon Valley cash. The goal was to build up the capacity of Facebook and throw the doors open to whoever wanted to join.

Originally, Facebook worked by invitation only. You needed to be a member of a "network." Your hosting school was usually your network. You could invite "friends" by sending them an email invitation; when they received the invitation, they had been officially friended by you. If and when they accepted, you were friended by them.

In 2005, realizing it could and should add more potential "friends," Facebook swung open its doors to high-school students. Each network was organized by school affiliation. Soon students were deserting MySpace in droves and "friending" each other on "FB." It was a totally closed system free of cyberstalkers and marketeers — but that didn't last long.

Why did Facebook work? Here are some reasons:

Universal Directory

It allowed a non-committal email reach-out to people using real names instead of unknown email addresses. A request for friending is simply accepted or ignored.

No Need to Build a Page

It was the polar opposite of Second Life. You could be up and running instantly. It cut to the chase. Comparatively, MySpace was much more complex.

Blended Multiple Media Types Easily

It provided a simple, single interface to upload and share photos, video, and links to other media. Formats and standards didn't matter since FB glued it all together for the user.

Friends Invited Friends

Could there be a more disarming method to sign up users? The product was already endorsed by the people you knew and trusted.

It Was Easy and Free

In the digital economy, people **expect** free.

In its first 18-month period as a commercial business, Facebook grew to over 300 million users. As this book goes to print, there are approximately 500 million FB users. With numbers this massive, it's going to attract the attention of marketeers and fast-company types quicker than you can say "monetize." Marketeers saw the potential of "friending" hundreds of millions of eyeballs with behavioral advertising. The girl who dumped young Mr. Zuckerberg and triggered his Facebook brainstorm may have had second thoughts when the fast-company venture capitalists made Mark among the richest 20-somethings in America. It would be a good guess that he probably no longer lacks for friends.

Friends Like This

For the rest of us, Facebook has become a common meeting place where you and your geographically disbursed friends and family are able to share the day's activities along with casual conversation. It delivers just enough information and social interaction for the casual user. Not as assertive or committal as a phone call, and not requiring an email or postal reply, it's more on the expressive level of a postcard — an effortless method of telling people what you're up to without burdening them with unnecessary information. Think about it: a postcard is inherently friendly and everyone likes them. And, mimicking its laminated-paper counterpart, FB can even include a colorful picture of where you are or what interests you.

Although some users feel compelled to tell us more than we want to know about the trivia of their daily lives, you can always respond to an FB post or ignore it entirely. Neither is mandatory. Among my circle of friends, it has become a vehicle for fast two-line reviews of the film they have just seen or book they have just read, pictures of what they have just cooked or dishes from restaurants they're just about to enjoy, and images from trips. Since most of my friends travel a lot, FB is a live feed from around the world, with lots of pictures of kids.

My media business has been part of a virtual community for better than a decade, with conference calls replacing the location-based meetings that used to be the norm. So Facebook has become our virtual "water cooler" — a place to discuss the events of the day, pay tribute to the latest fallen cultural icon of our youth, and argue about politics.

For those so inclined, communities of interest spring up as "fans" of everything from bands and causes to places and authors. No matter how esoteric, it is easy to find someone among hundreds of millions of people who shares your interests. Communities can easily form around political or social issues. Even the fire pits on the beaches of San Diego warrant a fan page, which might well become a community effort to save them from going down the municipal-budget drain.

A particularly compelling trend (although I must admit it seemed stupid and invasive to me at the time) was called *25 Random Things About Me.* The process starts when a person is tagged by friend, then compelled to offer up 25 personal qualities or events that have shaped their lives. I was constantly surprised to read the movingly honest statements, almost confessions, related in just 25 lines. If psychologists started with something as simple as this, they might cut their task down considerably (but probably their income, too).

One of the most touching aspects of Facebook is how people are reconnecting with friends and family with whom they have lost touch over the years, especially if they live half a world away. Everyone has a story to tell, including rekindled romances and long-lost family members. Despite its origins on a college campus, the majority of FB users are now baby boomers. Probably because it's a near-perfect combination of free, simple, and useful, no digital application has ever grown at the rate of Facebook.

There is a lot of good human interaction taking place in this virtual world. Unfortunately, however, not all is right with Facebook. Opposing forces are at work behind the friendly face and there are fundamental conflicts, including private vs. public information, and social vs. commercial orientation. Overall, Facebook fosters valuable human connections, but what is the hidden cost for this social utility that is free to all users?

Brains Behind the Face

Why are supposedly "savvy" investors throwing down huge piles of money to own even a small percentage of Facebook? Do they know something, or are they foolish investors taken in by what they think is the next big thing? Or does that matter for us?

Jason Benlevi

These numbers about Facebook might get your attention:

- $240 million — the amount Microsoft paid for just 1.6 % of Facebook
- $200 million — the amount Russian investors Digital Sky have poured into FB
- $500 million — the amount Goldman Sachs spends for a share of the action for its wealthy investors
- 54.7 % — the percentage of 12–17-year-olds who use FB every day
- 10 billion minutes — personal time spent on FB every day
- 200 billion — page views per month (reportedly bigger than Google)

While we are playing checkers with our friendly social network functions, marketeers and fast-company types are playing chess with FB behind the scenes. And yes, once again, it's all about the advertising. Yet, looking at FB, you don't see pages plastered with lots of hideous ads — at least not like MySpace or Yahoo. Ad rates are low but click-through rates (a measure of effectiveness) are also very low.

Today, it's a different ad world from that shown in *Madmen*. We moved beyond having just three big TV networks available to capture attention and sell products. Attention is the watchword — and digital magic actually makes attention harder, not easier, to get.

The Attention Economy

Although digerati often push the idea of multitasking as an inevitable and desirable part of modern life, marketeers are not dreamers. They are realists. There is realization among neuroscientists that humans have a rather finite ability to absorb information. Human attention is, in fact, a fixed quantity — it has something akin to a "budget." With the avalanche of advertising messages

323

thrown at you, the consumer, marketeers are looking for ways to grab a bigger slice of your attention budget.

TV advertising works by going big. Dominating the senses. Creating a buzz. But it is a shotgun approach that wastes impressions (and money) on people who are not potential customers. The web presents a more specific target by using "cookies" to mark the affinities of the user. Web-activity tracking is still just a guess based on assumptions from the sites you visit. Sometimes keywords in the story you are reading deliver hilariously ironic ads. Most people are hardly aware that the ads they are seeing on a website are totally different from what a different visitor might be seeing while viewing the exact same page. Still, click-through rates are extremely low on these web banner ads, too, so these methods are not particularly effective.

The ideal advertising "platform" is a network that knows all about you because you have told it all about yourself. It knows your age, your location, your level of education, your line of work, where in the world you have traveled, and what specifically you are interested in. It even knows who your friends are. Have you looked at your Facebook profile? You've filled the bill.

Social media provide the ideal mechanism for what is called "contextual" or "behavioral" marketing. In a world with limited attention and an avalanche of information, Facebook has transformed your personal relationships into a sales tool for marketeers. Your friends become the funnel for channeling information toward you. All of the data you have voluntarily provided for social purposes is being hijacked to feed marketing efforts directed at you.

The most blatant and controversial approach was Facebook's "Beacon" application that was linked to major online merchants. My experience with Beacon was buying a pair of shoes at Zappos and having that purchase announced in my newsfeed the next day on Facebook. I had no way of knowing that Zappos would be linking my purchase information to Facebook. Amazingly, no one at Facebook perceived this as a problem. It was only when users complained that they ceased the practice.

Naked on the Net: Let's Get Social!

If you look at Facebook, you will notice a few ads on the right-hand side of the screen. There are some linkages to your interests. But these ads are hardly compelling and it's obvious these cheesy little messages can't be enough to pay for Facebook's operations. So what else is making it run?

Facebook thinks about their business as something larger than a website and larger than a single application. They consider it a platform, which means that they are open to, and encourage other companies to develop, apps that run on top of that platform. "Platform" in the tech world conventionally describes an operating system/hardware combination. "Real" platforms are Windows/PC or OSX/Mac. So, while FB isn't *technically* a platform, for our purposes we'll pretend it is. Although you pay nothing to use Facebook, developers of apps that are "running" on the Facebook platform have ways of collecting money from you and splitting the money with Facebook. These are not apps in the conventional sense; most are simple quizzes, games, and entertainment.

If you are a Facebook user, you know there was a period of time when there was a new quiz almost daily. Examples include: "Which Star Trek character are you?" "What kind of shoes are you?" "Which president are you?" "Which Beatle are you?" At the time, it seemed a harmless exercise and people had fun as they posted their results to compare with friends. What wasn't clear was that every time you took one of these whimsical multiple-choice quizzes, you were submitting your profile — and all of your linked friends' profiles — to third-party companies gathering information about you.

Keep in mind how much information you have profiled and what you might have said in chats and posted on walls. Be aware that your friends haven't authorized you to share their personal data nor have you authorized them to share your data. The same marketeers who have been filling your mailbox with spam and scams for decades now have a better list to work from and sell to other marketeers — courtesy of you and your friends. Oh well, at least you'll know "Which Brady" you are.

Community and Faux Community

Many people like the ability to mobilize around a cause on Facebook. There are political, community, and charitable causes. These actions are generally well-intentioned and FB provides an excellent method to seek out like-minded individuals to form communities of interest. However, for every real cause there are several cynical marketeers leveraging the good will of these networks of friends to water their astroturf community.

It becomes easy for faux causes fomented by marketeers to ride on that wave of good intent. In December 2009, JPMorgan/Chase Bank came up with a program called "Chase: Community of Giving." Set up to capture the positive vibe of holiday do-gooderism, Chase and Facebook announced a program that would dole out $5 million dollars to charities nominated and voted on by Facebook users. Although Kim Davis, president of the JP Morgan Chase Foundation, called it "innovative," it turned into a contemporary *Queen for a Day* pity parade of otherwise worthy causes. In the event, it was called "crowdsourcing," a rather ugly sounding and stupid digerati term for people nominating and voting their preferences.

Elliot Schrage, vice president of global communications and policy at Facebook said,

> *"The program is unique in that a person can leverage their vote on Facebook — in addition to their wallet — to collectively help those in need during the holidays or support a cause important to them."*

But keep in mind that JP Morgan Chase, one of the masters of the Universe behind this charade, had nearly driven the global economy over a cliff, fired U.S. workers in droves, foreclosed people out of their homes, taken a huge government bailout, paid its executives hundreds of millions in bonuses, and compensated its lobbyists and politicians generously to avoid having to account for its actions. All this was on top of refusing to renegotiate underwater mortgages because it would be a "moral hazard."

Now, for a relatively cheap $5 million, Chase was putting a

positive spin on itself while harvesting massive amounts of personal information about participating Facebook members. Put that "generous" contribution in the perspective of the hundreds of millions of dollars that Chase spends on TV advertising and direct mail. How many impressions were made of a benevolent Chase that in reality was screwing customers while taking taxpayer's money?

As your friends urged you to participate in the voting, the marketeers managed to invade your private relationships to sell their "brand" as benevolent — all on the cheap. Because Facebook is not a public company we don't know how much Chase paid FB to place the campaign. It could well be more than the size of the fund that was being awarded. Unfortunately, we can expect more of this same type of activity and, probably, more idiotic terms like "crowdsourcing."

Hooked on the 'Book

Unlike any other medium, Facebook is extraordinarily live, with multiple channels coming at you in real time. The channels are your friends. Real people you know telling about what they are doing in real time. It is fascinating, charming, irresistible, and distracting. It is a discussion that goes on all day, often tied into breaking news events. You want to stay plugged in. Yet it can be a black hole where time disappears as you chatter, share, and browse away. How social can we consider an application that has people spending their time glued to screens and not interacting with other live human beings in physical spaces?

There are numerous stories of students putting their accounts on hold or having friends change their password and withholding it from them during finals or while completing college applications. Still others have deactivated their service entirely. Vastly more are addicted, continuously maintaining their interactions by mobile phone throughout the day. Deactivating an account requires checking off one of six reasons. One is "I spend too much time using Facebook." If Facebook is the cocaine of social networking then social gaming would be the crack.

Zynga & FarmVille: The "Fertilizer" That Makes Facebook Grow

At a 2009 industry conference in the UK, Facebook founder Mark Zuckerberg stated that, "Applications make up a huge part of Facebook. There are over 90,000 applications on Facebook. 69 million active users are using FarmVille alone."

As I said earlier, Facebook had a rough go of trying to make banner ads pay for keeping the lights on. Something more was required. Enter Zynga and the world of social gaming. It's probably a misnomer to call these "social games" because the play is usually quite solitary. The games, most of which are blatantly "inspired" by other existing online games, are created with a child-like simplicity and graphic style, much like their predecessor, the crooked ring-toss challenge at the carnival.

"Social gaming" companies such as Zynga are making hundreds of millions of dollars with games such as *FarmVille* and *Mafia Wars*. On the surface, these games are free. Anyone can jump off of a Facebook or MySpace page into a game, but that's just the come-on. For example, you can plod along growing your cartoonish simulated garden for free. Much like Second Life, Zynga games have an "in-game" currency that allows you to buy seeds and such. However, in order to move up to the next levels and have a better gaming experience you are going to need more tools and supplies than your in-game currency allows.

If you want, you can buy virtual tools and supplies that, once again by virtue of digital magic, cost Zynga nothing to make. They are infinitely replicable and very profitable. One of the big sellers was the tractor for *FarmVille* that sold for $20. In the U.S. the daily sales volume of these virtual tractors has at times exceeded the sales volume for real tractors. There are also more people farming in *FarmVille* than on real farms.

If you don't want to pay real cash for a tool, you can get in-game currency in exchange for signing up for various services, such as a trial of Blockbuster. You get the valueless cartoon garden tool, while Zynga collects actual cash from you, or from Blockbuster for getting you to sign up. Users sign up and drop their personal information, including credit card numbers, into the hands of marketeers. Then, Zynga puts a bounty on getting your friends to sign up for the service as well. You think you are helping friends out on that cute little *FarmVille*, but in reality you will find yourself signing up for some sketchy service. The entire "social" network gaming system is built to do two things; provide "lead generation" for global Internet-based scammers, and sell virtual objects for *real* cash.

Pitches are made for game currency in exchange for filling out an IQ survey. Four simple questions are asked. When the users get to the last question they are told their results will be text-messaged to them. They are asked to enter in their mobile-phone number, and are texted a pin code to enter on the quiz. Once they've done that, they've just authorized a $9.99/month subscription to some mobile-based scam service. Often nothing in the offer says that users will have to pay a monthly charge. Then, users have to figure out how to deauthorize the scammer. When you try to get out from the scammy contracts you tend to wreck havoc on your credit scores or find yourself the subject of identity theft.

There are legitimate companies like Netflix using the service, but they are far outnumbered by the scam artists. In fact, the scammers are scaring off the legitimate companies, leaving people to turn over their credit card numbers to organizations with which, were they not in game mode, they would probably not choose to do business.

The more money Zynga makes, the more they plow back into advertising for the games on Facebook which again feeds more lead generation for scammers and more cash for Zynga. Consequently, the company is a cash-fueled growth rocket booster pushing Facebook into the ionosphere. Meanwhile, Zynga's addictive games have people hooked and annoying the hell out of their Facebook friends. How much money are these cute little games generating? In December 2009, the Russian group Digital Sky ponied up $180 million for an unstated percentage of Zynga, which puts the estimated value of a company that makes nothing tangible into the billions.

The question remains, then: If social networking is a positive human activity, must it be dependent upon dubious and deceitful companies for financial support? Certainly there must be better alternatives that leave the deceptive games behind.

TWITTERATI

Given that mobile phones and laptops have built-in cameras for video calling, and that tech giants HP and Cisco are pushing communication with life-size video imagery called "telepresence," why is text still the most popular medium for human communication? Perhaps it's because text effectively cuts to the chase in lives with too much activity, where even a phone call is too much of a commitment — especially if it involves having the patience to listen to another human being.

Brevity: The Soul of Twit

Once again, we find social networking getting back to its most basic form, text-based chat. Twitter, as we now know it, first appeared on the scene in 2007. "Back to basics" would be an understatement in describing this minimalist application. Adapted from taxi-cab dispatch software, Twitter only lets the user send 140 characters (including spaces) of text. The innovation was allowing chatter to occur between mobile phones, computers, big-screen TVs — anything that can connect to the Net in any way can easily be made to send and receive messages, called "tweets," broadcasted through Twitter.

From the beginning, Twitter was designed as a "one-to-many" short-message system that allowed communications to be broadcast to a group of interested parties, called "followers." It was also designed to be adaptable enough to be a part of other applications, comparable to an engine that could be interchanged among many different car models. Twitter is amazingly simple. Users set up an account, which allows them to send messages through the Twitter servers and also to "follow" other Twitter members as they post messages. "Following" is the equivalent of subscribing.

When you choose to follow other Twitter users, their tweets are displayed in reverse chronological order on your own Twitter page with the most current message on the top of the page. If you follow 10 people or organizations, you'll see a mix of tweets from those 10 subscriptions scrolling down the page as they are tweeted by posters. This was a change from the standard text message, which was usually part of a one-to-one conversation.

Much like blogging, Twitter attracted people who had something to say, but did not know exactly to whom they were saying it. Unlike blogging, though, not much deep thought or authorship was required. Twitter is ideal for an increasingly attention-deficit-disordered culture that doesn't want to spend much time writing or reading. In their search for a name, the developers looked up "twitter" in the dictionary.

"...a short burst of inconsequential information"

Bingo! They had found their brand. Almost immediately, the most attention-consuming members of our culture, celebrities and politicians, started tweeting. With only 140 characters and easy input from a mobile phone, we were reminded how painfully self-absorbed and illiterate most young celebrities are. Much like MySpace, Twitter became a playground of self-promotion and narcissism that put middle-school students and Hollywood pseudo-glitterati on an equal footing. Almost immediately, rapt followers are bathed in the daily banalities and alleged "thoughts" of Lindsey Lohan, Larry King, and mega-Twit Ashton Kutcher.

Corporations that have younger, allegedly hipper or savvier members in their corporate communications or PR groups quickly realized that they could tap into what nasty truths were being spread about their bad customer service and poor quality products. Opening their own accounts, corporate Twitmasters went on the offensive to try to steer the buzz with counter-tweets. They remain vigilant on spin control by search word.

There is also a customer service aspect for corporations. Tweet a compliant about Comcast's sub-par service and "ComcastBonnie" will pop on and ask you what the problem is. While the traffic is still relatively low compared to traditional call centers, this approach is fairly effective, but personal responsiveness will not easily scale to the huge volumes of complaints Comcast can generate on a daily basis.

At this point, blasting tweets is insanely cheap advertising with an aura of hipness, novelty and immediacy. Every ad agency and PR firm is jumping on this train for fear of missing out. Ad veterans are trusting newly minted social media "experts" as their guides, replicating the same mentality that brought the world the enormously successful Pets.com and Webvan.

One devoted user has called Twitter "a giant megaphone" for what's on her mind. Fortunately for the world she is well-informed, thoughtful, and worthy of attention. That is not the case for most others, but you are under no obligation to follow idiots (though they might choose to follow *you*). And of course, there is the TwitterLit of Sarah Palin.

DimTwits

For some indeterminable reason, Kutcher, one-time cast member of a TV mediocrity called *That 70s Show* and cougar-bait for actress Demi Moore, has over 4 million human beings following his life on Twitter. Those are the kind of numbers that marketeers like to see, especially when they reveal a demographic profile that is loose with cash for sugary drinks, video games, and fast foods. We are seeing Kutcher being heralded as the Don Draper of Twitter-based advertising. Along with his business partner, Jason Goldberg, the pair is pursuing opportunities as the inexorable convergence of Hollywood and Silicon Valley takes place. Good luck with that, guys. The good news is that anyone can use Twitter; the bad news is that anyone can use Twitter. Take for example this Tweet from superannuated corn-state Senator Chuck Grassley attempting to reach out to his public on a matter of national importance:

> *"Pres Obama while u sightseeing in Paris u said 'time to delivr on healthcare' when you are hammer u think evrything is NAIL. I'm no NAIL."*

Twisted Twits

Twitter's low-cost, low-literacy standards allow any and all demi-celebrities to broadcast their profoundest ruminations for all to share. Take for example this work of moving prose by Tila Tequila after the death of girlfriend Casey Johnson:

> *"Why do I tweet so much? Even BEFORE Casey passed away? BECAUSE I HAVE NO FRIENDS! THERE! THE TRUTH COMES OUT!"*

> *"PPL say I need 2 get off twitter & grieve with friends & family... WHERE? I DONT HAVE ANY! Casey was my only family & my Dogs! Worst day ever."*

Even the unknown can shoot from fleeting micro-fame to notoriety. Take, for example, Shellie Ross. Ms. Ross had an online presence called "Blog4Mom" and "MilitaryMom" with a Twitter account that had in excess of 5,000 followers, an audience with whom she shared her life. There were 5,000 strangers who voyeuristically eavesdropped on the banal life of this ordinary mom. Then, like going to a car race waiting for a crash to happen, a true drama did tragically unfold from the routine.

At 5:22 p.m. December 14, 2009, Ross tweeted about a rare fog that had rolled over Brevard County while she was working in her chicken coop. While she was passing that important tidbit to her followers, her two-year-old son slipped into the family swimming pool and drowned. According to 911 records, a phone call from Ross at 5:38 p.m. indicated she had found her son at the bottom of the pool. Without missing a beat, there she was at 6:12 p.m. with more grist for the Twitter mill:

> *"Please pray like never before, my 2 yr old fell in the pool."*

Too Much Magic

I don't know about most other parents, but if this happened to my child at that age, the shock, pain, and anger would have been so overwhelming that sending a "tweet" would have been the last thing on my mind. Nevertheless, Shellie is indefatigable. At 11:08 p.m. she posts a photo of the deceased child and tweets:

"Remembering my million dollar baby"

Another blogger, named Madison McGraw, responded to the event:

"Anyone that has ever spent any time on Twitter knows that answering replies and sending out messages can literally eat up your time...a ten minute check of Twitter can turn into hours...Perhaps if Mrs. Ross had spent less time Tweeting and more time playing with her son, this would not have happened."

A harsh criticism, perhaps, but it contained a ring of truth. Another Twitter user named "jalynsandoval" tweeted:

"(her) fault for not keeping an eye on her son while he was next to the pool. she was to busy with twitter i guess. RIP kid"

This did not go down well with Mrs. Ross:

"@jalynsandoval you are an ass, I was outside w/him and it took 2 sec for him to slip away, I hope U never feel this pain u ass"

The fact that she even spent a millisecond pouring through responses, much less bothering to defend herself, is telling indeed. At last report, she had finally taken herself out of the public space with an unintentionally ironic blog banner stating her wish to be allowed to grieve in private. Amazing that it wasn't her first instinct.

As incredible as this episode may seem, it's not very far from the family of teary faces always found on local TV news after a tragedy befalls a relative. After all, years of Maury Povich, Jerry Springer, and "reality" shows have prepared everyone to be ready for their close-up. Never let a tragedy go to waste when it's your 30 seconds of fame.

(Warhol pegged it at 15 minutes, but that was before YouTube and our ever-shortening attention spans.)

Have people completely lost the concept of privacy and discretion? The line between what's on TV and real life has been obliterated. At the same time, everything you see on TV is a complete fabrication of reality, especially since it generates false intimacy. People erroneously believe that they know these stars and politicians they follow or watch on TV. "O.J.'s a murderer? You've got to be kidding. He was really funny in *Airplane*."

Do we really care about all the crap coming at us from all these sources or is it just ways to fill up the little time we have on this planet with trivialities that seem less trivial than our own? Do we need to hear from them on a live-update streaming basis such as Twitter so easily allows?

TwitWits

True tweets. Honesty in 140 characters or less:

> *"@Franzulla: I mostly use twitter for inebriated ramblings. I'm sure I can't be the only one out there."*
> *(You're not. Zappos created a video instructing employees not to "Drunk Twitter.")*

> *"@theconnor: Cisco just offered me a job! Now I have to weigh the utility of a fatty paycheck against the daily commute to San Jose and hating the work."*
> *(At Cisco, they were not amused. Bye-bye fatty check.)*

> *@Marielhemingway: We are in a high technology ridden world. Good to back off of it on a daily basis. Turn off technology from time to time.*
> *(…umm. Okay.)*

Pro Twits

Although it started with dim celebrities figuring out how to send text from their mobile phones, now the importance of the tweets is too big to leave to chance. A cottage industry of dubious "social media consultants" are swarming the famous and well-funded, taking over the twittering duties. This is a job for professionals. The trick is learning to write badly enough to imitate the star — even the odd, incoherent tweets of Sarah Palin are ghostwritten by an allegedly professional writer.

Twittering is moving from a fun ad-hoc peek-a-boo game to yet another element targeted at a media-saturated audience. The human attention budget is being overdrawn. Ad agencies and marketeers are cramming to fabricate social media strategies. It is becoming yet another prong of "integrated marketing." That being said, text remains as powerful as ever.

News Twits

Is Twitter also a legitimate news medium? It does seem to allow people to cover a lot of ground as a headline service.

As Stompk291 tweeted:

> "I resisted for a long long time. but i've been using it for about two weeks and I use it for breaking news ...my home town is on there. my current town, my employer, CNN, Fox, NASA and tons more. it's nice to get a constant flow of updates in one place."

Twitter is a two-way medium, and therefore provides a conduit for citizen journalism. A two-way dialogue is emerging between paid journalists and citizens who fortuitously happen to be where news is occurring. Having hundreds of millions of eyes and ears on the ground, camera-phones ready, is a remarkable development for news gathering. It comes just as news-media organizations have been shuttering local bureaus and shifting their shrinking budgets to talking-head formats. Anchors as overpaid celebrities are absorbing resources that once went for field reporting. Social media can help to fill the gap in coverage that the news media has abdicated.

News from Mumbai in 2008, Tehran in 2009, and Haiti in 2010 reported via Twitter gave the world a head start on images and even intelligence about what was happening on the ground. During the Mumbai attack, various eyewitnesses sent an estimated 1,200 tweets every minute. Twitter users on the ground helped compile a list of the dead and injured, and sent out vital emergency phone numbers and the location of hospitals needing blood donations. CNN called this "the day that social media appeared to come of age."

The late CBS/CNN/NPR correspondent Daniel Schorr correctly critiqued tweets as sources that lack verification. Nonetheless, Twitter is now a direct channel into existing news organizations and the blogosphere, but its first drafts are still subject to error and abuse. When it comes to tweeting, the libertarian digerati mantra is to trust in "the wisdom of crowds" — in this case, multiple sources reporting the event equals instantaneous fact checking. But they also trust in "the wisdom of markets," and history tells us that crowds have delivered lynchings, and that markets have delivered panics. Verification of events (fact checking) by responsible individuals is still a necessity for news.

We have already seen bad actors working en mass to create falsehoods. In 2009, for example, the Connecticut GOP set up fake Twitter accounts in the names of 33 Democratic members of the state legislature and sent out fraudulent tweets in their names. Did they think no one would notice, or were they just super savvy about how hard it is to unring the bell in people's memories? In another instance, Tea Party activist Daniel Knight Hayden was arrested by the FBI after tweeting threats in connection with his attendance at a protest event in Oklahoma. He made history as the subject of the first criminal prosecution to arise from a tweet. Unfortunately, we should continue to expect fallacious use of Twitter from spinning corporations, politicians, rogue governments, and even dumb criminals (though these groups can be hard to differentiate from one another.)

Tweet, Meet Wall Street

Even if Twitter is a viable technology for short messages, it doesn't mean the company is a viable business. Much like Facebook, it is going to have to do something to support itself. It's going to have to "get a job" at some point. The *Industry Standard*, a technology journalism endeavor, has remarked that Twitter's viability is threatened by a lack of revenue. The *Standard* folks should know what they're talking about, as the publication that set a record for advertising pages during the dotcom boom, then went belly up after the bust, they've seen this movie before.

Being free is expensive. Twitter board member Todd Chaffee believes that Twitter could make money from e-commerce, suggesting that users might buy items directly from Twitter since they already use it to get product recommendations. The question is, with the access to online shopping already so easy, why would people bother with Twitter? No matter what innovations start-ups think they are creating, each business model seems to repeat the same tired "monetization" strategy — advertising and selling people more stuff that they probably don't need. They'll just call it "engagement." The latest buzz word that marketeers can't get out of their small minds.

As is true with every other "social media" company, Twitter collects personal information about its users and shares it with third parties. Twitter considers the information you create through its application as its own intellectual property and reserves the right to sell it if the company changes hands. While Twitter displays no ads, advertisers can target you based on your tweet history and they reserve the right to quote you in ads for any product or service they see fit.

Obviously, there is a proliferation of really annoying ideas as the Cult of Tech looks for the next big thing in the social media realm. Again, Twitter is just a way to share text. It is not a revolutionary concept. Most " innovative ideas" are really about integrating information into mash-ups rather than creating anything fresh and useful.

Blippy, Gowalla & Foursquare...We Don't Friggin' Care

New ventures are running head-first into the land of Too Much Information. Foursquare, Gowalla and Blippy are social-media apps that intend to inundate the friends of users with a non-stop stream of trivial information about where users have been and what they've bought.

Foursquare posts your visits to locations, including stores and restaurants, on the social-media platform of your choice. They motivate you by offering badges for "checking in" when you arrive at the location and notify them. Foursquare then uses the GPS in your phone to show your location on the map embedded on whichever platform you've chosen and you collect points. What are the points are for? Foursquare hasn't exactly stated yet. For "the look-at-me generation" of video gamers and kids who grew up with the "everyone's gets a trophy" mindset, this might be an attractive incentive even though there are no actual benefits for users. Oh, wait! The one with the most visits to a particular spot is declared "mayor" of that location. Thrilling, indeed.

Blippy picks up where Facebook's Beacon went awry, recording your purchases at specific stores and websites, then blasting that information across your Facebook page or Twitter account. That way your friends and associates can see how much you just paid for toothpaste and Pringles. Take it from me — your friends don't want to know *that* much about you.

Both of these schemes, which are masquerading as apps, are essentially data-collection companies assembling behavioral marketing profiles about you for sale to third parties. They didn't even bother to think up a plausible reward to induce people to participate. They believe (with good reason, sadly) that people will sign up because it is the latest thing. Even when these ill-conceived start-ups fold and go bankrupt, they'll retain your personal behavioral data, which they can then sell to anyone, whether you approve of it or not. They own your profile, not you.

Balancing Social & Commercial?

From the beginning, the web has been about free and open. Because content can flow everywhere at once, there was no value derived from scarcity. Early web culture was academic and curious, filled with people who wanted to share knowledge. It was why the World Wide Web was invented in the first place.

Social networking was always offered as a free service, except in the days of AOL (and you know what happened to them). Social networking is an appealing method to provide just enough information-sharing among friends, family, and associates, yet no one has created a self-sustaining business model. That doesn't mean it is not possible. However, it *will* require an honest and transparent method of self-finance that doesn't involve the subterfuge of data mining, profiling, and deceptive games with shady third parties.

There's already a model for building a web-based utility that incorporates commerce while maintaining integrity. Whether it was by naïveté, brilliance, or both, Google found it. Google was not the first search engine, but it did several things differently. The most serious previous effort, called Alta Vista, preceded Google by many years. Alta Vista had a location in Palo Alto, California, only a few blocks from Google's start-up garage. Although Alta Vista wasn't the first search engine either, it was funded by a major computer company and was pretty good at finding content when it was a research project. Then Alta Vista made a critical mistake. It went commercial. Instead of delivering objective search results scientifically, it pushed companies that paid to be listed ahead of legitimate search results. It didn't take long for people to realize that the results were always being skewed. It was analogous to exchanging an encyclopedia for the Yellow Pages.

Google was designed by people who believed that sharing knowledge was a good thing. Their challenge was to help the users find information with an objective system of scoring results, while also trying to figure out how to pay for their own research and operations. They rejected display ads, and the existing paid search models that produced skewed results. Google specifically calls out and separates results paid for by advertisers. This was essential to Google's credibility as a search utility and is the reason that the interface remains clean and free of ads.

Users appreciated the difference and punished pushy search services that were advertising-centric, including Yahoo, Excite, and Microsoft. Credibility made Google the winner. Social-media companies should be looking for similarly creative solutions to balance social networking and commerce. Advertising is acceptable, but sifting through your personal communications and relationships as marketing fodder is not.

A Bill of Rights for Users of the Social Web:

A group of rather knowledgeable web veterans has proposed a "Bill of Rights for Users of The Social Web." Authored by Joseph Smarr, Marc Canter, Robert Scoble, and Michael Arrington, and published on September 4, 2007, the document states:

> *We publicly assert that all users of the social web are entitled to certain fundamental rights, specifically ownership of their own personal information, including:*
> *- Their own profile data.*
> *- The list of people they are connected to.*
> *- The activity stream of content they create; control of whether and how such personal information is shared with others; and freedom to grant persistent access to their personal information to trusted external sites.*
> *Sites supporting these rights shall:*
> *- Allow their users to syndicate their own profile data, their friends list, and the data that's shared with them via the service, using a persistent URL or API token and open data formats;*
> *- Allow their users to syndicate their own stream of activity outside the site;*
> *- Allow their users to link from their profile pages to external identifiers in a public way; and*
> *- Allow their users to discover who else they know is also on their site, using the same external identifiers made available for lookup within the service.*

Regrettably, no matter how well-intentioned and sensible, these ideas are non-starters because corporations are not democracies and there is no governing body to enforce these rights. Ironically, there is no social contract in social media.

Social Network as Public Utility

There are also lessons to be learned from the Wikipedia and the Mozilla communities. Perhaps the next social media venture will develop as a public utility in the same model. Facebook and Twitter are not complicated technologies in the slightest. They were cheap to develop, are cheap to maintain, and, since the users create all of the content, there is no cost for that at all. Just like the not-for-profit browsers, email applications, operating systems, and other apps that are made available for free, social networking should serve users and preserve their privacy without having to return profits generated from the exploitation of their personal information.

There needs to be a social utility that lets people connect to each other with no governing intermediator, much as the Internet itself has never forced the use of any particular application for web access or email. Just as in the web model, you would pay for simple connectivity rather than for the application itself. The obvious way to support this model is to have a small surcharge on Internet services much like the 911 fees that are levied on your phone bills every month. Since the dominant web-serving application is Apache, which is open source and free, this is not a naïve notion. It is proven and successful.

There is already a spark of a public, open-sourced social network in development. The group of former NYU students developing the model, called "Diaspora," has some initial backing — unfortunately, among those providing the funds is Facebook CEO Mark Zuckerberg. So it remains to be seen whether this will be a genuine effort that can both successfully reach a critical mass of users and resist becoming yet another venue for behavioral marketing scams.

There is an obvious paradox between the laissez-faire posturing of the Cult of Tech and their avarice in wanting to own Net users' private information. Behavioral marketing and data collection are antisocial behaviors, especially when users are not adequately informed about how they are being tracked, recorded, and marketed by the social networking entity. At least there is some level of awareness and outrage when Facebook introduces some invasive new app, but we still have no idea what they are really doing behind that friendly face.

The Silence of the Café

As someone who has spent the past decades writing in cafés — first with a pad of paper and pen, then with the very first version of the Apple PowerBook — I have seen an amazing shift take place. Once upon a time, not too long ago, writers, artists, readers, and travelers converged on cafés to escape solitude and share the casual ambience of a social environment. There was talk in the air. The sounds of overlapping conversations drifted around the room from lovers at neighboring tables, people having a polite but heated argument about the film they had just seen, and a group of Germans looking through their phrasebooks and practicing together. In the background, the übercool barista was playing some underground music. A café typically was thick with atmosphere and ambience.

Nowadays when you walk into a café, in San Francisco or elsewhere, there is silence. Well, not exactly silence, it is the faint tapping of fingers on little plastic keypads. And, while there is still music selected by the hipster barista, what is missing is the sound of human voices — unless, of course, they are those blathering loudly into mobile phones. There are fewer conversations taking place between and among individuals at the tables. Even when friends or lovers are seated together, they are likely to have their laptops facing each other; they're close in physical terms, but digital miles apart. Not sharing the real social network that has always existed when people are face to face.

Even the background music is replaced by headphones that completely isolate these patrons from the ambience of the space. Frankly, with faces buried in screens and earbuds snuggly plugged, they might as well stay home. Still, they are lured to be in a public place, though not actually experiencing it.

All hope is not lost. Curiously, if you look at places where the Net was first adopted, a rebalancing is starting to occur. For instance, the owner of an Oakland, California café told a local paper about the evolution he has seen as of late:

> *"When we opened this place we wanted to create a community. Instead it's just been a room full of laptops. I don't have anything against technology, but it's not the same as looking someone in the eye and pressing the flesh."*

So now he is asking customers to leave their MacBooks and netbooks at home and actually engage in conversation. Patrons are encouraged to sit at communal tables and chat. These customers, when forced away from their computer screens, realized what a great idea it was. Two typical responses:

> *"When I get away from the computer, it's a relief."*
> *"Laptops cut people off... I think it forms a social divide. Technology's great, but there's a serious social impact."*

Another spot nearby that originally opened as an "Internet café," has literally pulled the plug by reducing the number of electrical outlets to one. The reaction? According to the manager,

> *"Chatting is now starting to overcome the keystrokes. It's really changed the feeling of the place. It's really nice."*

Ken Goldberg, a professor of robotics at UC Berkeley and director of Berkeley's Center for New Media, hardly a Luddite, offers this insight:

> *"It's now socially acceptable to text during dinner parties or stand alone at a party and check email — actions that not long ago would have been considered unspeakably rude. The result of having the world available at our fingertips, and likewise always being*

available to the world, is a general devaluation of information, ourselves, and personal relationships.

... people hop from one distraction to the next without focusing on real people or actual ideas. Paying attention, being patient, listening to people and concentrating on an idea not easily expressed in 140 characters are skills we're in danger of losing unless we learn to occasionally unplug. I love technology, but we need boundaries."

Social or Commercial?

As a once reluctant user of social media, I can see both their negative and positive aspects. It is excellent at maintaining what I'd call "just enough contact" with your extended network of friends without necessarily becoming invasive or annoying. It's all about having a conversation, at times rambling and random, at times trivial, at times pointed or heated. Connecting with people is always a good thing, and though new users tend to over-share, that soon fades away. Until it does, you may need to tell your friends you are not really interested in knowing what they are having for dinner. Then again, maybe you do want to know. Maybe that will create further bonding among individuals.

As I've indicated earlier, the real danger is letting yourself be hijacked by marketeers who exploit your personal revelations, preferred activities, and friendships by converting social media into just another marketing channel. You certainly wouldn't want anyone from the phone company listening in on your conversations and calling you back telling you about the great offers you might be interested in based on what you just said to your friends.

Is social media distracting? Yes. So is life. It only becomes a problem when it moves from enriching your life to substituting for life. It should not discourage people from interacting in the physical world.

Is it addictive? Yes. We all crave connection and mutual affirmation. Some people have even compared it to social grooming. It is still way better than having people glazed out on anti-depressants, or anti-anxiety meds because they are socially awkward. Social networking can be a bridge, but it should never be a destination.

Is it changing the world? Maybe. We can easily be fooled into thinking we have taken serious action just because we have said something about "change." A virtual life, a simulation, is no substitute for getting out and doing something physical. (But for those with physical disabilities the ability to engage on a level playing field with those who are fully mobile with all five senses and four limbs in fine working order is liberating.)

Originating from a decade that kicked off with massive unemployment, the social network could well be the glue that forms a new kind of social cohesion. It is part of the mutual temperature-taking, the job search, the collaboration and self-affirmation that may be needed to keep people connected to each other. Hopefully, it will not subvert the motivation for going out into the world and physically connecting with other people. Physical passivity combined with social connection can lead us to lives like those pictured in Wall-E, where we are plugged into a cycle of nonstop consumption, passivity, dependence, and lassitude.

We all have to determine for ourselves what our level of exposure should be in the social-media realm. For our children, it is critical that we get them engaged in the real world and reduce the amount of time they spend in front of a screen with their ears plugged by earbuds — or else they may well become hollow avatars of their truly human selves.

Section Three

TOO MUCH MAGIC

and

What To Do

About It

Too Much Magic

Jason Benlevi

3.1

Puncturing the Illusion of Progress

Since I began writing this book in 2008, a light year has transpired in digital life. Facebook and Twitter have become a huge part of daily life for hundreds of millions of people. Though they loom large in the culture and media, they are still miniscule in terms of revenue generated, which impacts their long-term viability. One can rest assured that a start-up company is forming to become the "Facebook-killer."

There is much that should have been accomplished but has not in these past years. We have not solved the big healthcare problems, and the lack of a coordinated medical information system has served as a source of byzantine frustration for patients and physicians. The economic situation that brought us to the brink of a global bank failure in 2008 was entirely facilitated by digital technology and computerized models that were either wrong, fraudulent, or both, and we have yet to see effective intervention to keep it from happening again. In May 2010, we saw the tiny keystroke error of a single trader almost bring down the markets again.

While writing this, the oil gushing in the Gulf of Mexico had finally been stopped, but, day and night for three months, the hemorrhaging of toxic crude continued unabated. The population of the Gulf Coast now has to assess and try to fix the worst damage to beset this nation short of war. Although BP had the wherewithal to put a deep hole in the planet, they hadn't bothered to develop the technology necessary to stop the resultant volcano that spewed crude from a mile beneath the ocean's surface. In a sense, the disaster was a decade-late swan song to the 20th century, which was, above all else, the Petroleum Century. The lesson here is that technology is better at starting something than stopping it when it goes awry.

Too Much Magic

We have now entered the second decade of what might be called the Digital Century. It was digital supercomputing that revealed where to look for deep oil, yet digital magic didn't reveal how to plug the hole in the seafloor. More accurately, preventive scenarios had not been developed for economic reasons. Oil clean-up technology has been arrested for decades due to lack of investment. The lesson of the Exxon Valdez spill in 1989 was (thanks to corporatist activist courts) that the company responsible for the damage was not compelled to fully pay those for the damages. Consequently, corporations have had no incentive to invest in clean up technology. For most of the new century, the U.S. Coast Guard itself has spent less than a million dollars a year on oil-spill clean-up research. This is less than what the TSA pays for one single full-body airport scanner.

The digital difference between Exxon Valdez 1989 and BP 2010 is that the latter delivered a live video feed of the gusher to our desktops, mobile laptops, and iPhones. We could watch multiple camera views in high definition, day and night. We were spectators to disaster and yet totally unable to do anything to arrest the wholesale destruction taking place before our eyes. Digital life is rich with opportunities to watch, but there is a huge technical gap between observing and having the ability to act. Keep in mind that since BP controlled the cameras of the live video feed, it could easily have been manipulated to mislead viewers as to the gravity of the situation. At a mile deep, there was no independent observer around to provide objective coverage.

The BP oil spill became a digital-media event of the first order. In the disaster's early days, PBS's *News Hour* even devoted a segment to the media impact of the BP disaster. The guests were oil lobbyist Amy Jaffe, TV personality Bill Nye the Science Guy, and Paul Saffo who has roots in the Institute for the Future, a Silicon Valley think tank. The oil lobbyist admitted to being dumbfounded by the lack of a solution, Nye offered some solid thinking, but Saffo went down a different path, typifying the digerati's bubble logic.

> *MARGARET WARNER: Paul Saffo, beginning with you, the public's fascination with this story, what is driving it? Is this like*

Jason Benlevi

other disasters, or is there something more at work here?

PAUL SAFFO: I think this is a new chapter. This is one of those McLuhan moments that would have seemed pure science fiction 10 years ago, watching in real time this spreading horror deep in the ocean below the level anybody can reach. It's part Titanic the movie and part 1950s The Blob. It's just strangely compelling. I know all sorts of people who just can't stop watching.

(Analogizing life to a movie — a common sensibility in our entertainment-centric culture.)

AMY JAFFE, Well, you know, we, in the American public, we are a big believer that there's a science and technology solution to everything — everything.... So, to sit here night after night and watch all these scientists unable to close a simple pipeline, even though it's a very complex engineering problem, as a layperson, when you sit here and watch the oil just spewing out of this pipeline, it's just this horror movie, like we cannot believe that there isn't a technology to close this pipeline.

(Again, real life looks like a movie. Remember this is someone, ostensibly intelligent, from the oil business saying this!)

MARGARET WARNER: So, Paul Saffo, do you — do you agree that it's shaking our faith in technology and in Americans' ability? I mean, usually we think — part of our whole ethos is, if there's a problem, Americans can fix it.

PAUL SAFFO: Well, we have had an uneasy accommodation with our faith in technology for the last 10 years. It was shattered first with the popping of the dotcom bubble. And the whole climate debate circles around us right now.

(Perpetuating the misconception that the dotcom crash was a technology story instead of greed-gone-wild story.)

Too Much Magic

PAUL SAFFO: In fact, you see two camps in the climate debate. There are the druids who say we need to turn the clock back because we can't solve it, and the engineers who say we need to accelerate because we can solve this with heroic engineering.

(A false argument: you can either trust science — no matter how misguided — or be dismissed as a throwback.)

BILL NYE: OK, everybody, look, technology doesn't come from outer space. Humans made this thing.

AMY JAFFE: I work at a university that's known for its math and science departments and its engineering. And it — we find it very depressing that a lot of young people who are good in mathematics in this country have chosen to use that to develop financial derivatives that have actually hurt our economy — and we see it here in Houston with all the people who rushed to work for Enron — instead of going into concrete science that could be used today to shut this pipeline.

MARGARET WARNER: Paul Saffo, what has been the role of the web in all of this in — in creating a kind of community that's tuned in to this all day every day, or at least part of the day?

PAUL SAFFO: TV brought the world into our living rooms. And the Internet has done something that's vastly more intimate. It brings it to our desks and to handheld devices. And, so, I think people feel an emotional connection with this that is much, much, much deeper than television. And the fact that it's real-time and it's unedited and at any moment something completely surprising could happen just has people captivated.

You know, the only thing that would become more captivating is, we have got a dozen or so robots, telerobot ROVs down there, running around. If one of those got tangled in some cable or stuck in the Christmas tree blowout preventer, and the name of that robot got out, then you would have a drama of the first order.

While people are losing their livelihoods, their homes, and their lives, Saffo is bubbling with childish glee about deep-sea robots and what their names might be. In his flawed judgment, the name getting out would be a "drama of the first order." I guess wholesale destruction of sea life in the Gulf for a generation is just a musical comedy to him — but oh those robots, that's a story!

Then again, nothing personal against Saffo, but digerati such as Saffo don't have much of a track record for calling it right. Did they predict this one any better than the web-enabled refrigerator that would talk to our web-enabled oven, cook up dinner for us and order our food from Webvan? Oh yeah — that must have been a different future.

The Future You've Been Promised Has Been Cancelled

It's startling to arrive in the second decade of the new millennium and realize that, for all the technology we are carrying around in our pockets, we no longer have the ability to do important things in which we once took pride. Those ambitious landmark accomplishments were made when our personal technology was limited to wired telephones and TV sets that pulled a half dozen channels out of the air.

While we are all agog at the launch of the iPad and newest iPhone, for the first time in 50 years we are no longer launching Americans into space. Only two generations ago, we could send a person to the moon. Starting in 2011, an American will be unable to reach the International Space Station without catching a ride on an antiquated Russian space capsule. Keep in mind that these are the people we "defeated" in the race to the Moon and the Cold War. While we short-change real exploration and research, there is no problem obtaining venture-capital funding for trivial and banal activities that have been repackaged as "tech" ventures.

With untold billions spent on games and movies that make us feel that we are cruising around the galaxy and engaging in battles with aliens, the sad fact is that in reality we are falling behind as we inhabit our digitally generated illusions. Watching and pretending will have to suffice. Modern America's business model is illusory and virtual — we digitally design products, but they are made in factories out of our sight and out of our country. We are not making real things. We are making illusions. It gets more abstracted all the time, and now it's extending to the political realm, as well.

Our citizens think that they can have government services without paying taxes. That we can have clean air and water while still driving everywhere in 6,000-pound cars. That our kids will somehow score above average in specious academic tests even when they are glued for increasing hours to screens awash with always-on entertainment.

Although fantastic aircraft appear in movies and in games, our airlines are stuck at the gate, or at subsonic speeds with us, the passengers, crammed in like sardines, while the most heralded current innovation in air travel is being able to have web access on the flight.

Our wars take place against enemies that are vaguely defined with unclear objectives fought by soldiers who have been trained since childhood on video games. Video games famously have reset buttons, thin premises, one-dimensional villains, and faulty logic, as does our present set of wars. Yet our military soldiers on with limited awareness. They are living the game but dying in reality. Real victory requires territory. Terra firma trumps ideology and technology. Reality rules over illusion.

Change You Can Pretend In

The digital age is an era of watching and pretending more than doing. From gameplay to movie special effects to the news, the fidelity of illusion grows more convincing and more compelling every day. We have warriors "fighting" who are seated comfortably 7,000 miles from the battlefield. Most citizens watch our wars long distance, on demand, sacrificing nothing, not even paying taxes to cover the costs. It is painless. Battle-weary, laptop-toting soldiers fighting in the war zone recreate and pass their free time by shooting it up on video games. Is there even a recognizable line between these experiences?

On the screen at home, real war is indistinguishable from

entertainment carried on the same networks. Technological warfare is a complete abstraction that doesn't even have an identifiable enemy and certainly no ideas about what victory should look like. Yet modern history tells us that local boots on the ground tend to win every time over technology. No matter what anyone invents, territory rules. Real estate is real.

Reality beats virtuality, too. Take, for example, the thousands of bloggers penning polemics and tracking political stories. On the surface this phenomenon looks powerful, and politicians have learned to play to it. Then compare that power to a few dozen lobbying firms set in close proximity to the Capitol Building in D.C. When it is millionaire lobbyists versus bloggers, who do you think will win in the end?

Yet, there is a deceptive power in unreality. Actors become politicians to typically bad effect. Pretending to be a leader in a scripted fantasy has zero relationship to running the machinery of government. Candidates are similarly scripted, filmed, and edited to create a persona that is only partly theirs; the rest is blow-dried hair and an empty designer suit. It is not surprising that a radio biz showman like Glenn Beck, is able to pull off his tear filled jingoistic charade with his viewers none the wiser.

Pretend banks move pretend money and crash peoples' real lives. We've seen highly computerized banks that don't have sufficient hard assets or cash in their vaults fail, yet never go out of business and are instead sustained by a digital stream of numbers transmitted from the Federal Reserve. No consequences for failure. In most cases the bankers were rewarded with bonuses.

Customer service is increasingly delivered on phone lines, or through online chat, by digitally synthesized personalities posing as other sentient humans. These faux "conversations" are meant to sideline us from speaking to a real live person who might cost a few dollars to employ or, worse yet, have empathy and a desire to be helpful. So accustomed are we to the abysmal level of "service" today, we are almost glad to hear these fake voices rather than having to punch dozens of buttons on our phones to get help.

Companies push virtual conferences for employees because

they sell the technology, not because it makes any sense. Yet the CEOs of these companies put on hundreds of thousands miles in business travel in their own jets. Why? Because "being there" counts. Obviously, there is more value to presence than they want you to believe. Real presence. Not "telepresence."

Say "It's Magic"

Although this book never set out to critique any specific technology product, and this author has the highest affection and admiration for the creativity of Apple Computer, there is one innovation that has entered popular culture that seems to illustrate our current crossroads. This particular device, from this particular company is a watershed event. I am referring to Apple's introduction of the iPad.

Although some might say it's an iPhone on steroids, the rationale for the iPad is not as a communications device with extra capabilities. It is an entirely new species. When personal computers were first introduced, they allowed regular people to do things that they could never do before. Technical users had a machine that allowed them to develop innovative software, and creative users had a new tool to help them design or produce things. People could communicate and learn in new ways. Personal computers were all about creation, making and doing — even if that creation was just a new way of doing businesses as an entrepreneur.

The iPad is a sea change because it is a consumption device, not a creation device. It is for purchasing and viewing media. Although it's capable of rudimentary document creation, that's not the point of the device. It's not so much a tablet computer as a display screen with wireless access to a wide array of purchasable media. Instead of an empowering device for thinking individuals, it's merely a screen where people can view stuff to buy. It's a vending machine for digital media. Of course, I was most struck by the word used to market it: "magical."

Apple's iPad features brilliant engineering and design, but there is something disturbing about the business that it has spawned. As a part of its package, "iAd" will be integrated into the platform to help marketeers advertise to iPad users. The iPad and other digital-media delivery devices are inciting a huge flurry of development activity. But to what end? Do we really need more entertainment and media coming at us?

Where is a similar flurry of development activity for, say, hybrid cars? Unfortunately for the environment, there were more iPads sold in a one month than hybrid cars in an entire year. Two million iPads sold in its first two months on the market, while less than 300,000 hybrid cars were sold in the U.S. during all of 2009. In just one quarter, Apple sold 3.25 million iPads, which is more than the total of hybrid cars sold in an entire decade.

Where is the flurry of development for an educational curriculum that moves us out of the early 20th century? Just adding computers to schools is the equivalent of putting a TV in every classroom — it becomes huge distraction that does nothing to encourage unique, insightful thinking.

Where is the clever and effective way to clean up an oil cataclysm, or a plan to move beyond fossil-based fuels altogether? The answer, pathetically, is that is considered a lower priority than knowing what brand of toilet paper is selling best at any given moment.

The Best Minds of a Generation

There is a driving reason that we find ourselves in possession of "magic" like the iPad and yet unable to solve our more pressing problems. There is no lack of talent to make real substantive change in the world using technology but, just as in the dotcom days, the best minds of our rising generations are being attracted elsewhere. Technical talent and academic minds are following the money, as the fast-company few wave magic wands and beckon. In digital technology and medicine, people of science are being compromised by financial promises. Just as no great art was ever done for money, great science is done for curiosity rather than cash.

It's not that oil disaster clean-up technology is impossible. It's just not attracting technical talent because few investors saw the profit opportunity. There is abundant technology to drill deeper chasing oil because that is where the money comes from. With oil often hitting records prices it did not take a great business mind to know that there was money in helping oil oligarchies to seize and extract the gooey stuff.

Just as our business students are being siphoned off to fashion sophisticated Ponzi schemes on Wall Street, our science students are being drafted to create the latest web and mobile application sensations, or ways to stamp a patent on nature. It's hard to resist the economics. For instance, the brainiac team gathered at Google could be doing real science. Instead, almost the entirety of Google's business — and the scientists' brainpower — is focused on matching viewers and advertising, because 90% of its revenue comes from that one activity.

When it's just about the money, society tends to do the wrong thing. In this age when we are supposed to believe in the "wisdom of markets," we have seen consistent failure, along with the perversion of science and engineering. Markets have rewarded unproductive risk, abandoned productive factories to chase cheap labor overseas, while in the meantime weakening domestic demand with massive sustained unemployment.

An argument could be made that it's good for the makers of things to connect with their potential customers. But what is being offered? A closer look at who spends the most money on advertising shows a predominance of cars, sugary drinks, fast foods, beer, diet programs and pharmaceuticals for conditions often brought on by our own excesses.

When it comes down to it, how many exposures to McDonalds, Chevy, or Cialis do you need to get the message? You already know about Coke — how many times a day and in how many places and ways do you have to hear about it?

Technology for cleaning up spilled oil is not as readily lucrative as finding a new way to shovel advertising into a person's brain or giving customers a "one click" method to make a purchase.

Adformation Week?

In the age of digital magic, technology and science have become subservient to marketing. Current issues of the trade publications *Adweek* and *Information Week* reveal much of the same content regarding iPads, Android OS, and location-based ad services. As in the dotcom era, so much of what we call "technology" and "innovation" is really just merchandising and marketing. Target media have shifted from newspapers and TV to computer screens, phones, and in-store video displays. This is labeled "interactive," but the only activity offered is a way to buy yet more stuff. The biggest "tech" stories of the day are Twitter and Facebook, which use very little technology innovation except for a few lines of computer code. Technically, next-generation applications like Foursquare, Gowalla and Blippy are even more yawn-worthy, yet have created buzz among the Cult of Tech. There is no real genius in any of the social/marketing applications. But they keep sketchy social-media consultants and industry conferences busy extracting money from insecure Fortune 500 executives terrified of missing the wave.

Our citizens believe they have become more sophisticated as users, but don't mistake that for being tech savvy. After all, you probably drive a car competently, but that doesn't make you a mechanic or an expert on internal-combustion compression ratios. A user is just a user. No matter how smart and technical you think your kids are, it's likely they probably don't even know how a light switch works. There's an effect, which is apparent, but little attention is paid to the cause.

The distance between our digitally enabled illusions and real life grows by the day. We are becoming mighty in our own minds, but enfeebled by technology. That is the desired effect, the desired addiction — an addiction fed by the Cult of Tech, that cabal of digerati, fast-money types, and old-line marketeers in advertising agencies.

In the Beginning...

Let's revisit the quotes that opened this book. Beginning with that of Dr. Arthur C. Clarke, who brought the world *2001: A Space Odyssey* and invented communications satellites:

> *"Any sufficiently advanced technology is indistinguishable from magic."*

The process of making amazing things ridiculously small does seem like magic. The complexity folded into a thin package of glass and metal no bigger than a scratchpad is beyond the comprehension of all but a small group of engineers. For the other 99.999% of the world, our current digital age has indeed achieved magical proportions.

Where Clarke foresaw the high ground of the technology proposition, the low ground was exposed by the late social comedian George Carlin.

> *"Everybody's got a cell phone that makes pancakes so they don't want to rock the boat. They don't want to make any trouble. People have been bought off by gizmos and toys in this country. No one questions things anymore."*

The infatuation with digital devices is far in excess of their practical utility. In fact, they do far more than they need to. We have hundreds of thousands of applications available. Now, for some people, it's hard to imagine life without these digital accouterments. Unhealthily attached, these folks are willing to pay whatever it takes and stand in line overnight to possess new devices that, until they appear, have no real necessity for life. One must always get the model that — despite differing in only the most minimal way from the model they already have — is an upgrade.

Simultaneously, the political climate has grown contemptuous of people who work for a living. There is not a working-for-living person in America, or in the rest of the industrialized world, who is not working harder than their parents did a generation ago. Unions and political systems that they pay for have done little to serve them, and despite all the blogs and cable news noise, not much change takes place. Yet toys of technology distract us from what we are losing or paying in the real socio-economic world. If you gaze into the future, the devices look more gleaming than life itself does.

There is going to be ever more cool-looking stuff, but a higher price for citizens to pay for their basic needs of housing, education, and healthcare — all the things that used to be possible with one-earner households and very little technology. Is this the root of the dystopia always portrayed in our movies about the future? Are people secondary to technology, with authoritarians gaining tighter control of the mechanisms for oppression? We inherently understand that this future doesn't jibe with our humanity, but admittedly it is hard to see it clearly with so many bright shiny objects glowing in the foreground.

3.2

All Things Being Digital, Is Your Life Any Better?

Here's a question, modeled on the all-too familiar political query: *"With all things being digital, are you better off now than you were before?"*

Sure, you have more stuff and more options, but can you think of anything the digital world has made fundamentally better in terms of human existence and your personal happiness?

Earlier in this book, we discussed *seven aspects of life* that have become radically changed by digital technology. Although considerably *different* from before, it is hard to make the argument that life today is *better* because of digitization. You have to continually ask yourself the question "Is it better for *me*?" Let's reexamine these topics in this light.

1. Always-on Entertainment

You can watch whatever you want whenever you want. But are you any happier? Are the entertainment choices any better, or does everything start looking the same. Originality, personality, locality in entertainment seems to be trumped by easily and instantly distributable product, much as local and regional street foods have been pushed out by mechanisms of McDonalds and KFC. It's sad when people burn their own free time watching what happens to *other* people on TV. That same faux life entertainment follows people everywhere as they watch on their phones. At the same time, it is good to have the film treasures of the past available to new generations. Classic films and music need never die — and even narrow fan bases can be reached and served.

2. Mobile Communications

You've got the world in the palm of your hand with a smart phone and a car full of electronic gear, but are you communicating any better with those whom you know? Are your relationships any better or more successful? Are you understood any better? Do you feel more secure? Are you helped or inconvenienced by the constant buzz of contacts from work, family, and friends? How much of your time is truly your own, compared to the days before you had a mobile phone? Do you feel more busy but getting less done? Are you even fully aware of the space and time you actually occupy? A mobile phone can keep families connected through the day, but at the same time, kids need to learn to be independent and trust their own judgment without checking every decision with parents or friends. And of course, the level of distraction afforded by these devices is a massive concern in our attention-deficit culture. Still, the potential for bonding across distance and time is very compelling and human.

3. Electronic Gaming

Play used to be practice for life. Life was the real deal where reward was found, or at least sought. Life had its own way of keeping score. Now gaming has exceeded the thrill and experience of many people's personal lives — they live to play in a fantasy world and don't bother to venture very far beyond it. Ask yourself: Are your kids any smarter from playing video games? How many car crashes and shootings do they need to witness by the time they are 15? And why are they still playing at 30? Or 40? Outside of hand-eye coordination, what skills have they ever mastered with a video game? How much irreplaceable childhood or young-adult time could be better spent in creative and personal pursuits instead of being cocooned in games designed by Asperger's afflicted programmers who spend day and night in rabbit-warren cubicles? Have movie-fantasy and military-simulation technologies blended together to develop professional killers who experience little remorse after so much practice mayhem? Along with these questions, ask yourself this last one: How many hours of yours or your children's lives do you consider completely expendable? Except for those who have a physical circumstance that makes it difficult to venture far beyond four walls, what does this narrow band of pretend provide that enriches life?

4. Moving Images

We're used to moving images creating fictions, falsehoods, fantasies, challenging perceptions, and a shared alternate reality. But for both the artful storyteller and the Hollywood hack there is the danger of a massive erosion of both wonderment and veracity. Soon CG imagery will be identical to reality. So everything will be visually possible, but nothing will appear special since everyone knows it's just CG effects. How does a flyover of the Grand Canyon compare to an extravagantly rendered James Cameron movie canyon of unlimited dimensions and colors? Are characters and story taking a backseat to the effects? Has randomness and vibrancy been extracted from the art of acting because CG dominates the film making process?

While we expect motion-picture entertainment to be fantastical and fictional, we find ourselves in a position where what we see as "news" can be altered. Filmed reality has always been editable, but only recently has it been possible to edit and manipulate that visual reality in real time. What will this mean to our political and legal systems when photographic reality is no longer proof positive of anything?

5. Personal Rights and Privacy

Nothing else displays the inequities of legal and legislative systems driven by corporate interests more clearly than the issues of rights and privacy. Vast, publicly financed yet privately owned machinery is sorting through the laundry of your life and passing your personal "dirt" on to various soap-sellers. Is your dignity as a human being protected or completely expendable for a few cents to anyone who wants to sell you more stuff you don't need?

Too Much Magic

Do you feel any freer than you did before the dawn of the digital age? Do you harbor feelings of dread about the future? Does anyone have the right to know everything about you? When you buy music, do you think it is it yours? Why should descendents be entitled to be paid for works authored by great grandparents whom they never could have met? How much of our common cultural heritage will be locked up to enrich those who have done nothing to deserve it? Why do corporations have a right to patent your DNA and hide these natural facts for almost a century? The problem with all of these questions is that the answers are not favoring the ordinary law-abiding citizen, but rather the Cult of Tech.

6. Freedom and Democracy

Everything else depends on this. We can't have representative democracy when the system has been hijacked. Are you better informed? Are you annoyed by carpet-bombing political ads from ultra-wealthy candidates? Has the Net delivered more freedom anywhere in the world just once? Is democracy on the rise or are we just fooling ourselves as the powerful grow even more so by controlling the flow of information on the Net, as well as the banks and the armies that they have traditionally controlled?

Although it is an issue that is still under the radar for most people, the issue of Net Neutrality looms large in the wings. It stands to be the defining act of digital democracy when it crosses the stage of public opinion. Right now, the Net *is* neutral. You can have any content from any source and your service provider delivers it to you without prejudice. If big media and telecom companies have their way, they alone will decide what it is possible for you to see or read online.

Much good comes from the chaos of press freedom. Do you want it to be squelched by those who provide basic communications services like Net connectivity? How dangerous will it be when service and content networks merge into a single company with its own agenda, undeterred by regulation?

Even if you can get information out and ensure a fair and tamper-resistant election, cash and presence will win. The reality of lobbyists offering martinis, cigars, and checkbooks beats any blogger. Even faced with the big electoral results of November 2, 2010, this is not a fight we can give up — we need to do everything in our power to ensure Net Neutrality if there is even any chance of democracy, digital or otherwise.

7. Social Media

With social media, technology is at last addressing a core human need (other than porn). Why have we allowed them to turn it into yet further methods for marketeers to crawl into our consciousness? Social is a good thing. It's people getting along with people, doing things together, conversing, but do we really want marketeers leeching knowledge about us, and our relationships with others to drive yet another advertising gimmick? Social media needs to be a public utility, not a private reservoir of information to be exploited by marketeers. At some point, Facebook will be facing the MySpace dilemma: The more commercial it becomes, the less socially appealing it will be. Right now social media is newish and enjoyable. It's hard to predict how it will ultimately fit into our lives, or which model will work, but it's safe to say we don't want advertisers exploiting our personal information and relationships to sell us yet more stuff. The marketeers may want to "engage" you, but you should call off the wedding plans. In short: Social utility apps should be free of commerce.

Jason Benlevi

3.3

Breaking the Spell

WHAT *YOU* CAN DO ABOUT IT!

As much as you have been sold digital technology as a solution for everything that ails you and society, you are not obliged to buy it or to believe the story you've been told about it. People have gotten along without digital magic for 99.99999% of our existence on this planet.

Here are some suggestions on how to disengage from digital life and yet stay engaged as a human being in the modern world. Choosing to remove your self from digital is not an all or nothing proposition. You can make your own terms. The first step is awareness. This book has been a look into the agenda of the Cult of Tech to give you an understanding of what motivates them... money and power. Unless you're aware of the forces trying to control you, you'll never be able to free yourself from them. Ultimately, in your life, you have more control than you think, but you need to break off some of the automatic behaviors and bonds that you have been sold. The good news is that most of it is easy and enjoyable. You know about reducing your carbon footprint: Now it is time to consider lowering your "silicon footprint."

Get Real: The Steps to Owning Your Own Digital Life

1. Be your Own Story

Entertain yourself. Learn to play an instrument. Be a storyteller or seek out those who are and encourage their participation in your life. Make things, tangible things that involve your hands and senses, and give them away to people you like. Take the time to talk to strangers. Bake bread, learn another language, take a painting class, ride your bike. Don't watch TV during dinner. Converse, argue, and amuse.

2. Be First Person

To the extent of your ability, go places, and while you're there, pay attention. Don't fiddle with your iPod, answer your phone, or text a friend. Multitasking is dead. *Total*-tasking is where you want to be. You want to live 100% of every experience. Listen to the ambient noise. Walk in a random direction. Devote your attention to the people and experience those who are sharing the same space as you. Close the laptop. Talk to the person at the next table. Make eye contact. Ask questions. If you have small children, park your media player and phone and talk to them, sing to them, be a first person. Spend less time through the camera lens. Lose the two-dimensional view of the world. Treat anything you see on a screen with skepticism.

3. Be an Island

It's good to be connected, but do so on your own terms. Don't be afraid of seeming out of touch because you aren't using the latest social networking or mobile app. You don't need to check your phone every five minutes. You can pick and choose what you want. Islands are good places for vacations and, contrary to John Donne, every person is an island. If there's nothing currently concerning you, turn off your mobile phone. Whenever possible, keep your phone number to yourself.

4. Get Physical

You are not meant to be a passenger in life, you are meant to be a driver. You are supposed to use all of your senses. "Touch" is more than what you feel on a trackpad or screen. Life is not a spectator sport.

5. Ignore Public Opinion

You are not a throwback or a Luddite if you eschew the digital world. Obviously, you're going to have to master whatever technology is required in your professional life. But that doesn't mean you need to pay attention to anything else. Be a "post-techie."

6. Beat Them at Their Own Game

Reduce the amount of digital breadcrumbs you leave for marketeers. Provide bad information to keep them guessing. Make up stuff. Regularly dump the cache and erase the cookies on your computer. Click the ads that you're not remotely interested in and quickly abandon the pages.

7. Be a Friend

Try the original social network — talk to the people you meet in your daily life. Strike up a conversation on the bus or in the supermarket. All those people standing in line with nothing to do but stare into their palm are bored and isolated. ***Don't Forget... You Can Always Pull the Plug!***

When the magic isn't there for you. And sometimes even when it is...just because you feel like it.

Two Last Words : Net Neutrality

No matter whether you lean libertarian, conservative, moderate, liberal, or progressive, you want to protect both freedom of expression and freedom of commerce. Let's not turn it over to the worst elements within the Cult of Tech. Freedom in the immediate future will depend on two words that are first becoming familiar to many. This is the next chapter to be written in digital life. Know and fight for these words as if your future freedoms depend on it. They very well might.

(Now go out and do something real.)

Thank You to:

Ariel & Kasha for love & inspiration
Richard R. for patience & intelligence
Sharon W. for a careful eye & loving heart
Lisa C. for forever friendship & encouragement
Dar Plone for mindreading & mindediting
Bill G. for art, both fast *and* good
Tricia A. for reading things right and rightful outrage
Bruce & Sonya
Edward S. just for being Edward S.
Roger H. & Everyone at Farley's, SF
(especially Evan & Naharu)

Index

Index

Index

About the Author

Born in Brooklyn, New York and transplanted against his will at a young age to Southern California, Jason Benlevi found himself channeled into the sciences by the launch of Sputnik and the L.A. Unified School District. It was a trajectory that was enjoyable until intersecting with the twin evils of geometry class and the Vietnam War (which did unsavory things with science.)

From that point forward Jason was on a different course, one that ultimately won him the disaffection of the L.A. school system and an escape to the San Francisco Bay Area. Living a dual academic life in creative arts/film school and computer geekiness, Jason authored what was probably the first feature film about computer hackers, well in advance of anyone in Hollywood having the vaguest idea what he was talking about. This was years before *War Games* and *Sneakers* (which no one remembers anyway.)

Back in the Bay Area, Jason was engaged in numerous creative ventures, but kept tinkering with electronics and computers. Deciding that he couldn't live on art alone, or afford the electronics, Jason became involved in advertising, where creative ideas are sent to die, but at least the artists and writers get paid. The timing was fortuitous since Jason was among the few creative individuals who actually liked talking to engineers and could translate what they were saying into language that any normal TV-watching, newspaper-reading individual could easily understand.

In past decades, while working at the will of the world's leading technology companies, he has blogged heavily under many aliases about politics, culture and technology. Now he has summoned the courage and recklessness to put a name to his work…and an end to his career.